CREATIVE CONTROL

Creative Control

THE AMBIVALENCE OF WORK IN
THE CULTURE INDUSTRIES

Michael L. Siciliano

Columbia University Press
New York

Columbia University Press
Publishers Since 1893
New York   Chichester, West Sussex
cup.columbia.edu
Copyright © 2021 Columbia University Press

Library of Congress Cataloging-in-Publication Data
Names: Siciliano, Michael L., author.
Title: Creative control : the ambivalence of work in the culture industries / Michael L. Siciliano.
Description: New York : Columbia University Press, [2021] | Includes bibliographical references and index.
Identifiers: LCCN 2020045830 (print) | LCCN 2020045831 (ebook) | ISBN 9780231193801 (hardback) | ISBN 9780231193818 (trade paperback) | ISBN 9780231550512 (ebook)
Subjects: LCSH: Cultural industries. | Creative ability. | Creative ability in business. | Work—Psychological aspects.
Classification: LCC HD9999.C9472 S525 2021 (print) | LCC HD9999.C9472 (ebook) | DDC 658.3/14—dc23
LC record available at https://lccn.loc.gov/2020045830
LC ebook record available at https://lccn.loc.gov/2020045831

Cover design: Noah Arlow
Cover image: Shutterstock (seesaw)

CONTENTS

ACKNOWLEDGMENTS

The production of a book, like any cultural product, is an immensely social process involving many people, all equally important. Sociologists have known this for quite some time, yet most studies of cultural production focus on only the most visible, most obviously "important" contributors to the production of knowledge, information, media, and the arts. Among my many aims with this book, I hope to correct the absence of routine workers in studies of media and the arts by including both expressive and routine forms of work in this ethnography of creative labor. With that in mind, I want to begin by thanking all the people whom I met while conducting ethnographic fieldwork for this book. All the people involved with the recording studio that I call SoniCo as well as the freelance recording engineers and the many YouTube creators who invited me into their workplaces and homes were incredibly generous with their time and candid with their opinions. This book could not have been written without their valuable contributions to my research project and my life.

I also, like a ghost, owe much to my haunts where I did much of the writing for this book, and so I would like to acknowledge the importance of cafes in Los Angeles; the East Bay; Kingston, Ontario; Pittsburgh, Pennsylvania; and Steubenville, Ohio. Even though they may never read this, I would like to extend a big thank you to the many baristas who served me countless cups of black coffee while I wrote. These unsung heroes include the bean slingers of Stories, Chango (RIP), and Cafecito Organico in Los Angeles; Lili (RIP) in Pittsburgh; Leonardo's in Steubenville; and the Elm in Kingston. Though I mostly wrote in these places, it also felt a bit like ongoing fieldwork as I watched people use Slack to chat with their coworkers, share their latest PowerPoint decks via Dropbox, or use their laptop to work on their latest mix of a song for some geographically distant client. Even after I left the offices at SoniCo and The Future, I was still surrounded by their modes of work whenever I decided to plunk away at my computer's keys in public.

This book would not be possible without Ching Kwan Lee, whom I thank for her robust and ceaseless support as well as rigorous criticism. I owe her much for her years of mentorship, a debt that I cannot begin to repay. While others might have reined me in, attempting to fit a square peg in a round hole, she gave me a rather long leash during the early stages of this project. I would also like to thank Edward Walker, Stefan Bargheer, and Christopher Kelty at UCLA. I do not think I would be the scholar I am today without their support and guidance.

Early drafts of several chapters benefited from thoughtful feedback provided by Joan Donovan and other participants in Chris Kelty's Part.Lab as well as by the UCLA Sociology Department's working groups in Ethnography and Movements, Organizations, and Markets, which were headed by Kyle Nelson and Lina Stepick. Likewise, Nina Eliasoph's Politics, Organizations, Ethnography, and Theory (POETs) and Paul Lichterman's Ethnography of Public Life (EPL) working groups provided me with an important social and intellectual anchor during my time as a postdoctoral scholar in the Department of Sociology at the University of Southern California. Thoughtful comments and collegiality from Thomas Abrams, Martin Hand, Annette Burfoot, and all my colleagues at Queen's University provided much needed positivity during the final stages of writing in the coldest months of my first Canadian winter.

I thank my good friends for their continued friendship, reading of early drafts, and providing positivity during my fieldwork and writing. I was always excited to have Pat Reilly show up at my door while in Los Angeles to discuss sociology, records, and comedy over coffee and lunch. Although Steven Tuttle resides in Chicago, he never felt far away as he offered thoughtful comments on my work and continued emotional support, providing a friendship that I highly value. Alexandra Lippman's invitation to

ACKNOWLEDGMENTS

participate in her Sound Ethnography Project opened me up to the incorporation of sound recordings in my fieldwork while also introducing me to sound studies, STS, and incredible friends such as Nalika Gajaweera, a familiar face who made USC less intimidating, and Alessandro Delfanti, with whom I continue an ongoing discussion about the future of labor. I also want to thank Neil Gong and Brooks Ambrose for their patience when we lived together and for their continued support of my research. I miss the countless hours we spent in traffic talking about social theory and research methods. I thank Wisam Alshaibi for being supportive and generous with his time, offering both commentary on my research as well as superb drumming for some of my more recent creative pursuits. I also want to thank my good friends Ashton Leech, Frank Fornsaglio, and Jeff Gentle for sharing their perspectives on work with me and for letting me bounce ideas off them. I also want to thank my mother and my family for offering their support in the ways they know how.

This project benefited from funding generously provided by the National Science Foundation (Grant Number 1636662) and from time spent discussing my work with Melissa Gregg, Hannah Landecker, Gabriel Rossman, David Halle, Zsuzsa Berend, and William Mazzarella, whose course Commodity Aesthetics at the University of Chicago left a lasting mark on my thinking, making a starting point for this project.

I would like to thank Eric Schwartz and the editorial board at Columbia University Press for taking on my project and providing guidance through the publishing process. This project also benefited from three anonymous reviewers who provided thoughtful comments on earlier drafts. Portions of chapter 3 appear in a significantly truncated form as an article in *Organization Studies* published in 2016.

Last but not least, I thank my ever-inspiring partner, my love, Ariel Pittman, for attempting to keep me sane during the final year of writing this book and for sharing her experiences as someone in a "creative" career. I finished this during the COVID-19 pandemic, and walking with Ariel around our neighborhood in Los Angeles and taking trips to the beach (staying inside the car the whole time of course) eased some of the anxieties brought out by 2020's perpetual crises. I will forever cherish all those times she convinced me that yes, it was OK to take a break from this book to go for a walk outside.

CREATIVE CONTROL

PART I

Introductions

Chapter One

CREATIVE CONTROL?

Creative control usually refers to the power to exercise final authority over the planning and execution of a film, a song, a performance, or some other cultural product. The guarantee of creative control is often a hard-fought clause in contracts of musicians, writers, filmmakers, and other "creatives," and there exists an entire mythology around the pursuit of creative control—fabled stories of directors, musicians, and even pro wrestlers who dared, fearlessly, to wrest creative control from the clutches of executives and all those who might pursue profit over artistry. Depending on your point of view, those stories elicit either admiration or a laugh. Either way, my point is not to draw an imaginary line between the artistic intentions of "creatives" and corporate profiteering but to highlight the *work* involved in cultural production and, in doing so, highlight tensions between capital and labor in the culture industries.

Struggles for creative control are ultimately struggles over who controls creative labor, placing creativity front and center as part of the contested terrain of work, especially today when creativity no longer finds its sole remit within the gilded lives of auteur filmmakers or visionary songwriters. As a wide range of scholars have said for the past forty years, jobs that involve "knowledge," "information," "cognition," or "creativity" play a central part in the global economy,[1] and today, roughly 25 percent of the

U.S. workforce finds itself employed in the fields that constitute Richard Florida's "creative class" (science, technology, finance, higher education, and media), the same people whom Robert Reich dubbed "symbolic analysts" in the early 1990s.[2]

Work in these fields requires "creativity," a job requirement that supposedly offers us the chance to "do what we love" so as to "never work" and, in the process, perhaps "change the world." Presumably, we will love whatever it is we create and, hopefully, earn a tidy profit as part of a passion-filled career in a growing creative class of "entrepreneurial" workers. Put differently, work in these creative industries seems to offer up the chance of meaningful, potentially lucrative employment, one in which capital invites labor to be creative, but this still leaves the issue of creative control. Who controls workers' creative labor?

In this book, I examine creative labor in two organizational contexts, one fairly conventional (a music recording studio) and the other firmly embedded within a digital infrastructure (a YouTube production and management firm). I leverage this comparison to develop an empirically grounded theory of creative labor, one attuned to similarities across divergent cases, and to explain how each organization's infrastructural context shapes creative labor processes. Here, recording studios represent a more conventional mode of organizing creative labor, emerging in their current form, independent of any *single* infrastructure, during the latter half of the twentieth century.[3] In contrast, firms that manage the production of social media content represent a newer mode of organizing creative labor, one firmly embedded within digital infrastructures and, in this book, tied to a single such infrastructure: Google's YouTube. I use this ethnographic comparison to extend sociological theories of control over labor and worker alienation, explaining how these organizations control and capture creative labor as well as how these processes vary by organizational context.

The workers whom I met while writing this book perform creative labor, but who possesses creative control? Who controls their creative labor and the ends to which they put their efforts? No longer separated out from work, creativity and the use of judgment now appear as vital, requisite skills for work within knowledge industries, or "cognitive capitalism."[4] For cognitive capitalism, the key source of value lies in the organizational appropriation of generically human capacities to act through, upon, and with symbols by way of complex technological systems—what I call *creative labor*. The peculiar thing about labor is that it is always bound up in the bodies of human beings and all the uncertainty that comes with them. Once hired for a job, there is no guarantee that a person will actually provide their labor—creative or otherwise. Workers may simply refuse to perform their jobs, watching the clock tick away while they do nothing. This happens less often than one might expect which is why discussions of labor often focus on why it is that people do not simply sit idle on the job. For sociologists of work in the labor process tradition, this becomes a question of how organizations maintain control over labor. Control tends to fall into one of five categories: simple or direct oversight, technical direction as in the assembly line's mechanical governance, bureaucratic control through rules, normative control wherein beliefs propagated by management govern the labor process (e.g., "corporate culture" or company slogans), and organizational aesthetics or the material culture of an organization, a central theme in this book.

Creative labor somehow seems different, less subject to control. After all, creativity tends often to be thought of as beyond or even antithetical to control. This way of understanding creativity may be seen in romanticized descriptions of a painter's brushstrokes upon a canvas or any "wildcat" workers' strike. For labor scholars and critical scholars of media, "creativity" supposedly resists power—the "soul"[5] or personal "integrity"[6] that remains ever eager to burst free from any cage. If one leaves these assumptions behind, there remains no reason to assume that creative labor should be any different with regard to capital's need to control, and therein lies what I find so puzzling.

If cognitive capitalism depends upon creativity or the generically human capacities to freely invent, express, and render judgment, then how does capital discipline or control creative labor? Typically, the absence of creativity at work results in worker dissatisfaction, or what Marx called alienation—and, often, resistance. This process varies in shape and form depending upon the sort of labor power required for work. So, for example, Arlie Hochschild in *The Managed Heart* draws a distinction between the experience of physical laborers breaking their bodies in the service of enterprise and the managed emotional displays of flight attendants and debt collectors (the smiles and anger that are not their own).[7] In Hochschild and, more broadly, sociological theories of the labor process, each type of labor experiences particular modes of control and alienation along with sociohistorically specific forms of resistance. Control, alienation, and resistance need to be included in any theorization of creative labor, and so I ask: How does capital control creative labor, and how does the inclusion of creativity shape workers' alienation and the possibility of resistance?

I take creative labor to refer to human capacities for interpretation, action, improvisation, and judgment using symbols and signs within the context of waged work. To be clear, I am not attempting to use this definition to arbitrate what does or does not count as "creativity." My intention is quite the opposite insofar as I use this definition to draw together two critical traditions—labor process theory and British cultural studies—that focus on the relationship between creativity and class power in capitalist economies. From the former, there is Harry Braverman's classic argument in *Labor and Monopoly Capital* wherein capitalism progresses by removing creativity from work, by separating planning from execution or mind from body, as in Taylorist factories.[8] Though still readily used by scholars studying "digital labor,"[9] Braverman's argument runs rough against capital's increased demand for "creativity" in paid employment, a trend most clearly seen in this book's empirical subject matter: (un)paid work performed within the culture industries. Heightened capitalist demand for "creativity" runs counter to labor process theory's conceptualization of power within capitalist labor processes, and this stems, in part, from this tradition's overemphasis on factory or service workers. Studies of factory and service work do little in explaining how capital commands creative labor, and so if capital tends to invite rather than banish "creativity" from the labor process, how does capital control creative labor?

This brings me to the other strand of critical scholarship underlying my project, one that ought to be familiar to those in cultural sociology and neighboring disciplines who concern themselves with creativity and inequality. My definition of creative labor borrows rather directly from British cultural studies, specifically Paul Willis's definition of "symbolic work" in *Common Culture*.[10] Symbolic work consists of everyday meaning making, all that we do when we interpret the increasingly dense array of sensations, images, sounds, and words in our social worlds. Creative labor refers to these activities in the context of paid employment. Willis's specific focus had been on showing how consumers and audiences of mass media possessed agency, specifically how the lived realities of the working classes and other marginalized groups pushed against earlier theorizations of the "masses" or working classes as "dopes," their cognition supposedly deformed by a singular "culture industry."[11] In stark contrast, Willis and other members of the "Birmingham School" showed how the working classes and other marginalized groups "resisted." Their resistance came in the form of everyday creative reinterpretations of cultural forms promulgated by corporate mass media and dominant cultural institutions. This creative resistance came, for example, in the form of the bricolage style of early punk rockers; people of color who invented hip-hop by reimagining turntables as instruments, vinyl records as raw materials, and street lamps as power sources; and "slash" fiction authors who appropriate fictional characters for homoerotic storylines. Though perhaps accepted today, these activities were initially denigrated and excluded by both capital and cultural institutions. These activities demonstrate creativity, which Willis called the "rare, irreverent gift" of the marginalized.[12]

Today, capital invites "creativity" from all, seeming to offer agency to anyone who engages in "creative entrepreneurship" and "self-branding." Arriving at this observation requires neither in-depth ethnography nor exceptional library skills. To see what I mean, you need only drift through some North American cities, observing their murals and advertising as fragments suggestive of work's new terrain. While in Chicago for a conference, I rode the Blue Line train to Wicker Park—the nexus of business and culture that Richard Lloyd calls "neo-bohemia."[13] There an advertisement invited people to become a "Creative Entrepreneur" by enrolling in a local college. A mural around the corner advised me to "Never Stop Pursuing Creativity!" Following the mural's advice, I ended up in Montreal to discuss some of the research I conducted for this book. There, I encountered another advertisement for something called a Gym de Creativitie, or Creative Gym. The gym offered "free and directed workshops for individuals and companies" seeking "expressive creativity." In Los Angeles—the primary site of my research—I regularly saw advertisements for "creative office space." These stand alongside billboards paid for by YouTube that invite passersby to "Be yourself" by producing content for the companies increasingly called the "Fearsome Five" (Apple, Facebook, Amazon, Microsoft, and YouTube's parent company, Google/Alphabet).

These fragments of contemporary urban life suggest a capitalist economy that invites "creativity." Just as this runs rough against sociological theories of the labor process, the invitation to "be creative" shifts the political stakes when it comes to questions of creativity and inequality. Rather than searching for "creativity," hoping to discover everyday acts of resistance among workers and marginalized groups, we need first to think through how capital invites us to be creative, to participate in our own exploitation whenever we accept the invitation to be an entrepreneurial worker flexing in a creative gym or inhabiting a creative office and producing content for one of the Fearsome Five's social media platforms.

The digital infrastructures that we commonly call "platforms" "disrupt" media work by enabling participation and innovation, supposedly undercutting the role of traditional media gatekeepers (e.g., movie studios, TV networks, book publishers, and record labels). How exactly do platforms shape creative labor processes? One narrative, popular since the first wave of social media platforms arose in the early 2000s, goes something like this: heretofore excluded peoples and publics may now let their voices be heard and their faces be seen as one hundred flowers bloom in the twenty-first century's wide-open fields of media production. Here, Google's corporate invitation to "Broadcast Yourself!" echoes yesteryear's transgressive call to "make a spectacle of yourself" in a way not unlike capital's recuperation of the 1960s' radical demands for participation described in Boltanski and Chiapello's *New Spirit of Capitalism*.[14] This narrative increasingly falls flat.

Platforms certainly expand opportunities for creative employment to anyone with a computer, microphone, and camera or even just a smartphone, but this rather obvious fact obscures how the corporate-owned, monopoly infrastructures that we call social media platforms structure users' paths to expression and remuneration. According to YouTube—one of the most popular of these platforms, with over a billion users—people produced more video content in the past ten years than was produced over the course of the twentieth century. Many pieces of content on YouTube generate revenue from paid advertisements that run before, after, or within the videos and music distributed by the platform. YouTube takes a portion of the advertising revenues and then distributes the remainder to content producers, or, to use the parlance of the platform, "creators." So, while this digital infrastructure provides for an abundance of "participation," the infrastructure's owner (Google) depends upon the globally distributed labor of its users, and these users constitute Google's largely unpaid, global media production workforce. To this, I again ask, how does capital control creative labor?

Put differently, how do organizations compel workers to their creative labor despite radically uncertain and, often, paltry economic rewards? Nearly forty years ago, Michael Burawoy, in *Manufacturing Consent*, asked why workers in factories seemed to participate actively in their exploitation.[15] Why did they work so hard in the absence of direct force or coercion? He responded by arguing that the organization of capitalist labor processes elicited consent to managerial hegemony, often by promoting localized forms of meaning making. Workers made a game of work, and so they did not need to be coerced. I am pressing the same question to creative labor processes, and I argue that any answer requires us to understand how workers come to be affectively invested and sensually engaged by their precarious, often alienating jobs.

CREATIVE LABOR'S ATTACHMENTS AND WORK'S AESTHETIC DIMENSION

Workers who perform creative labor also tend to be precariously employed, especially in the culture industries, where a few stars earn fortunes while most workers take home lower-than-average wages or nothing at all. Still, studies commonly find that culture workers "love" or enjoy their work despite lacking stable incomes and all the protections that come with "standard" employment. Some people might cynically interpret this common finding as nothing more than a mere rationalization or trivial ideological gloss. That seems much too easy an answer and much too dismissive of peoples' ability to reflect accurately upon their lives. I prefer to take these workers at their word and then ask how they come to enjoy precarious work, and, in doing so, I find a much more complicated and altogether more multivalent picture, one in which enjoying precarious work coincides with alienation.

Current explanations of creative labor's core contradiction tend to be predicated upon a rational, calculative individual, one for whom the opportunity to be creative functions as a fair tradeoff, a "psychic wage" that replaces stinging financial burdens and, ultimately, motivates workers to supply their creative labor to employers.[16] But how exactly does being creative offset the socioeconomic costs of precarious employment? Another explanation common to both economists and sociologists focuses on normative control or ideology—what Bourdieuian scholars might call the *illusio* of the "field of cultural production." Proponents of this explanation claim that an "art for art's sake ideology" motivates culture workers to pursue status or "symbolic rewards" rather than purely economic gains. In this explanation, the weight of reputation and the disciplining whip of radically uncertain labor markets discipline or control labor rather than management or capital.

The limit of this style of explanation becomes apparent when endeavoring to explain what actually binds people to their beliefs. A passage from Ashley Mears's *Pricing Beauty*—a Bourdieuian ethnographic study of fashion models—clearly illustrates this limit. An informant explains to Mears that he pursues low-paying gigs because he genuinely enjoys his work and wants to be part of a "masterpiece." Mears dismisses her informant's explanation and instead claims that culture workers merely say that they work "for the chance to be a part of something *magical*. But the magic . . . is an illusion," or *illusio*, the field's guiding ideology.[17] In this explanation, *illusio* or ideology supposedly explains both why people work so hard for so little (control) and their persistence in uncertain careers (attachment).

Anyone familiar with even the cheapest of dollar-store magic tricks ought to find this interpretation odd. Illusions, after all, do not produce magic. If the magician conjures illusions and the sorcerer's spells bind, then what spells bind creative workers to their *illusio*? Less magically wrought, how do workers become affectively attached to precarious employment, or, to use my informants' words, what makes these jobs so "cool?" Drawing from Mears's example, it seems rather easy to point to the magic of cultural products as a source of power over their producers. After all, the anthropologist of art Alfred Gell was not without reason when he theorized cultural objects as "technologies of enchantment,"[18] and of course, there is a long history of considering the culture industries' products as tools of "mass deception" or "distraction."[19]

In this book, I tell a slightly different story, one that ought to be of interest not just to scholars of work and media but to anyone concerned with the materialities that support and enable capitalist power as well as the potential political possibilities of affect and aesthetic experiences. Workers in the culture industries often feel deeply attached to their labor processes, but as I show in this book, they also report a distinct type of alienation vis-à-vis their products, often likening the fruits of their labor to trash, garbage, or excrement. In the same breath, they emphasize embodied pleasures derived from "being creative"—often pointing back to sense experiences in relation to technologies—and so I want to press a bit further on Gell's "technologies of enchantment." For Gell, aesthetic objects (e.g., art, media, music, etc.) mediate social relationships and exert power over us by virtue of our fascination or ability to figuratively "disappear" into them as we search for meaning. This constitutes the "magic" that an object has over us, and to disappear into or "merge" with an object is to have what a range of philosophers and social scientists describe as an aesthetic experience.

Mobilizing my extensive ethnographic fieldwork alongside theory and research from the social sciences and related fields, I argue that contemporary work technologies provide us with aesthetic experiences, enchanting work as workers "disappear" into these objects in search of meaning. No longer appendages to disenchanting machines of mass production or slaves to bureaucracy, creative workers appear enchanted by the machines that enable and extend their ability to perform creative labor. In presenting technology as part of the material, embodied experience of work—one that both enchants and enables work to be done—I hope to provide a more full-bodied and ultimately more satisfactory answer to the question of how workers become so deeply attached to precarious employment. As I argue, explaining creative labor's attachment to precarity by pointing only to ideology provides an incomplete, disembodied answer. Ideology depends upon distinctive, often technological aesthetics or materialities found in creative workplaces. The objects or artifacts that enable and extend creative labor provide a bit of "magic" or ineffable "cool"—a distinctive "structure of feeling" that binds workers to their work.[20]

In discussing how organizational aesthetics and materialities shape how work feels, I am gesturing toward what, in critical cultural theory, has come to be known as "affect theory."[21] Here, a diverse array of theorists defines affect as our "ability to affect and be affected" through nondiscursive forms of meaning caused by a variety of sensory impingements upon the body—not quite emotion, more vague and inchoate: a feeling. This resembles how organizational scholars define aesthetics, or "what is thought and felt by the body's sensory and perceptive faculties," in relation to objects.[22] A key assertion from Brian Massumi, one of affect theory's leading voices, has been that these "asocial but not pre-social" embodied meanings lie below the level of discourse and outside ideology.[23] As such, affect supposedly provides an "outside" from which one might resist dominant and dominating meanings and thus a basis for political mobilization.

In this book, I describe an altogether more ambivalent situation, one where aesthetics or sense experiences vis-à-vis objects enroll workers in capitalist projects of profit making. Workers often experience the sort of effervescent moments that Émile Durkheim claimed to bind believers to their beliefs while using technology at work.[24] Repeated interactions with technology make precarious work sensually enjoyable, affectively binding workers to their work. So, to be clear, I am arguing in support of affect theory insofar as I consider embodiment and sensation to be of causal import, but rather than positing the affective or aesthetic dimension of social life as a sort of asocial wellspring of resistance, unbridled by ideology or discursive qualification, I argue that affect or aesthetics may lead us down the path of consent to domination just as much as our felt experiences might nudge us toward refusal. Affect and aesthetics provide a basis for power to act upon us just as much as a bedrock upon which resistance might be built. My contribution lies in bringing these discussions into the sociology of work while standing alongside recent critiques of affect theory in anthropology,[25] highlighting how work's aesthetic dimension constitutes what Pasquale Gagliardi called the "fourth dimension of control."[26]

DIGITAL INFRASTRUCTURES AND CREATIVE LABOR

This book also addresses how digital platforms affect creative labor. In doing so, I extend outward from two fieldsites, always considering them within their broader infrastructural contexts—what Karin Knorr-Cetina calls the "microstructures" of economic life.[27] In extending beyond the local sites of my fieldwork, I am following in a tradition wherein sociologists of labor and work emphasize the effects of structure upon microinteractions—what Michael Burawoy calls the "extended case method."[28] In this ethnographic tradition, researchers begin with their "favorite" theory or explanation of a social process and then go into the field in search of anomalous cases in order to "extend" or make existing theory more robust. Both cases of creative labor in this book exist within the same country, and so, rather than examining the effects of different political economies and nation-states, as in so many extended-case ethnographies, my key source of variation lies a bit higher, way up in the "cloud." My aim in comparing two cases of creative labor is to explain how one of global capital's digital infrastructures or platforms (i.e., YouTube) affects creative labor processes.

If my focus on control begins with Marxian theories of the labor process and Bourdieuian theories of cultural production, I examine distribution infrastructure as a way of extending Paul Hirsch's organizational model of media production.[29] In Hirsch's model, gatekeepers (critics, curators, talent scouts, etc.) exert power over production (control) by determining what is available in the market. In conventional media, film studios and music publishers along with distributors have traditionally taken this role. As gatekeepers between producers and consumers, these intermediaries tend to shape or exert a structuring influence upon production much like an editor may shape the work processes of writers. The advent of internet distribution and production platforms such as iTunes, YouTube, SoundCloud, Spotify, and Bandcamp suggest a diminished role for traditional gatekeeping and thus, potentially, a more open and democratic future for media production.

Platforms like YouTube, however, perform a similar gatekeeping function. This function often goes unnoticed in discussions of culture industries but is already underway in discussions of politics and the public sphere.[30] Thus, I expected both cases—music production and YouTube content production—to exhibit a similar degree of influence from platforms. Instead, music workers experienced few, if any, direct effects of any particular platform, while both production and office staff in the YouTube case regularly grappled with Google's arbitrary governance. This core difference, I argue, stems from each case's political economy of infrastructure or concentration of infrastructural ownership.

CREATIVE LABOR'S AMBIVALENCE

These theoretical concerns emerged from situations I encountered during the extended ethnographic fieldwork that I conducted at a music recording studio and a YouTube management firm, which I respectively call SoniCo and The Future. Before explaining more about those two organizations, I want to ground my theoretical discussion by introducing some of the workers whom I met during my fieldwork, starting with my second day as participant observer with SoniCo, a recording studio that also runs sound for live music events. On a warm winter evening in Los Angeles, a crowd of fashionable, young urbanites stood outside waiting to see a pop singer perform at an "invite-only" event held in a corporate-branded art gallery. SoniCo had been contracted by the gallery to provide an engineer to oversee sound during the performance and a crew to set up the stage and backline, which included the PA system and musicians' equipment. I was inside with the crew setting up the backline beside a cotton-candy machine in the middle of an artificial grass field. The walls were covered with floor-to-ceiling images of that evening's performers along with stencil paintings of various instruments—saxophones, guitars, and the iconic Roland 808 drum machine.

On the eighth hour of that twelve-hour day, the crew and I went to the alley behind the gallery, taking a short break to eat from the catering table and smoke some cigarettes before showtime. That's when I first met Jerry, a sound engineer who worked freelance for both SoniCo and a handful of local music venues. Sound engineers like Jerry oversee the technical aspects of music recordings and live performances, using a variety of equipment to adjust, alter, and document the sounds produced by the musicians. Without their creative labor, live performances or recordings might sound dull, harsh, or lacking in sonority. Providing his creative labor in this job required technology, and during a typical gig in a studio or at a venue, engineers like Jerry mediated between musicians' demands for particular sounds and the technologies ("gear") used to achieve those sounds. Gear factored into how Jerry and the other engineers I interviewed for this book came to enjoy certain gigs. As he said, "I like working at those places because they're just beautiful places and I can work with really cool, new equipment. Like, they have these new [mixing] boards there and me and the other engineers are just like 'Whoa! Do you know how to work that thing? Have you ever seen one of these!?' It's really great." Good gigs, as he said, provided "cool, new equipment," objects that seemed to possess exciting possibilities, potentials that he might unearth if only he could use them. That's how he imagined them, at least.

If sound engineers like Jerry found beauty in the aesthetics of technology and its potential uses, what about the more routine workers in the crew? Crew members were largely responsible for loading, unloading, and setting up the equipment; building stages; and any other physical labor. They earned about ten to twelve dollars an hour, a small wage for skilled work, but accepted because they strongly desired employment with the company. Some even worked as office staff, earning the same hourly wage and performing many of the same tasks, save for the heavy lifting. These workers, too, claimed to "love" their jobs despite the low pay, or, at the very least, they preferred these jobs to other employment options that might pay more. For instance, Thomas, part of SoniCo's office staff, regularly sold plasma to pay rent but still emphatically voiced enthusiasm for the job, despite being fully capable of working in more lucrative and stable fields, given his earlier career as a barber.

What explained these routine workers' enjoyment? Before I met Jerry, I helped the crew assemble the stage and the backline. While we set this up, one of SoniCo's owners spent a few moments showing off equipment owned by the studio that had been rented by the gallery for the evening. He invited our gaze, asking, "She's a beaut, ain't she?" as he unveiled a vintage Rhodes electric piano, Vox amplifiers, and analog synthesizers. The crew responded with varying degrees of excitement, which left me wondering about the relationship between technology and creative labor. Were these simply tools? Or, as Jerry and the manager seemed to imply, were they also objects of beauty, sources of both aesthetic pleasure and imagined potential agency?

Technology seemed to offer temporary moments of enjoyment, but absent these small satisfactions, creative labor performed in the service of others, like a lot of jobs, seemed rather alienating. Jerry described the gig at the gallery where we met as "a big pain in the ass." Why? Well, first of all, Jerry lacked the tools he preferred, so the gig lacked a certain aesthetic satisfaction. Second, the musicians repeatedly challenged his ability to exercise creative control or judgment over the use of his creative labor. Earlier in the day, before our pre-performance break for food, Jerry ran a lengthy soundcheck to ensure that all the musicians could be heard loud and clear without feedback—the squealing, irritating noise that sometimes occurs during a performance. With upward of a dozen sound sources onstage, this required extensive technical skill and practical knowledge. After what seemed like hours, the musicians remained unsatisfied. One even came back to Jerry's mixing console, repeatedly pushed the sound levels into "the red," which would overload the system, producing feedback. The musician would then ask Jerry to fix the feedback, a dance of egos that continued for several hours. As a former touring musician, I was surprised. I had never seen anyone challenge an engineer like this in nearly twenty years of performing. Most live engineers ("sound guys" or "the sound man") never allow musicians to touch a mixing console. Save for microphones against the lips of a singer, they rarely let anyone touch any of their equipment. To touch the gear or challenge an engineer's use of it can be a major cause of friction during a recording session or live gig.

I asked Jerry if that particular musician was the band's personal "sound guy." Apparently, the musician had said, "Well, I am an *artist*, but tonight I am the sound man as well." Jerry repeated this several times in parody. "See, I'm an *artist*! See! I'm an *artist*." Jerry was not questioning the quality of the musician's work; in fact, he said he'd "liked the last group that soundchecked a lot." What infuriated him was the musician's usurpation of Jerry's ability to shape and exercise judgment over sound. "But I let him do his thing, and if he makes it sound crappy, what do I care? It's not *my name* on this bullshit." Alienated from his judgment, Jerry distanced himself from his contribution to the performance. He could be creative, but only within limits set by his clients.

Across town, Desmond worked for The Future—a company that earns its money through advertising revenue generated by views of videos made by its network of thousands of content creators located around the world. Sitting at an IKEA desk, eyes transfixed on the world coming through his laptop's screen, Desmond, like many of The Future's employees, searched for YouTube content producers or "creators" with hopes that he might convince them to sign a management contract. He and the rest of the staff then provided a minimal amount of career services to creators, offering advice on when to post new videos to the platform or "best practices" for lighting and video editing. I regularly did all these tasks during the ten months I spent at The Future. Less often, we tried to set up brand sponsorships, but only with the most popular creators. The Future received a percentage of creators' earnings, not wholly unlike a traditional talent management company, except at a global scale—and providing significantly fewer services to the "talent."

Desmond had entered the culture industries as an actor when he had been in his early twenties. He landed at The Future after deciding to seek a "steady" job behind the scenes. By the end of my fieldwork, he had worked there for two years. Most employees lasted under twelve months—a high level of churn thought normal by many in the office. Despite their rather fleeting time at The Future, Desmond enjoyed his job because he could "be creative"—something that nearly all the people I spoke to in my research cited as the most enjoyable part of their job.

What did it mean to "be creative" at The Future? The meaning of "creativity" varied quite a bit among employees, but for managers it usually meant improvising solutions to the organization's practical problems. Finding and securing a steady flow of new content producers, or "creators," was one such organizational problem, one Desmond could freely solve and thus "be creative." How did he choose to solve this problem? He tried to anticipate emerging trends in YouTube content, searching for untapped genres, or "verticals," by drawing together pieces of information he found on Reddit or Twitter, combing through data that The Future scraped from YouTube's servers, and chatting with friends about what they liked to watch.

When I asked him to explain this process, he described a rather ambulatory experience vis-à-vis his screen, what he called entering a "wormhole." Metaphorically, he entered the world offered up by his laptop screen in search of content that might prove lucrative for The Future's bottom line. Disappearing through the wormhole, he would end up in some unexpected part of YouTube and discover untapped sources of the types of content desired by his employer. He felt more "productive," seeming to lose himself in this process—a certain subjective absence that I quickly recognized as similar to my experiences when I performed the same tasks. These moments resembled what philosophers of art and social scientists might call an "aesthetic experience"—one in which the subject disappears into an object in order to unlock the meanings that seem to lie within. Again, the organizational demand for workers' creative labor coincided with a certain embodied engagement vis-à-vis technology, a situation similar to what I found at SoniCo.

YouTube content "creators" lie downstream from both the platform and The Future. Creators work in their homes all around the world and earn a piece rate tied directly to the metrics that so concern people like Desmond and companies such as YouTube. When I arrived at the Midwestern home of the creator whom I call Hank, he and his family greeted me warmly before he led me down to his basement production studio, where he had a green screen, a camera, audio recording equipment, and a professional lighting kit. He started creating video content in 2008 after being laid off during the "Great Recession." With no college education and no prior media production experience he said to himself, "I've got to do something that's flexible and that I can maybe make money at and just do when I can do it." He had read a number of news articles wherein people "make all kinds of money" making YouTube content. He imagined, "I can at least do *something* with it." A 2018 report presented to the World Economic Forum on British schoolchildren's most desired careers suggests that Hank does not imagine alone. In the report, schoolchildren ranked the occupations of social media celebrity and YouTube vlogger higher than work in music and the arts, law enforcement, law, medicine, or science.[31]

After coming home from his new full-time job in an unrelated industry, Hank spent most of his free evenings producing videos where he explained how to prepare for a nuclear attack or, heaven forbid, a zombie apocalypse. With over eighty thousand regular viewers, Hank earned about $30,000 a year, in addition to his salaried day job. Still, the flexibility and freedom of platform-based work came at the cost of stability. Only one-quarter of that $30,000 came from YouTube's piece-rate system. The rest came from a variety of side deals and sponsorships that Hank learned about on his own, despite being under a management contract with The Future. With these side deals, Hank could earn roughly 21 cents per view; he earned only six cents without them. Not counting the costs of his labor, Hank spends two to three cents to produce each view, so he works hard to retain the more favorable profit margin. Despite his contract with The Future, he said they do little to help, though they occasionally mediate on his behalf when YouTube removes his content or erases his view counts without warning.

Each of these jobs requires *creative labor*: broadly distributed yet historically specific human capacities for interpretation, action, and improvisation using symbols and signs. Like physical and emotional labor, all forms of employment require some creative labor, but as I show throughout this book, capital explicitly invited workers in each of the jobs I have just described to "be creative." Even in rather routine jobs, such as those performed by SoniCo's crew and by Desmond at The Future, I found management inviting workers to take "ownership," to devise strategies for routine tasks, to be, in a word, "creative," in ways not wholly unlike those in seemingly more clearly expressive jobs, such as Jerry and Hank. Despite management's exciting invitations, each worker remained economically precarious because of low pay, high churn, or the wide-ranging power of a platform.

Notably, all of this may be seen *within* the labor process, an empirical focus severely lacking in research on the creative labor of "informational" or "cognitive" capitalism.[32] In bird's-eye theorizations of cognitive capitalism, work is supposedly regulated or controlled by the capitalist mobilization of workers' passions, affects, or feelings. Put differently, power over work supposedly operates at the level of affect, of sensation, of feelings. This differs from more empirically grounded research on creative labor processes that instead point toward ideological mechanisms of control wherein "creativity," as a discourse, justifies precarious employment. A key argument I make in this book is that these ideological mechanisms depend upon distinct materialities or aesthetic structures that modulate workers' affect and allow workers to perceive and imagine possibilities within the working day. These aesthetic structures of work exert power or control over creative labor by affectively binding workers to their tasks.

THE CASES: SONICO AND THE FUTURE

The scenes I just detailed come from twenty months of extensive participant observation and interviews that I conducted from 2013 through 2018. During this time, I worked alongside or shadowed employees such as Jerry the engineer, office workers like Desmond, and music laborers. This includes eighty-four semistructured, in-depth interviews with managers, workers, and technology designers; a field survey of employees at The Future; and audio field recordings.[33] Men tend to be overrepresented in terms of employment in both conventional and digital media, a pattern present at both field sites and thus also in my data. Despite somewhat of a lack in gender diversity, my informants were diverse in terms of ethnicity, race, and sexuality, especially in the case of YouTube production. I mention this because my effort to maintain the confidentiality of informants' identities often obscures this feature of my ethnographic data. After concluding my primary fieldwork, I began interviewing YouTube creators in Los Angeles and then in the Midwest and Southwest of the United States. Sometimes I had known these creators for several months, but sometimes we only met for an interview. Creators were clients of The Future; I selected them with the aim of achieving maximum variation in terms of creators' genre, gender, race/ethnicity, and location. A few chose to speak with me only via Skype, but many were overwhelmingly generous with their time, often inviting me into their homes to see how and where they worked. In addition to qualitative data sources, I used descriptive statistics from the U.S. Bureau of Labor Statistics and economic census data to locate workers within the broader U.S. economy.

The primary aim of my research was to examine creative labor in two divergent organizational contexts, drawing out similarities between the two cases so as to develop an empirically grounded theory of creative labor. To address the theoretical issues discussed earlier in this introduction, I selected a fairly conventional mode of organizing creative labor (SoniCo, the recording studio) and a relatively new mode of organizing creative labor, one that depends upon a particular social media platform (The Future, a YouTube management network).

I also leverage this comparison to explain how each organization's infrastructural context shapes the creative labor process. As a music recording studio, SoniCo represents a more conventional mode of organizing creative labor, the current form of which emerged in the 1970s and has remained largely unchanged since the 1990s. Music production is relatively independent of any *single* infrastructure, and much like other industries marked by what Walter Powell and others refer to as "networked" forms of organization, SoniCo and its workers depend upon reputation and social networks in order to secure profits.[34] In contrast, The Future depends upon YouTube's global platform and thus upon global, technological capital. While digital distribution infrastructures or platforms exist in both organizations' respective fields, no single platform dominates in music, whereas YouTube content, by definition, exists on only a single platform. Thus, this comparison provides insight into how dependence upon a single infrastructure shapes work in the emerging field of cultural production around YouTube.

Both SoniCo and The Future generate revenue from the provision of production services. At both firms, production personnel such as sound engineers and creators (expressive creative workers) are considered independent contractors, while office staffmembers (routine creative workers) tend to be employed full-time by the firms. They differ insofar as YouTube creators tend to be under multiyear (and sometimes lifetime) contracts at The Future, whereas audio engineers tend to be employed on a project-by-project basis or self-employed. Like barbers or tattoo artists in their parlors, audio engineers worked at SoniCo but not for SoniCo. Management at both firms invited workers to "be creative," to improvise and integrate the planning and execution of tasks, yet workers' skills command very little power, given the large standing reserve of creative labor. This feature stemmed, in part, from SoniCo's location in Los Angeles, The Future's use of a globally distributed workforce, and the more general decline in unionization in the United States. These factors, which prevent culture industry workers from appealing to labor regulations, combine with management's attempts to extend the working day while paying relatively low wages.[35] Creative labor in the United States exists within what thus may be termed a despotic labor regime.[36]

Though similar, SoniCo and The Future differ in the logics that undergird how they organize production. I draw out what is common to creative labor processes through a comparison of these divergent cases. SoniCo exists within a network of organizations that operate under what Bernard Miège calls a "publishing logic."[37] Common to music and other conventional media industries (e.g., film, television, etc.), the publishing logic tends to organize work around short-term projects, with a networked organization of small firms producing a range of products with the hope that a few products may be successful enough in terms of sales or status to support other, less successful projects. The Future, on the other hand, exists within a network of organizations tied together by their dependence upon a single platform: YouTube. YouTube production tends to be

TABLE 1.1
Cases of creative labor in the U.S. culture industries

	SoniCo	The Future
Product	Music	YouTube content
Workers	Sound engineers	Content creators
	Office staff	Office staff

organized around a constant flow of new content produced by a globally distributed workforce, given the economics of platforms and their reliance upon increased growth in their number of users.[38] The platform determines the economic value of this content by way of various metrics and blackboxed calculations.

Surprisingly, I find that these two cases share more in common than might be expected, even if they still differ in one fundamental way. Both cases share a dominant managerial ideology ("be creative," a euphemism for self-management), requisite forms of labor, and workers' relation to technology. Many of the differences between SoniCo and The Future stem from the latter's structural dependence vis-à-vis global, technological capital (i.e., Google and its YouTube platform). The platform enables The Future (and Google) to capture the value produced by a globally distributed workforce of content producers.

SoniCo and The Future represent two regimes of creative labor: the social and the quantified. Each contains distinct but similar modes of control. SoniCo's social regime controls labor by managing how work feels through workplace sociality and the materialities or aesthetics of the workplace, whereas The Future's quantified regime governs first through metrics and quotas and second by managing how work feels. As an ethnographer, I aim to provide an in-depth view of creative labor in these contexts while generating theoretically transposable concepts, so I aim for conceptual generalizability rather than statistically generalizable findings. Though these cases may limit my theorization to the particular political economy of the United States, they raise broadly relevant issues that may prove useful in understanding creative labor processes in other sociocultural contexts.

STRUCTURE OF THE BOOK

Leveraging the ethnographic comparison of creative labor in two organizational contexts, I make three arguments in this book. First, a full-bodied understanding of creative labor under cognitive capitalism requires consideration of work's aesthetic structures in conjunction with work's social, economic, and technical structures. In this book's two cases of creative labor, I find that work's aesthetic structures engage and excite, exerting power or control over creative labor. These engagements—what I call aesthetic enrollment—increase the likelihood of workers' consent to precarious, often exploitative conditions of employment. This leads to my second major point. This distinctive mode of social control never fully resolves the contradictions of creative labor processes. The organization of creative labor produces neither full consent to exploitative precarity nor eruptive collective resistance. Instead, these engagements temporarily bind workers to work, enrolling them in capital's projects of profit making just long enough to secure their creative labor. When this process slips out of balance, workers exit or engage in simple refusals. Third, social media platforms may and do exert centralized control over creative labor much as other platforms exert power: by imposing blackboxed systems of governance along with quantified metrics that reconfigure or replace professional conventions.

I make these arguments across three parts. In chapter 2 I provide a brief genealogy of "creativity" discourses to better understand the variety of ways in which people used the term creativity while I was in the field. To be clear, this chapter treats creativity as an ideological formation or discourse, so my goal is not to find some "real" creativity but to understand the range of historical and contemporary meanings of the term and then to understand how creativity, as ideological construction, operates in this book's two cases of creative labor. Critical scholars of creative labor claim that the contemporary discourse of "creativity" functions as a *dispositif*, that is, a self-regulating ideological control mechanism that regulates. Bourdieuian studies of cultural production suggest much the same, that a field's singular *illusio*, or ideology, justifies what might otherwise seem exploitative. Based on these explanations, I expected to find minimal variation in the discourses employed by workers and capital. Instead, I found differences along class lines, with workers, managers, and global capital all offering up different definitions. Though still steeped in distinctly Western, often masculine discourses of autonomous self-expression, workers' accounts of creativity never appeared fully subsumed by the more instrumentally pragmatic views espoused by management and global capital (Google's YouTube). These divergent accounts, I argue, show how the discursive terrain of creativity appears too varied to provide either a stable source of normative control, as in critical feminist scholarship, or explain workers' affective attachments to work, as in Bourdieuian studies that point toward *illusio*. There remains a gap between classes, one that needs to be bandaged over if these extant theories are to explain why workers consent or become affectively attached to precarious employment.

Part 2 then focuses on the entangled processes of attachment, control, and consent. I begin the ethnographic portion of the book at SoniCo, where I delineate the contradictions of creative labor processes—what I call creative labor's positive and negative poles. At SoniCo's positive pole, I find dense social ties and embodied engagement vis-à-vis technology, which provide for workers' attachments to precarious employment. These features of work hang alongside the precarity and alienation of SoniCo's negative pole. Examining the working days of expressive audio engineers and routine office staff, I find that both jobs require creative labor, and so any empirical distinction between expressive and routine workers in these industries appears to be of less conceptual import than suggested by previous research. Across both types of workers, managerial power tends to be exerted directly through a soft form of simple, direct control and indirectly by managing how work feels and incentivizing professional networking opportunities. Managers shape how work feels by cultivating social relationships with employees and creating a "cool" workplace. I show how this ineffable "cool" tends to be intimately bound up in SoniCo's distinct materialities—most often through embodied engagement vis-à-vis the studio's technology. Here, I develop what I call *aesthetic enrollment*—a mechanism by which workers' come to feel "creative" even in the most mundane of jobs. Alongside the mechanism of aesthetic enrollment, management incentivizes tasks by framing the workplace as full of possibilities for professional networking and reputation building—crucially important parts of work in networked organizations such as those found in the culture industry. These strategies aim to secure friendly office staff and a stable group of freelance engineers while also encouraging labor to adopt an entrepreneurial disposition.

Focusing on the negative valences of creative labor, that is, precarity and alienation, chapter 4 asks how workers reproduce their labor power and relate to what they produce. I find that engineers and office staff both understand their jobs as just one of many income streams—not unlike theorizations of neoliberalism's entrepreneurial subject. Illustrating this entrepreneurial disposition toward work, engineers often view themselves as small businesses, while office staffmembers see their full-time jobs as enabling them to become a small business eventually. The lines between work and nonwork blur as this disposition leads workers to engage in constant professional networking within and without the formal boundaries of the organization in order to secure enough income streams to maintain economic solvency. Often failing to do so, workers rely upon networks of friends and family for economic and social support. In explaining how SoniCo's employees relate to music produced at the studio, I theorize creative labor's distinctive form of alienation, what I call "alienated judgment." While creative labor requires workers' use of judgment, they do so toward another's ends. Work is both immediately engaging, as in the previous chapter, and mediately unpleasant upon reflection.

Part 3 extends these concepts to a different organizational context by examining YouTube content production and office life at The Future. Doing so highlights the specificity of creative labor under conditions of monopoly infrastructure as well as the transposability of the concepts developed in part 2. Chapter 5 examines The Future's positive pole, tracing the production of YouTube content from creators' home studios to the daily rounds of employees in The Future's offices. Beginning with an analytic description of the platform's interface and training materials, I show how YouTube disciplines a global workforce. While the platform leaves creators free to choose the thematic core or message of content, the platform endeavors to discipline creators' formal choices as well as creators' production of metadata and use of preexisting intellectual property.

The Future's office workers reinforce the platform's disciplinary strategies by advising creators on platform-specific "optimization"—not unlike the process of formatting used in homogenizing other commodities. Within these structures, management and the platform invite workers to "be creative." I then descend from the platform to the working days of The Future's content creators and office staff to illustrate how control strategies described in earlier chapters reappear in altered form. Whereas management at SoniCo governed, primarily, through the socioaesthetic experience of work, The Future governs through quotas or metric benchmarks and manages creators by withholding projects and production assistance until creators meet monthly growth goals. Likewise, The Future governs office staff using a quota system linked to YouTube's metrics. The platform and The Future invite these workers to "be creative" within these quantitative structures.

Despite rampant quantification, The Future resembles SoniCo insofar as both firms attempted to manage how work felt through their distinctive workplace materialities. The Future accomplished this through unsettling, flexible office design and the use of communication technologies designed to re-create the aesthetics of social media. Among creators and office staff, I find that working on and through the YouTube platform elicits an ambivalent mix of frustration and fascination. Workers navigate the platform's blackboxed, algorithmic governance—often the cause of lost revenue and precarity—alongside the platform's ever-changing interface and opaque rule structure. Nearly constant changes in this infrastructural technology dynamize work, simultaneously engaging, captivating, and frustrating workers. Change is constant—a source of "cool" satisfaction—yet the platform's satisfying dynamism often results in heightened precarity. Paradoxically, workers appear fascinated and satisfied by that which heightens their precarity: the unknowable logic underlying changes in the algorithms and interfaces through which they work.

Chapter 6 examines The Future's negative pole in order to show how The Future's quantitative regime shapes workers' attempts to mitigate precarity and their use of judgment. In attempting to mitigate precarity, The Future's creators and office staff engage in constant learning aimed at consistently expanding their skills so as to maintain employability. Rather than learning from peers, as under SoniCo's social regime, they learn from YouTube content. As they view this content, they simultaneously learn and generate advertising revenue for the platform, and so the platform captures value from both their production and consumption of content. Relatedly, The Future indefinitely defers support to the majority of creators. This deferred support, along with YouTube's training and promotional materials, encourages workers to inventively develop new income streams. They do so by creating a dense web of revenue streams derived from YouTube and other digital platforms. The Future captures a portion of these revenues, and so, again, even in attempts to mitigate precarity and gain economic autonomy, workers generate value for The Future and YouTube, blurring the lines between labor performed for capital and labor performed for one's self. In the remainder of chapter 6, I illustrate the subordination of workers' judgment vis-à-vis the platform, arguing that the platform structures the creative labor process more loosely and more thoroughly than under SoniCo's social regime.

In the conclusion, I provide a conceptual map or theory of creative labor and discuss the implications of my findings for the sociologies of work and media production as well as for theories of cognitive capitalism and the relations among affect, aesthetics, and power. I emphasize the power of work's aesthetic dimension, the engaging everyday materialities that aesthetically enroll workers in economically exploitative work. In doing so, I argue that control operates at the level of sense and feeling, not simply discourse or ideological gloss. Embodied experiences vis-à-vis work's technologies allow for this to occur, illustrating how the ineffable "cool" that binds creative workers to their tasks depends upon distinct materialities. In other words, the aesthetic dimension of work exerts control or power at the level of the labor process, and this aesthetic dimension often obscures what might otherwise feel grossly exploitative, eliciting a partial and ultimately tentative form of consent that may at any time spill over into passive resistance or exit. Workers know and understand their economic circumstances, yet work feels undeniably engaging, dynamic, and, often, enjoyable. Based on this, I argue for a labor politics of judgment focused not on how work feels but on workers' control over the use of their creativity. Closing out the book, I suggest the potential policy relevance of these arguments to discussions about the blurred boundaries between work and nonwork and the power of digital platforms.

Chapter Two

CONFLICTING CREATIVITIES

"Well, I get to be creative." I heard a version of this answer nearly every time I asked workers what they enjoyed about their jobs, and managers often told me that they wanted "creative" workers. A match made in heaven, it would seem, but what did "being creative" mean to them? In this chapter, I interrogate "creativity" as an ideological formation, showing creativity's multiple meanings as they vary between labor, management, and global capital. To be clear, I am not attempting to define creativity[1] so much as I am concerned with how creativity, as a discourse, comes to be meaningful in the context of employment. As noted in the previous chapter, scholars of creative labor claim that the discourse of creativity and closely related ideological formations such as "innovation" and "art for art's sake" govern or control creative labor under cognitive capitalism, "pushing workers to internalize this system rather than oppose it."[2] This claim suggests that belief alone explains why workers willfully participate in precarious, often exploitative employment. In pursuing the meanings of creativity espoused by workers, managers, and a global media platform, I find conflict rather than conformity and contend that these classed creativities vary too widely to function as an ideological mechanism of control.

Creativity and its sibling "innovation" have been buzzwords in business and policy circles since the turn of the century, so much so that many claim "creativity" as the ideology of our times, a sort of secular "fundamentalism" with roots in the mid-twentieth-century advertising industry and Silicon Valley's "Californian ideology."[3] In this view, creativity often appears as a sort of cure-all for a variety of socioeconomic problems, with start-ups in the United States' Silicon Valley, Alley, and Beach (respectively, Northern California, New York, and Los Angeles) proffering radical, creative "disruption" as a supposed guarantee of our collective, economic future. Altogether, these creativity discourses represent forms of what Boltanski and Chiapello identified as the "new spirit of capitalism,"[4] one in which capital actively invites our creative labor.

In response, there exist two interrelated critiques of creativity. The one with which I most clearly engage claims the symbolic meaning of creativity to be wholly subsumed by the demands of capital. Mostly populated by critical essays assaying the fields of scholarly writing on the subject, books such as *Joy Forever: The Political Economy of Social Creativity* "scrutinize creativity as an ideology of cognitive capitalism," painting a picture of an uncontested discursive terrain, usually without a basis in empirical observation.[5] Among the more ethnographically grounded critiques, Angela McRobbie treats "creativity" as a *dispositif*, or self-regulating apparatus of social control, in *Be Creative*. Rather than direct control, capital supposedly relies upon dispositions that workers bring to the workplace, and so McRobbie argues that education programs in the arts which focus on "creative entrepreneurship" function as disciplinary vectors that supposedly propel young people to pursue precarious careers in the culture industries.[6] Disciplined by education, management supposedly needs only to invite workers to "be creative." This dovetails with research in sociology and business studies that suggests a diminished need for managers to actively control and discipline workers in the culture industries.[7] Dispositions formed via education or social milieu supposedly do much of the ideological and disciplinary functions traditionally associated with management.

In the other major critique, researchers highlight how "creativity" functions as an exclusionary discourse used by dominant groups to exclude along standard sociological fault lines such as class, gender, race, ethnicity, location, and occupation.[8] This critique dovetails quite clearly with an extensive body of research dating back at least as far the 1970s, when the early "Birmingham School" sought to highlight the "irreverent" creativity of working-class youth and Black communities in Britain. In more contemporary discussions focused on labor, "creativity" and "innovation" appear as universalizing ideologies of the Global North, which symbolically exclude the creative labor of workers in the Global South.[9] The labor of marginalized groups, though integral to culture industries and the tech sector, tends often to be unrecognized, such as in celebratory writings about the "creative class," which tend to ignore the physical and emotional labor, often performed by women and people of color, upon which creative labor depends.

While I touch upon the latter of these two critiques throughout this book, my primary aim is to expand upon claims that "creativity" functions as an ideological mechanism of control. These two critiques of creativity focus on two sides of the same ideological coin. If the second critique highlights how creativity operates as a universalizing discourse to the exclusion of marginalized groups, then the first highlights the degree to which this discourse operates upon privileged workers in the Global North, controlling their creative labor. Workers supposedly consent to precarity and participate in their own exploitation because they aspire toward "creativity," hegemonic and singular, cutting across the class lines of labor and capital. Instead, I find workers' understandings to be quite varied, differing from management yet far from innocent. When discussing creativity, workers draw upon romantic and universalizing discourses of autonomy and godlike power, often ignoring their actual social dependence.

Management invites routine workers (i.e., office staff) to engage in a sort of instrumentalized pragmatism and offers expressive workers (i.e., on-screen talent and music production personnel) the "freedom" to work. I call management's discursive and interactional practices *the managerial invitation*, one that needs to be accepted if workers wish to remain employed. Alongside management's open call for "creativity," workers in digital media receive another invitation from YouTube—one of many "platforms" that increasingly mediate everyday social interactions as well as markets for cultural products, labor, and services.[10] Platforms like YouTube tend to be owned and operated by capitalist organizations, and so the platforms' owners—as capital—possess interests separate from both workers and their managers in downstream firms. Thus, platforms each provide distinctive, structured invitations to particular sorts of activity, which

I identify as a heteronymous, or other-oriented, entrepreneurialism that stands in contrast to the sort of visionary autonomy usually ascribed to entrepreneurs and artists.[11]

Workers' accounts of "creativity," universalizing though they might be, illustrate class divisions, suggesting a slippage or gap in meanings between labor and capital. Because of this classed gap in meaning, I argue that the theorizations discussed in chapter 1 regarding how workers consent and become attached to their precarious jobs provide incomplete explanations. These incomplete explanations emphasize belief or ideology rather than labor's material experiences. As I show, many workers' accounts of creativity revolve around tasks performed during the working day, and so this chapter sets the stage for parts 2 and 3, where I argue that the material, sensual experience of work provides something of a temporary fix, papering over this gap.

A BRIEF GENEALOGY OF CREATIVITY

When I asked people what they meant by "creativity," their responses did not emerge from thin air. Managers and workers alike often paused before responding—an indication that they lacked a well-rehearsed answer. After gathering their thoughts, they offered up definitions steeped in the oft-criticized, universalizing definitions of creativity found in Western philosophical and religious traditions as well as social theory and contemporary managerial scholarship. To draw this out more clearly, I want to begin with a brief genealogy of creativity. My goal is not to lock down the term in some operational definition but to sketch a few distinct ways that creativity has been imagined. I do so to better understand the broader discursive field from which the classed accounts of managers, workers, and platform emerge.

It should come as no surprise that the word "creative" comes from the word "creator," usually of the divine variety. After all, most world religions contain some sort of origin myth, often one involving an original act of cosmological creation. In Christianity and Judaism, for example, the first creative act preceded the oft-studied social processes of naming and classification—a power, according to this particular myth, bestowed upon humankind by a benevolent creator. Creativity remained the sole possession of divine beings or heavenly creators until relatively recently.[12] For example, humans remained creatures—the created—in the English language up until the sixteenth century, and in German, the words "creative" and "creativity" retained their strictly religious connotations until the early twentieth century.[13] Creativity's divine associations live on among many of my informants, but, of course, other metaphors abound.

Hans Joas identifies four modes or metaphors for creativity that include expression, revolution, and production.[14] Production tends to be most clearly associated with work and, for Joas, the writing of Karl Marx. In Marx, creativity appears nowhere as a core conceptual term; however, Marx did claim that to be human is to be diversely and indeterminately *productive*. As he said in his *Economic and Philosophical Manuscripts*, "an animal forms things in accordance with the standard and the need of the species to which it belongs, whilst man knows how to produce in accordance with the standard of every species, and knows how to apply everywhere the inherent standard to the object. Man therefore also forms thing in accordance with the laws of beauty."[15] Put differently, the capacity to be creative—in the sense of performing a diverse array of actions in order to satisfy one's needs or the needs of others—is a fundamental, essential aspect of being human. Though we might debate whom Marx included under the category of "man" or "humanity," his definition seems aimed at highlighting the diversity of human potential. Humanity may be special because of our potential for following the "laws of beauty," but that potential appears as a generic and nonspecific capacity of humans.

Marx assigned neither rarefied status nor emancipatory promise to what we now call cultural production or "creative" work. Bailing hay, lifting pig iron, refining coal into coke, or producing a painting all appear as potentially creative activities, and all appear equally human for Marx insofar as they represent the diverse array of activities in which humans may engage. In Marx, humanity's natural inclination toward creativity, one dominated by capitalism, requires emancipation, but creativity does not, itself, provide for emancipation. The problem, for Marx, appears in dividing labor, compartmentalizing activities so as to remove or require just a portion of an individual's capacities to create, invent, devise, and perform diverse production processes. This much appears in the famous and oft-quoted passage in *The German Ideology* wherein Marx outlines a communist style of life in which humans might one day "hunt in the morning, fish in the afternoon, rear cattle in the evening, [and] criticize after dinner."[16] Whether it be Braverman's deskilling thesis or the consumption-as-resistance theorized by the Birmingham School,[17] the lack or abundance of creativity appears as a central theme in twentieth-century Marxian social science.

This brings me to expression, another major metaphor for creativity highlighted by Joas and more explicitly theorized by John Dewey, who placed everyday expression (e.g., speech, communicative interactions) along a continuum with and thus of a kind with creative expression embodied in objects (i.e., art and other forms of material culture). Expression, argued Dewey, begins from an "impulsion,"[18] some feeling had in relation to one's environment that provokes an emotional response. A simple, knee-jerk response does not, according to Dewey, constitute an expression so much as a simple release, a sloughing off of feeling. "A gush of tears may bring relief, a spasm of destruction may give outlet to inward rage. But where there is no administration of objective conditions, no shaping of materials in the interest of embodying the excitement, there is no expression."[19]

For Dewey, creative expression required additional work, distancing one's self from and reflecting upon an initial provoking or impelling sensation. "Between conception and bringing to birth there lies a long period of gestation."[20] Privileging reason or rationality, he claimed that without this reflection through which the actor develops an in-order-to motive and a plan for embedding an idea into some interactional or artistic medium (e.g., words, gestures, paint, clay, etc.), there is no creative expression, simply socioculturally structured reflex. Dewey's expression requires judgment, or what Kant described as the mediating reflection of "reason" upon inchoate sensation.[21] Setting aside Dewey's hierarchization of reflection over sense, I want to highlight how he portrays creative expression as generically human, something possessed by all—of course, some may be more skilled or better trained than others. Despite their philosophical differences, Marx's creative production seems rather similar to Dewey's creative expression.

The everydayness of creativity found in Dewey and Marx resonates with Raoul Vaneigem's *Revolution of Everyday Life*,[22] a book described by Luc Boltanski and Eve Chiapello as "the most concentrated version" of the "artistic critique" of capitalism.[23] This artistic critique focuses on capitalism's supposed lack of "meaning" and "authenticity." According to

Boltanski and Chiapello, capitalism's recuperation of the artistic critique led to the contemporary demands of cognitive capitalism: heightened worker participation and required creativity. Even if he mostly concerns himself with the loss of meaning and lack of "authenticity,"[24] Vaneigem's version of creativity appears remarkably similar to Marx's productive activity.[25] For example, Vaneigem says, "People usually associate creativity with works of art, but what are works of art alongside the creative energies displayed by everyone a thousand times a day?"[26] Vaneigem's examples of everyday creativity include daydreams, unsatisfied yearnings, and spontaneous acts of expression that either result in the revolutionary building of a "passionate life" or are channeled into consumption and self-destruction.[27] Despite Boltanski and Chiapello's claim that Vaneigem exemplifies a heightened individualism, Vaneigem and others in his milieu, such as Guy Debord, called for the *collective* production of new ways of living.[28] Like Marx and Dewey, Vaneigem's creativity appears as a generic, human capacity, but, like Marx, Vaneigem finds creativity everywhere bound by the demands of capitalist production and consumption.[29] In this variant, creativity appears as a common, generic human potential. While these authors' social positions as educated, white men certainly shaped and even limited their perspectives, I want to highlight how theirs is a discourse that brings creativity down from the heavens to the level of the everyday.

This everydayness appears absent in Joseph Schumpeter's discussion of entrepreneurs and Theodor Adorno's discussion of "autonomous" artists. Though at first glance this might seem an odd pairing, their portrayals of entrepreneurs and artists share a common understanding of creativity as socially transformative and, potentially, emancipatory. In *Capitalism, Socialism, and Democracy*, Schumpeter refers to entrepreneurs as "geniuses" and "visionaries," presumably great men of industry, willing "to die if necessary" on the steps of their factories, who represent the "small fraction of the population" capable of envisioning a world beyond that which exists. In Schumpeter's writing, the decidedly male entrepreneur dashes off to create new markets, believing in his (and this is certainly a masculine imagining of creativity) vision of a business plan beyond the "familiar beacons" of routine production while risking financial ruin and physical attack.[30] As competitive capitalism gave way to monopoly capitalism, argued Schumpeter, so too went the entrepreneurial spirit and the potential for radical, transformative, capitalist creativity.[31] For Schumpeter, creativity provides critical redress to an otherwise boring world, a rare capability that leads to socioeconomic transformation ("creative destruction"). Taken as such, Schumpeter's entrepreneurial critique of monopoly capitalism bears more than a passing likeness to Boltanski and Chiapello's "artistic critique," but Schumpeter's creativity significantly differs from Vaneigem's. Rather than a basic feature of humanity, Schumpeter's creativity is possessed by only a select few, most often male, *capitalist entrepreneurs* capable of envisioning a world beyond. As unlikely as it might seem, Schumpeter's entrepreneur bears more of a likeness to Theodor Adorno's discussions of autonomous artists than to Vaneigem's "artistic critique." For Adorno, art—often "autonomous" or avant-garde art—provided critique through a negative vision of utopia.[32] This understanding aligns reasonably well with contemporary imaginings of creativity and the role of the arts in social change. For example, Nigel Thrift and Ash Amin consider the envisioning of a world beyond that which exists to be a lost "art" of leftist social movements—what Stefan Nowotny calls "cre-activity."[33]

Considered together, the scholars discussed here illustrate two of three variants, the generic and the transformational. A third variant—what the communication scholar Marc Deuze calls the "rational" approach— presents creativity as both rarefied and pragmatic: the skillset of the "creative class" or workers in information, technology, research, finance, and entertainment. This appears in Richard Florida's writings, where the "creative class" produces "new forms and designs that are readily transferable and widely useful" or, alternatively, engages in "creative problem solving." Far from being possessed by all, creativity must be learned or, as he says, it comprises "distinct habits of mind and patterns of behavior that must be cultivated on both an individual basis and in the surrounding society."[34] In this line of thought, creativity improves society not through transformation, as in Schumpeter or Adorno, but through what the organizational psychologist Theresa Amabile and her coauthors call "the production of novel, useful ideas or problem solutions. [Creativity] refers to both the process of idea generation or problem solving and the actual idea or solution."[35] What these two rather different scholars share is a vision of instrumental creativity, one aimed at providing "novel, useful" solutions to organizational problems.[36]

Intended *for* management, research and theory operating under this definition of creativity tend to focus on workers' efficacy in producing controlled novelty in the service of capital. In this light, one might interpret Amabile and Florida as part of what the sociologist Pascal Gielen describes as the discourse by which "neoliberalism makes us believe that change is in itself morally and operationally *good*."[37] By and large, the measurable, calculable, and ultimately subordinate creativity described by Florida and managerial scholars dovetails quite neatly with what Hans Joas and his colleagues call an instrumental and reductive pragmatism. This reductive understanding treats creativity as mere "problem solving . . . a very trivial thing."[38]

Returning to this chapter's central question, what do workers mean when they speak of their creativity? Recent theorizations of creative labor under cognitive capitalism suggest that workers and managers share a common discourse of instrumentalized pragmatism. For example, the sociologist Pascal Gielen argues that "cognitive" capitalism invites "creativity without substance . . . stripped of its critical potential"[39] because capital demands an instrumental pragmatism rather than the singular, imaginative, and critical dimension of creativity found in Schumpeter and Adorno. For Gielen, the neoliberal creativity, or "creativism," of teams and the postbureaucratic, networked production found in the culture industries effectively shuts down the possibility of Schumpeterian entrepreneurs or Adornian artists through the discipline of teams and expanded forms of quantification and measurement.[40] For Gielin, the goal of management becomes ensuring that "all creativity is also at least 'lu-creativity' [lucrative creativity]."[41] Similarly, Angela McRobbie argues that educational programs comprise part of a *dispositif*, or self-regulating apparatus of control by training students to become "creative entrepreneurs."[42] As in much sociological theorizing of freelance contractors or "boundaryless" work,[43] disciplining or controlling labor appears less a task for management and more a function of ideology and dispositions learned and formed before entry into the workplace. The *dispositif* of creativity supposedly regulates behavior, eliciting effort in the pursuit of symbolic capital or prestige and psychic rewards.[44] This performs much the same function as the "art for art's sake" *illusio* in Bourdieuian research of creative labor.[45] These theorizations suggest a shared understanding of creativity across classes, and so one might expect to find identical or similar accounts of creativity among workers and the organizations that consume their labor. Instead, I find considerable variation, which I now illustrate beginning with the managerial point of view.

MANAGEMENT'S "CREATIVITY"

When I first met one of SoniCo's owners, he described the recording studio as "a truly *creative* space" for his clients and employees. Specifically referencing books such as *Learning from Las Vegas*[46] and Richard Florida's *Rise of the Creative Class*, he said that both the studio's interior design and the building's exterior represented a "critical mass of creativity" that lay within. SoniCo's brochure described the facility as a "creative space that feels creative," inviting clients to rehearse and record music in the studio's "magical" rooms. Later, he told me that he tried to make employees "feel creative" at work. Expanding upon this statement, he said, "We just really have to encourage creativity in the work environment." His managerial strategy included "managing people in a way that they *feel* empowered and are empowered on some level, but still things get done that need to get done" (emphasis added).

So how did he ensure that things "get done?" SoniCo's owner-managers tended to be physically absent from the workplace, leaving day-to-day oversight to supervisory employees. These workers were advised to "take ownership" and use their departments as vehicles for their "creativity." As one manager said, "Instead of believing that I know the best way to get things done, I'd rather give them goals. Okay, your division needs to cover its expenses and be profitable." He further elaborated, describing an anti-managerial approach to management:

> I respect the fact that most people don't like being managed. That's part of the hiring process. I'm trying to ascertain, "is this someone that can really take ownership of their job, or is this a guy that the second something goes wrong they're going to pick up the phone and call me?" That's not helping anybody. Those two things: the hiring and the managing are really tied to that personality type. [I'm looking for a person] who can be a fixer.

In practical terms, managers granted supervisory employees authority over day-to-day operational decisions and control over the material arrangement and adornment of organizational spaces.

All said, SoniCo's management afforded workers a good deal of autonomy in the execution of tasks and completion of projects. This applied "directly" to supervisors and indirectly to their subordinates. As one supervisor said, "The whole business feels a little bit more like a partnership than an owner/employee relationship." He then explained how he and the other managers built relationships and invited employees to participate:

> One thing that has been awesome about working at SoniCo, since the day I got started there, is if somebody has a really good idea, then you never get brushed off, you know? For instance, you mentioned the ads [for services offered], which is a simple thing we have to do every few months. One of the owners could just go ahead and make a decision; he does design. He could just tell us this is the ad this month or we'd just see it in the newspaper and be like, "oh I guess that's how we're going to advertise right now." But instead, he'll send an email to the two other owners and the two supervisors, me and Robert. He's basically like, "we need a new ad, what should we do?"

While management "could" produce these materials on their own, they invited employees to complete this task and thus invited them to be creative in accomplishing organizational projects.

Similarly, The Future's managers expressed a desire for self-governing, instrumentally pragmatic employees. Requiring workers to engage in what labor scholars call responsible autonomy, management expected workers who would manage themselves while also being adaptable, inventive, and capable of anticipating managerial needs[47] or, to quote one of The Future's job advertisements, "manage up." These abilities—hallmarks of what Paolo Virno calls the "virtuosity" of workers under cognitive capitalism[48]—depend upon cognitive-linguistic skills, capacities for creative labor developed over the course of workers' diverse, socially patterned biographies. These demands, however inviting they might seem, ultimately conceal class divisions between managers and workers as well as a clear gender hierarchy, which I discuss in more detail in chapter 6.

Like SoniCo, The Future's managers attempted to compel routine workers to "be creative" with minimal, direct supervision. They tended to frame this approach as necessary for their ever-evolving organizational structure and their intention to phase out rigid hierarchies and titles. SoniCo and

The Future were both relatively "flat" firms, with minimal hierarchies save for the division between executives or owners and everyone else, suggestive of a need for more expansive and inclusive class typologies, ones that include white-collar professionals as part of the working class.[49]

More importantly, this situation said something about how management envisioned themselves as antimanagement, as open and inviting. For example, The Future's hiring manager introduced himself in a meeting by saying, "Titles, titles, I'm bad with those, but I'm one of those hippie people that thinks people should be known as who they are and understood to be good at whatever it is they do." A former business consultant, this "hippie" sought to construct a new work environment where "hierarchies are less important. It's not a factory." Unhappy with the rigidity of titles and roles, his face soured when I asked if he handled the organization's "HR," or human resource, functions. "You don't like that term?" I asked. "No," he said firmly, his lips curling downward as he rolled his eyes. Initially he preferred "People and Organization" but later changed his title to manager of "Workplace Experience" or head of the WE team. Managers with whom I spoke often echoed the WE leader, frequently reminding me that we were not in a "factory." Often, they voiced a desire to phase out hierarchy, while acknowledging clear, often rigid divisions between executives or "C-Suite" and the rest of the staff. He said, "You're important if you have an office, but to attract the talent we're looking for, we're going to need to move away from that." As he explained, "Openness is good for being flexible."

So how did management engage workers in this "open" organization? Ironically, many "open" managers refused when I asked if I could record our conversations,[50] so I took copious notes during our talks. One manager said that he could not afford to be "precious about structure." Instead, he said that the firm provided "exoskeletons," offering workers the autonomy and freedom needed to improvise. In this way, he claimed to "empower" employees by removing controls, removing managers, and allowing workers to manage their time and resources "on the fly." In doing so, he explained that the company hoped to motivate people to "be creative"—a phrase he emphasized multiple times. Another manager at The Future did not want "rank-and-file follow-orders" employees. He wanted "real ambition." Rather than direct orders, he set goals and aimed to provide the resources needed to meet said goals—not unlike the aforementioned "exoskeletons." Keep in mind that biological exoskeletons both support and constrain an assemblage of organs, suggestive of an enabling, technological form of control. Speaking specifically about working in a global company with employees around the world in different time zones, the manager said,

> I don't really care what time they're in the office so long as, if there's a meeting we have set, you're there for the meeting. But, if you're coming up with your own path that's delivering successes, let's make sure that our structure accommodates that. The biggest issue is when somebody is not coming in on time and they're also not hitting their goals. Then it's like, well now I need to babysit you because you're not doing what you're supposed to *and* you're not accomplishing anything.

Ever the considerate manager, he wondered "is there something that I did wrong" when his subordinates failed. A man who left a successful career in a more lucrative profession[51] so that he could "have an adventure" and do "something more creative" ended up at The Future in an undefined, ad hoc position. He handled a wide range of tasks, such as analyzing revenue data, arranging merchandise production, and, occasionally, casting and managing digital video shoots. Was this creative work? He thought so, but he never felt sure where to focus his efforts, so he asked his boss for direction. The boss's response? "Just pick a lane." In other words, he had to "be creative" and devise his own job while ensuring that his actions produced profits for the firm.

Another manager's demand for "passion" echoed all the reminders I had heard about not being in a "factory." As she said, "You're not just on an assembly line. Like, you have to have passion to get it done right, because I'm not going to be breathing down your neck. I don't have time." Indeed, one is not on the assembly line. Rather than the deadening rhythms of technical control,[52] this manager relied upon the visceral, affective prod of "passion" to goad workers toward organizational goals. Beyond passion, her desired worker had to be willing and capable of performing ad hoc duties that might not strictly be associated with a particular position. As she explained, "It's really important to be flexible. I'm supposed to be the director, but I'm uploading videos or [handling] duties that others consider to be administrator or assistant duties." Another manager referred to this as being a "chameleon," capable of running errands one day and crafting an executive presentation the next.

Given these common themes of "not having time" to "babysit" or "breathe down workers' necks," I often wondered what, if anything, managers do. Aside from setting goals, much of management's work seemed to revolve around managing how workers feel. As another manager explained, he attempts to "empower" employees so that they feel valued:

That's kind of, my management style is like, a lot of things aren't going to go right, but that doesn't mean I'm going to think of you less. And if I not only empower you but make you feel valued, it's going to make me look better in the long run anyway, right? This is really the bottom line. So that's why I never understood people that are nasty to their employees.

Another claimed to take a caring approach to his employees, offering conversations about employees' progress toward organizational goals, never outright accusing employees of failure. As he said, "You gotta have the first meeting, and the first meeting is figuring out, is there something that I as a manager am not providing you? Is there something that's impeding you from being successful in the process?" He explained how this might go on for several meetings before deciding that all options had been exhausted and letting the employee go. This strategy of conversation and negotiation with employees further blurred distinctions between boss and friend. Other managers with whom I spoke played videogames with their employees to "bond," fulfilling much the same function. At both SoniCo and The Future, social interactions between managers and employees obscure traditional class divisions, and so workers perceived any social distance between themselves and management as less salient than might be expected.

These statements from managers reveal a striking similarity in approach. They described their ideal employees in much the same terms as managerial scholars who discuss creativity as "useful" and oriented toward organizational problems—what I term "instrumental pragmatism." When management speaks of creativity, they speak of instrumental pragmatism, which they expected and invited from office staff and content producers ("creators") with whom the firm held contracts. In addition to management's invitation, these creators receive an invitation from global capital or, more specifically, YouTube, a global production and distribution platform.

"DARE TO BE YOU" ON THE PLATFORM

YouTube creators whom I met while researching this book produced within and for a platform while also producing under contract with The Future. This structural difference sets them apart from workers in conventional culture industries and results in creators being invited to "be creative" by both The Future's management and global capital (i.e., Google/Alphabet). The goals of platforms and the people and organizations who use them rarely align,[53] so, if management at SoniCo and The Future wanted instrumentalized pragmatism, what did YouTube want?

Figure 2.1 shows one of YouTube's billboard advertisements, a common sight in Los Angeles. I came across this one in Marina del Rey—a few miles from "Silicon Beach," home to a Google campus and a concentration of smaller tech startups in West LA. YouTube's advertisement invites potential producers to "dare to be" their authentic selves. This suggests that Tyler Oakley—one of the most famous and financially successful YouTube creators—dares to be himself and is successful, just as you might be if you use YouTube. Another billboard referred to the platform as "Where

FIGURE 2.1 One of YouTube's many public invitations to be creative in West Los Angeles.

the Self Made Make It!" Notably, the value of this supposedly self-made authenticity may be rather precisely measured. Unlike advertisements for film or television that might make appeals to quality based upon awards or the praise of critics, YouTube displays a more precise measure of value: "7,278,892 Fans." This number refers to the number of "subscribers" to Tyler Oakley's YouTube channel as of the advertisement's printing.

These advertisements are just one of many invitations from the platform to potential creators to provide a creativity oriented toward audiences and an established market—what Pierre Bourdieu termed "heteronymous" cultural production—rather than toward other, perhaps artistic, considerations. For Bourdieu, cultural producers followed some combination of heteronymous and autonomous logics. The former refers to cultural producers who orient their actions toward established market demands, catering to audiences of consumers. In contrast, producers following an autonomous logic orient, primarily, toward valuations specific to their particular fields (e.g., awards, critical praise, admiration of peers, etc.). The advertisement portrays Tyler Oakley's content as valuable thanks to its measurable popularity, a stark difference in comparison to ads for films and television shows that highlight favorable reviews from critics or award nominations. Subscriber counts and other metrics such as views and minutes watched, or "watch time," translate rather directly into an income for both the platform and the content creators. Essentially working for a piece rate based on advertising revenues, creators receive a variable rate per one thousand views (CPM, or cost-per-mille), from which YouTube and The Future take a cut—keep in mind that YouTube's parent company (Google/Alphabet) is the world's largest seller of advertising.[54]

Taking this into consideration, YouTube, The Future, and creators have clear economic interests in generating as many views as possible. YouTube offers a whole series of training programs designed to aid creators in the generation of views. The Future respectively requires and strongly encourages routine employees and their thousands of creators to enroll in these online courses. In one such course, YouTube provides a strategic program by which creators may manage their emotional investment in content production while maintaining a steady production schedule. YouTube tells creators, "If your content is engaging, our discovery systems will handle the rest." YouTube's search algorithm is designed to "surface [find] content that keeps viewers engaged, not just good-looking content."

As part of the advice on how best to match content to the platform's algorithms, the training programs revolve around the creation of a personal brand. This includes advice to "think like a TV programmer" by creating content that is shareable, accessible, collaborative or interactive (i.e., inviting audience participation such as sharing, clicking, liking, commenting, etc.), discoverable (i.e., searchable), conversational, targeted, and consistent. For each attribute, YouTube provides "best practices" based, presumably, on internal behavioral research and knowledge of their proprietary and, for those downstream, largely unknowable algorithms. For example, YouTube advised creators to involve their viewers in promoting content by including a cursory course in a sort of pop anthropology. Specifically citing Patrick Hanlon's book *Primal Branding*, YouTube's training videos explained that "deep down everyone wants to belong" and that viewers want to belong to creators' brand communities.[55] According to the training video, such a community requires, a "creation story" or "authentic" narrative of the creator, a "creed" or "higher purpose" to inspire fans, "leadership" or charismatic authority, "ritual" or repeated elements in video content, and "language" or a brand-specific argot that supposedly allows fans to "feel like insiders."

These guidelines invite an entrepreneurial creativity, a pitch to potential creators that bears more than a passing resemblance to the sort of mass entrepreneurship offered by labor platforms such as Uber.[56] Of course, these invitations to entrepreneurship differ from the sort of macho visionaries portrayed by Joseph Schumpeter, and YouTube's encouragement to follow the numbers seems a far cry from Adorno's lofty discussion of "autonomous" artists. Different as they might be, Schumpeter and Adorno both spoke of creativity as socially transformative. In contrast, YouTube and managers seem rather drab and banal, content with problem solving and increasing the number of eyeballs drawn to screens through self-branding.

WORKERS' CREATIVITIES

If the tamed creativities espoused by managers and the platform fail to thrill, workers were both more vivid and more uncertain in their accounts of creativity. Even though workers used the term "creativity" all the time, most had difficulty pinning down what they meant by it. They laughed, perhaps nervously, or said "that's a good question" before a long pause and, finally, an answer. The meaning of "creativity" seemed equally puzzling to those whom I had known for years, months, weeks, or just a few hours. Creativity seemed a peculiar thing, meaning both too much and too little when prodded and probed. Workers often found it easier to explain what made their jobs creative—typically the day-to-day tasks of work—but here I focus on the ways that they understand the meaning of creativity before providing a fuller rendering of their everyday experiences in parts 2 and 3. In what follows, I illustrate two rather colorful ways that workers commonly discussed creativity and their less common adoption of management's instrumentalized pragmatism.

The Many Little Gods

YouTube creators and audio engineers often attempted to define creativity by referring to the act of creation—suggesting godlike powers. Felix, a recording engineer, said:

> Well, okay. So, it's like—it's fairly easy to explain. It's like there's—today is Monday, 10:44 a.m., okay? In three hours, a new song will be coming into existence. This particular song doesn't exist today, right now. It will exist in three hours when we start the session. You create something, that's creativity. And I get amazed still to these days whenever I realize at the end of the day, wow, this thing didn't exist eight hours ago and now we're all here, singing along, or, you know, it creates an energy that's undeniable. I mean, you can't say it's, "Oh, it doesn't affect people." It does. And if you think about how a few hours before, the day before, it wasn't there, it's weird because sometimes you—I listen to songs in the studio, and it feels like, oh, I feel like this has always been a song. It's always been there, it's natural. You know, you don't think that minds come together, came together maybe, to create that.

Felix saw creativity rather romantically as making something that did not previously exist. To borrow from the book of Genesis, the studio had been silent, formless, and void until Felix arrived for work. After creation, his creature (the song) confronted him as something alien—not alienating, but external, a magical or fetish object brought into being from the unordered chaos he found in the studio that morning.

"*Creation*! It's channeled creation. This is a taste of the beyond. Art is a taste of the beyond," exclaimed another recording engineer. Sitting in his studio, surrounded by comic books and the blinking LEDs of recording equipment, he said, "I'm trying to experience that god stuff here. Is it creative work? It is creation! There was nothing here when I woke up. That used to freak me out. I used to go to the studio and think I'm going to write a beat and I'm going to sell it. That beat doesn't exist yet! Where does it come from? You know what I mean?" Creating or conjuring some *thing* from "beyond," from the void, this engineer thought of himself as a channel for the godly powers of media production technologies—something of a frightening, exhilarating experience that hints at the sorts of enchantments I will describe in later chapters.

According to Peter, a YouTube creator and technology entrepreneur, "You have to conjure things out of thin air." Echoing Schumpeter's imagined entrepreneur, he elaborated, "That's essentially, if you're creating content, you're literally creating something out of nothing. I would also say it takes creativity to put the pieces together on the business side. You have to think about things that maybe other people aren't seeing the connections. Use your instincts, put them together, and make it work. That seems to go OK for me." Peter demonstrates the romantic ex nihilo explanation of creativity but includes "business" in his definition. One must be able to conjure, to use one's instincts in order to see "connections" that remain unseen—to envision a world beyond what exists. Peter's explanation includes something akin to the critical entrepreneurial and artistic creativities noted earlier and thus suggests an association between contemporary discourses of artistic and entrepreneurial creativities. Likewise, Kevin—another YouTube creator—said, "You know, entrepreneurship is creative work because you don't have a blueprint for success."

Harvey echoed Peter's sentiment, offering an equally esoteric description of imagination and conjuring:

I guess like being able to execute some sort of inspiration or coming up with something out of thin air that wasn't there before. It could be a song, painting, poem, whatever. I think everything is creative in some way. We're seeing shit being created all the time. Even real-estate developers, I guess.

We could call them creative. They're imagining a condo development being on this property that they demolished or whatever. In terms of music, I guess, just being inspired by some idea and making it into something.

In these accounts, creative workers describe both business development and artistry as of a kind; however, Harvey expressed some hesitation ("I guess"), voicing an unease with "business" or "the biz," which he imagined as a music industry executive. Peter described an earlier part of his career as follows:

Back in my hometown, having that indie rock, '90s, underground punk, whatever you want to call it, that way of doing music, it's definitely not cemented [in] any music biz label relationships. Even when I came to LA, I was still thinking that way. Like working with some band, yeah, the label guy wants to come by and listen to the mixes. The A&R [artists and repertoire executive] guy wants to come and play what we've been working on. I'd be like, "man, this ain't no jukebox. Fuck *that* guy. We'll send him the CD when we're done," kind of thing. That's all well and good but in LA that shit doesn't fly. You can't be a dick like that.

Unlike Peter, Harvey did not identify as an entrepreneur. He had to learn to accept the point of view of "the biz"—half-heartedly acknowledging the creative role of the entrepreneur. On the other hand, Peter—a YouTube creator and technology entrepreneur—identified both business dealings and video production as creative, expressive actions. For him, both required an imagining of as-yet-unseen potentials and possibilities in order to call forth an object into existence. His discussion of creation ex nihilo comprises a double act of imagination and conjuring or calling forth. As Tammy, a YouTube creator said, "I think [creativity is] having a thought and creating something with that thought into a tangible thing."

While these examples highlight the belief in creation from nothing, other workers defined creativity as involving the reinterpretation and rearticulation of preexisting objects. Wanda, the only female recording engineer with whom I spoke, said, "Creativity to me means the ability to play and literally generate newness or generate deviations of like one singular thing into a multiplicity of other things. Yeah. I guess that's kind of a generic, creationist definition of creativity [laughing]. I didn't mean it that way before I said it, but I guess it's applicable." Rather than creation ex nihilo, Wanda described her process as the production of difference, wherein a "singular" object becomes a "multiplicity" through human intervention. Likewise, Lucy, an office worker at The Future, recognized the necessity of preexisting materials. She began by likening creativity to creation but added, "Being creative isn't necessarily always building things from scratch. It's building upon basic ideas that other people have already founded, and it's the sharing of culture and visual mediums and music and all sorts of other different forms of media." For them, one creates by bringing some *thing* into the world, but this creation builds upon available cultural and material resources within a particular historical constellation.

Though these examples all came from expressive workers, office staff who had educational backgrounds in fine art or media production offered similar responses. For example, Jeff—one of SoniCo's office employees with a background in audio engineering—said, creativity is about "creative possibilities. You know, anything. Like, it doesn't matter. To me it's just building something out of nothing." Jeff, unlike the expressive workers, sees his job as "not a bit" creative. As he said, "I think you are facilitating creativity through these jobs." Miles, another of SoniCo's office workers, also provided an ex nihilo definition. "You know, [you can do] anything. Like, it doesn't matter. To me it's just building something out of nothing."

It is worth noting that the least godlike versions of creation ex nihilo came from women. While all suggested a struggle to wrest form from some abyssal void, men seemed less likely to acknowledge how the ability to pursue their personal *chaoskampfs*[57] depended upon unevenly distributed resources and socially produced tools. That men might describe themselves this way comes as no surprise. Despite their godly inclinations, workers did not produce their statements ex nihilo. They relied on ready-to-hand ideas that include the discourses of creativity I outlined earlier as well as romantic myths of (often male) artists, lone geniuses, or visionaries. Even if workers' understandings diverged from those promoted by management and the platform, these ways of thinking about creativity illustrate a way by which male "creatives" might ignore their dependence upon others at both the local and global levels.[58]

Measured against the power of a god, most "creative" work falls short, yet management still claimed to invite workers to "be creative." As one of SoniCo's owners said, "For better or for worse, my managerial style is to provide guidelines and encourage creativity in work. Even if it's a failure. It's the one thing that I value." He might have offered them practical problem solving while YouTube offered a chance at entrepreneurship, but workers believed themselves to be little gods. Between these competing discourses, there remains a gap, a chasm between capital and labor.

It's All About the Freedom, Right?

When not invoking the divine, workers described creativity as autonomous expression, what many called "freedom." As a content creator in the western United States said, "The limitless freedom of creation. Just being like today I can make whatever I want and it can be, can come from all these different worlds, can create all these different worlds, and it can lead to another thing, and I just love, like, not knowing what I'm going to do tomorrow and not knowing what I'm going to do today."

Likewise, a video blogger from the eastern United States said that for him, creativity "means expressing myself in the way that I know best whether it's through words or sights or music." Moreover, he enjoyed creating content because it allows him to use his "creative freedom whenever" he desired. Similarly, a YouTube blogger who aspired to work as a screenwriter defined creativity as "happiness" before adding, "I think freedom maybe? [long pause] If I were living in a poor country, I could never do this, so, freedom." Like others, he described creativity as a sort of free, limitless expression while also, perhaps superficially, noting his relatively privileged position as a U.S. citizen working full time as a YouTube creator.

The meaning of autonomous expression differed a bit for Kevin—a thirty-something on the East Coast who made YouTube content with his wife in the evenings after they came home from their day jobs and had put their children to bed. He said, "The opposite of creativity is having rules that tell you exactly what to do and you simply go about that." He went on to explain that companies known for rigid rules such as McDonalds are "phenomenal" because they allow anyone to "do something amazing because they don't have to be creative about the work." As he explained, "You're told 'no you put the hamburger together like this and you make the milkshakes like this and you do this and this.' . . . The creativity, I believe, is just the exact opposite. Look, here's all this stuff [makes circular gesture with hands], make me something awesome. Figure that out and then just come back and show me something. I think that ultimately creativity is undirected, creation of something unique kind of a thing." Rules may allow anyone to provide "phenomenal" food or customer service, but according to Kevin, rules do not facilitate creativity. As with management, Kevin draws a line between his creative activities and those in other, more regimented forms of work (i.e., "not a factory" or "not on the assembly line"). To be creative is to work autonomously without direction and create "something awesome." Similar to other content creators located outside of major production hubs, Kevin viewed his work as a content producer as a potential means of escape from the doldrums of office life. Referring to the work he and his wife do on YouTube, Kevin said, "We know that this is what will get us out of that because we believe that starting our own business [as drone videographers] will give us opportunities that we seek and that we want to live and how we want to change things for our lives."

Though routine workers offered similar takes on creativity, they sometimes described their day-to-day tasks with less enthusiasm. James, a twenty-eight-year-old office worker at The Future, explained that for him, "True creativity is a boundless expression of the self, and that's not something that can ever exist in this context." Despite being asked to "be more creative" by his boss as he produced data-driven PowerPoint presentations ("decks"), James never saw his work as particularly creative, given the subordination of his labor to organizational goals:

> I guess it's hard for me to think of creativity in a professional context because ultimately everything I do is aimed at helping a company. Which is, if I stripped away the world and money wasn't a thing and all of these things that are required of me that inherently force you to have a line of work, I wouldn't be making things for The Future. I wouldn't be trying to be creative for this entity. . . . As creative as I can imagine a deck being, I don't know if it's something I would ever, like, tout as, like, "look at how creative I am." There's an element of creativity in it, but I don't perceive that as true creativity.

Educated in art history, James drew a sharp line between the sort of "lu-creativity" or instrumental pragmatism[59] on offer at The Future and the autonomous, disinterested expression he claimed as his.

Some among SoniCo's staff offered similar distinctions. For example, one employee defined creativity as "a level of freedom." Despite acknowledging his sizeable degree of autonomy at work, he said that in "[these] peripheral jobs, when someone's telling you what you need to do, yeah you're putting your touch on it or whatever, but I don't know if I would consider that necessarily creative." Jeff, another of SoniCo's staff, whom I introduced in chapter 1, drew a more forceful line between the instrumental pragmatism invited by management and what he deemed to be "true" creativity:

> [Creativity] means that you're willing to give up the ability to live a normal life to make actual, real money and to support any kind of family unless you're already well off and just decide well I'm stinking rich and I'm going to be creative and I'm going to be a rock star or a movie star. You're going to get in through your money. That's how it works now. Creative people? Do you know a lot of creative people that own their own homes? I mean, most of them are fucking drug addicts and drunks crawling around, got no money [pause] ever. You're always buying them a beer and, like, that guy's a talented motherfucker, but sadly he wasn't born into a rich family, so here we are at the bottom [laughing]. I hate to say it like that, but it's the truth.

Like SoniCo's other employees, Jeff barely earned enough to pay rent. Often from blue-collar backgrounds with high-school educations, he and his coworkers were "at the bottom" despite possessing "talent" and, in many cases, years of experience as musicians or audio engineers. Jeff indicates that his struggle to survive results from his understanding of what it means to "be creative," a product of his limitless expression without the support of wealth. Still, when discussing his working day, he complained about coworkers' lack of initiative in a way that more closely resembles the everyday creativity found in Marx, Vaneigem, and Dewey. Jeff told me that his coworker never bothered to learn how to fix anything around the studio—a core aspect of the job. "I mean, no one ever told her to, so you can't fault her, but if you're a competent human being, why not try? That's the beauty of being human, right?"

Both autonomous expression and creation ex nihilo refer to similarly individualistic, romantic accounts of creativity shot through with relations of power, most obviously gender and, more central to this discussion, class. These accounts reveal the continued cleavages between worker and manager, labor and capital. These two variants both include a distinction between autonomous and organizationally circumscribed or subordinated creative labor.[60] Considered against existing explanations as to why workers in the culture industries persist in precarious careers, this gap between these classed creativities suggests a need for closure, a binding of worker to work that ideology does not seem to perform. Before turning to this issue in the next chapter, I provide some examples of the few workers who seemed to share management's point of view.

The "Steven Spielberg of Airfare Booking"

A few workers fully adopted management's point of view as their own, voicing the sort of instrumentalized pragmatism one finds in management and business research. Most common among The Future's office workers, these descriptions of instrumentalized pragmatism appeared both less individualistic and, often, less critical when compared to the rather romantic ideas discussed earlier. For example, Albert, a "talent search specialist," or web-scraping talent scout, at The Future said, "Creativity to me means—that's such an interesting question—being able to work efficiently and in tandem with a like-minded person or group of people to reach a desirable result." Elaborating, Albert explained that "really creative people can work with anyone and anything and reach that desired result without any hiccups or issues along the way." Here, creativity includes smooth sociality, affability, and, perhaps most importantly, a "desired result" or goal—but neither divine touch nor autonomous, potentially critical expression. Freddie at The Future offered a similar response. As he explained, his work is creative insofar as his team "dictates creative" (i.e., content production) through data analysis. Though perhaps benevolent dictators, Freddie's team asked a simple, instrumental question: "Quite frankly, is something working, or is it not?" In answering this question, the team used data provided from YouTube and cloud-based systems such as Google Analytics, BentPixel, Social-Blade, and Comscore. With these numbers, Freddie could "look and see what content is working, what isn't. Even within that content that is working, how can we improve that? All of that is dictated by [our] quantitative research. But maybe in that same vein, you also have the qualitative aspects, you come out with by being agile and ready, you have to be able to think outside the box." Anchored to the numbers, he could—cliché as it may sound—"think outside the box." Phrases such as "agile and ready," "achieving goals," "teamwork," "solving problems," and "self-learning" were common to workers' accounts of instrumentalized pragmatism.

Desmond, another of The Future's office staff whom I introduced in the previous chapter, spent between eight and fourteen hours a day in front of a computer screen watching countless hours of YouTube content as a sort of digital talent scout. His eyes hurt by the end of the day. Through he mostly watched content that he personally disliked, he found his work enjoyable, even interesting. Why?

> Because it's not like, a cut and dry [sic] position. You can do whatever you want. It's like I'm getting involved with these guys and telling them what they should be producing and making and linking them up with other like-minded people that boost their popularity and their talents. Just like, being responsible for that and having that stuff happen. It's definitely a creative position because you're thinking of outside-the-box creative ways to like, make these people blow up.

Desmond described autonomy ("you can do whatever you want") as in the other workers' accounts, but he expressed his autonomy in reference to organizational goals. One thinks "outside the box" while working with a group ("these guys," "like-minded people") to generate increased revenue for The Future ("make these people blow up," or gain popularity as measured by the platform's metrics). Nothing earth shattering. No romance, and none of the unique "visions" or godly struggles against nothingness. Instead, he defined an instrumental pragmatism, what Pascal Gielin calls "lu-creativity."[61]

Katherine, an executive assistant, likened creativity to the translation of information and facilitation of group communication. After stating that she felt that she performed creative work, Katherine explained what makes her job creative:

I think that the best way that I would describe my job and most of the company's job is that it's all an exchange of information, right? You go to a meeting, what happens in a meeting? Everyone just tells each other what's going on. Then you have the next week and you all tell each other what's going on in the next step and then someone might have some advice to contribute on how to make it go smoother or a warning or a previous experience. All that is exchange of information. There's so many phone calls that happen. To build a [YouTube] channel, for example, I want to make one. That all started with either a phone call, an email, and a [PowerPoint] deck. Then it grew into more conversations. Then it grew into an exchange of contracts, which is information and then, you know, creative. You know, the show started being made; that's all information too. It's entertainment, but it's all, it's not tangible.

She identified her rather mundane tasks with creativity while describing something like Paolo Virno's definition of the skills within cognitive capitalism. As Virno argues, skills demanded by cognitive capitalism include embodied, virtuoso-like communication skills.[62]

Some workers drew a line between artistic creativity—often autonomous and free—and "business" creativity. Describing himself as the "Steven Spielberg of booking airfare," Lawrence drew such a distinction while also espousing an instrumentalized pragmatism: "Creativity in this role or any other role is really coming up with solutions that are not your typical solutions and kind of having fun with it." Giving an example of work that might fit his criteria, he said,

If maybe I was looking to expand a department here or, like, if I wanted to start a department, I think that exploring another genre of what we do here with finding talent on YouTube, if I was to find a genre that we're not working with and go out and explore it and then bring it back and say I could do this, this and this with it and it's maybe not our typical way of doing things, I would say that that would be an example of creative work.

Despite drawing this distinction, Lawrence offered an account similar to that of management. Invention, novelty, and change were circumscribed by predefined organizational problems. Within this boundary, Lawrence and other workers at The Future could "explore" and "bring back" their findings in order to provide novel, atypical ways of achieving organizational goals. Performing rather routine work using spreadsheet and data analysis software, The Future's workers defined creativity in managerial terms, seeming to give credence to dystopic visions proffered by recent critiques of capitalist creativity,[63] but none were wholly subsumed by managerial ideology. There remained a gap, one that highlights the partial explanations given by theories that point to the discourse or ideology of creativity as key to explaining how workers come to be attached to precarious employment.

CONCLUSION

"Creativity" may be the "fetish of our times,"[64] part of the dominant ideology or "spirit" of capitalism, but this "fetish" remains polyvalent, open to interpretation along lines of class and, though not dealt with here, other dimensions of social position such as gender, ethnicity, race, and place. In this chapter, I illustrated this point by comparing accounts of creativity from workers, managers, and a platform's training and promotional materials. Workers' accounts were not identical to those of management or the platform. I never found workers' accounts to be so completely bound in by dominant discourses so as to appear "subsumed" by capital. Most workers offered vivid and dynamic accounts. Even the few workers in digital media who closely aligned with the managerial ideology retained a certain critical point of view. Only management tended to come out all one color, narrowly concerned with limited problem solving while the platform invited heteronymous entrepreneurs to secure viewers and profits.

These invitations to "be creative" form *part* of a strategy for controlling creative labor; however, there remain significant gaps between capitalist and worker understandings of what it means to accept them. This gap in meaning suggests that ideology alone fails to form a fully functional, self-regulating control mechanism. Workers require something more than simply labeling their work as "creative." Over the course of the next four

TABLE 2.1
Class and Creativity Discourses

	Workers	Management	Platform
Discourses	Creation ex nihilo; Autonomous expression	Instrumentalized pragmatism	Heteronomous entrepreneurialism

chapters, I present evidence from extensive ethnographic fieldwork to show that this certain something occurs at work, often in the everyday interactions between workers and technology. To borrow from Alvin Gouldner's *Dialectic of Ideology and Technology*, technology exerts power over workers by way of the "sheer experience of gratifications" that it offers.[65]

PART II

SoniCo's Social Regime

Chapter Three

SONICO'S POSITIVE POLE

Aesthetic Subjectivities and Control

Early on during my fieldwork at SoniCo, I met Robert, the supervisor of the studio's front office. He arrived just before the start of an 11:00 a.m. shift, dressed in a sort of indie country style, common among a certain subset of LA musicians—tight dark jeans worn thin and faded at the knees, cowboy boots, and a Western style, snap-up shirt. The office doubled as what Robert described as a "musician's pro shop," so there is usually a baseline level of foot traffic as musicians stop in to buy drumsticks or guitar strings on their way to record or rehearse. This particular morning had been especially quiet. A few Australian musicians checked into an hourly rehearsal room. After Robert and I took care of their needs, I sat listening to music play over the lobby's PA system and watching Robert type on a computer keyboard, receiving and responding to emails from clients, brand representatives, and other employees. A heavy smoker, Robert kept working even on his cigarette breaks, continuously checking emails and taking calls on his phone between drags. "I do this even when I'm not here. It's OCD," he said, thumbing his phone's screen.

Later, the studio bustled with musicians on their way in for a rehearsal or on their way out to smoke and chat with the studio's staff. Musicians walked in about every fifteen minutes, each receiving a greeting from Robert. Two women walked in wearing cowboy boots and denim. One of them carried a Fender guitar. They asked to rent a room where they could hammer out the details of their songs while an engineer finished editing their recorded songs in ProTools (a popular brand of digital audio workstation software, or DAW). Robert checked them into one of the smaller "songwriter" rooms and asked, "Oh, how's the record coming along? When's your next gig? Is it at the same venue as your last one?" Robert excelled at these interactions, always taking time to inquire about a client's music and career, occasionally offering encouragement to those stuck in a rut. After we checked the two women into a room, we checked in Guillermo, a solo guitarist, for a two-hour rehearsal session. "Found a band yet, Guillermo?" asked Robert with a smile. He had not, but even so, Robert cheered on Guillermo's frequent practice sessions. Later, Robert asked if I played music. "Yeah, but not right now. Not in a few years, actually." Ever the positive guy, Robert replied, "Ah, well, you'll find someone to play with soon."

Not every day in the office had been so client-focused and calm. A few months later, Jack, another supervisor, arrived with newly purchased costumes for a performance that evening where he, Robert, and another employee would play country music at a nearby restaurant. "Did you get a ten-gallon hat, Jack? A twenty-five-gallon hat?" asked Marcus, another staff member. "Forty-five-gallon hat!" said Jack. "Wow you can fit a lot of—" began Robert. Jack cut him off, "Yeah, a lot!" while donning the newly purchased "forty-five-gallon" cowboy hat. Most of the staff planned to attend the event, and I had been asked to join them by Marcus, who said that their friendship was important for me to see. "Most places I've worked, I wouldn't want to drink with the people, but here, it's different." Earlier that day, Marcus had complained about his ulcer, claiming to vomit every day before he came in to work. "Maybe I just can't stand working. Nah, maybe it's just the world," he said with a laugh. Ulcerated and alienated, he still claimed to enjoy working at SoniCo, as did many others. Employees formed a rather socially cohesive group, their relationships spilling over to outside the workplace, but what made the working day tolerable, even enjoyable? Was it simply their friendships, or was it that in their jobs they could, as management claimed, "be creative?"

In part 1 I discussed how management invited "creativity," but how do workers accept that invitation? How does management's desire for "creativity" articulate with Robert's unexciting day or Marcus's contradictory relationship with work? Service interactions, funny hats, and vomit offer stark contrasts with the owners' glossy claim of a "truly *creative* space that *feels* creative." If the previous chapter showed how "creativity," as ideology, means both too much and too little, this chapter focuses on the materialities of the working day that make that ideology feel true. In doing so, I begin to work toward a theory of creative labor, examining managerial power and control in the small enjoyments of the working day, the "bandages" that bind workers to their jobs.[1]

A LONG STAY FOR LOW PAY

Founded in 2008, SoniCo was a relatively "flat" firm, with minimal layers to its hierarchy, save for the gap between owner-managers and employees within three horizontally differentiated departments: recording, rent-by-the-hour rehearsal spaces, and offsite events. Owners granted substantial autonomy to each division's supervisors, preferring to manage by inviting employees to "be creative" and through careful hiring choices rather than direct control. Each department drew from Los Angeles's standing reserve of aspiring musicians and audio engineers for its pool of potential employees. When hiring, owners relied upon their judgments of applicants' character or disposition and referrals from current staff—what Robert described as a "pretty organic" process, where "it always just seems to come to light that there's this guy that we really like and we think has a good work ethic, and we hire him."

Because of these dispositional and network-based hiring practices, supervisors and regular employees tended to be homogenous in terms of gender, education, class background, and wages, with ages ranging from twenty-one to thirty-five. This made for a cohesive, organic workplace culture but also one thick with heteronormative masculinity, suggestive of a series of interacting micromechanisms that reproduce the culture industries' overwhelmingly male workforce. The distinctively male work culture appeared most clear in everyday, often sexual, humor around the studio, such as when a group of employees on a cigarette break were discussing a dilapidated, vintage bass drum. Hersch, a supervisor that moonlit as a professional drummer, said, "Looks great! The heads are busted, so I'm going to change 'em. Imagine playing a gig with this thing. You'll definitely get laid!" Another employee, Jeff, said, "Yeah, you'll go home with a middle-aged single mother." Robert arrived and, overhearing the conversation, laughed. Pretending to speak to the hypothetical woman, Hersch said, "Yeah, I hope you got a sitter, because I'm about to sit, you're going to sit. Dammit! I was going for some mustache-riding joke but fucked it up." In other instances, they delivered misogynist jokes that, ironic or not, added to the studio's overtly masculine atmosphere.

Unlike closed-shop studios in the 1960s and 1970s, SoniCo's workers were not union members. In this, the studio resembles 90 percent of the U.S. music industry and the majority of private-sector workers in the United States.[2] There were comparatively few full-time office employees (ten), alongside a fluctuating number of part-time employees and contractors. Part-timers generally worked in the office, while contractors worked as audio engineers in the recording room or as manual laborers on live

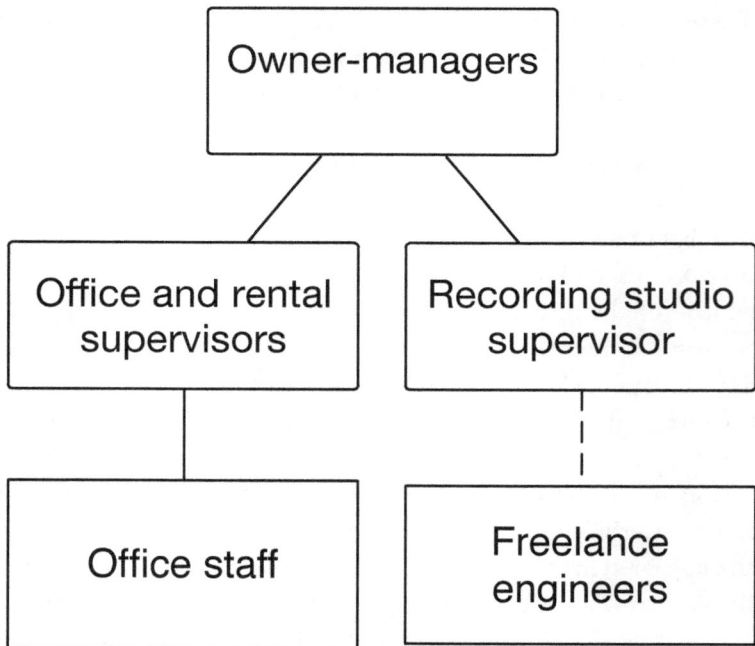

FIGURE 3.1 SoniCo's organizational structure. Solid lines represent full-time staff. Dashed line represents freelance employment.

events held offsite at music venues, museums, and public spaces through-out Los Angeles.

Though office staff and engineers perform relatively invisible jobs from the point of view of music consumers—analogous to "below-the-line" work in film and television[3]—audio engineering required the use of professional expertise as a means of *expression*, often embodied in a product. Similar to other expressive jobs (e.g., actors, writers, designers, etc.), engineers work as independent contractors, earning a living through a patchwork of "gigs" at SoniCo and other studios or as employees in the studio's office. Most office employees started off with that position being their "day job," one that pro-vided a low-paying, precarious solution to problems stemming from their unpaid or intermittent employment as musicians or engineers.

Both jobs required technical and tacit skills developed through formal education and apprenticeships. As a skilled occupation, audio engineering requires a minimum of a certificate or an associate degree, supplemented with internships. Less frequently, engineers developed their expertise by recording friends' music for free and through less formal, often unpaid training. Only one of SoniCo's engineers held a university degree in music composition and audio production; a few others had interned in studios after earning degrees in unrelated fields. Engineers at SoniCo typically received between $15 and $20 per hour for a recording session, slightly below the industry average of $23.[4] As freelancers, their incomes varied widely, with an average of $48,000 in gross earnings per year, not account-ing for overhead expenses or taxes.

Most office staff had completed high school or some college—often associate degrees or certificates in audio engineering—but only two held college degrees. Often trained as musicians or recording engineers, the office staff had acquired comparable sensibilities, dispositions, and levels of education to the engineers, yet management consistently equated the

TABLE 3.1
Years worked as an audio engineer by gender

	Median years worked	Respondents
Male	10	13
Female	8	1

office staff to food service workers, claiming that office work required "few skills." Though undervalued, management desired employees who could provide an instrumentally pragmatic creativity and, ideally, possessed skill sets comparable to musicians or engineers. As one of the owners stated, SoniCo manages by hiring "problem solvers" who can "really take ownership of their job." Discounting the specificity of worker knowledge, this owner went on to say, "Someone that works [in a coffee shop] has about the same amount of experience needed to work at SoniCo." He then acknowledged the skills and training involved in service occupations, noted their low wages, and said, "We pay at least a little bit more than that." Hourly employees earned $10 to $12 per hour, and salaried staff and supervisors earned $25,000 to $28,000 per year. For a forty-to-sixty-hour workweek, this shakes out to $8.68 to $14.58 per hour. The lower end of that range fell below California's minimum wage while I was in the field. Alongside these low wages, SoniCo provided no healthcare or other traditional fringe benefits, such as paid leave. Instead, perks consisted of the use of music equipment and facilities at no cost. When hiring new employees, managers made sure to highlight these perks, likening them to a supplemental income.

By the sociologist Arne Kalleberg's rubric, these were not "good jobs,"[5] yet management expected some degree of commitment, and workers tended to stay within the firm for an average of two years, roughly on par with the industry's median length of employment (2.4 years). Earning less than the national median wage, staff frequently cited their other job options in more lucrative service occupations such as barbering, waiting tables, and clerical work. Management assumed that employees also gigged as engineers or musicians and often allowed senior employees to take unpaid time off for extended touring or one-off performances at annual music festivals such as SXSW in Austin, Texas, or Coachella in

TABLE 3.2
Office worker tenure by gender

	Median tenure (years)	Respondents
Male	2	13
Female	1	2

nearby Indio, California. Management expected workers to return, hoping to retain employees after they concluded seasonal tours in the spring or summer. Highlighting management's expectation of retention, employees suggested that SoniCo hire me as a replacement after one of the few firings. Jack, a supervisor, said that I would be fine for the job, but he hesitated because I might not stay very long. Here, we have routine workers with relatively low wages at an organization with a relatively high retention rate (for the culture industries, at least).

So why did they stay for low pay? Both engineers and office staff expressed deep attachments to their work, claiming to "love" these relatively low-paying, "cool" jobs. Now, this is not to say that workers never expressed dissatisfaction. Some even shared my astonishment at their coworkers' professed "love," drawing this puzzling situation into clear relief. One disgruntled worker said, "Well, it's cool. I mean, you basically get paid to hang out and they do very simple things. . . . For everyone it's like 'Ah, I've never had a better job!'" Even after citing his low wages as grounds for hating his job, he pointed to something ineffable. Even if he appears to be critical of SoniCo, the job remains "cool." As I argued in chapter 2, ideology may explain how workers interpret their situation but not how it comes to be palpably meaningful. So, what bestows the working day with that certain ineffable, resonant quality that we call "cool?" The divergence of workers' and managers' meanings suggests a potential lack of consent to managerial hegemony or, at the very least, a gap between the two. Bridging or papering over this gap begins with a managerial invitation.

HAMMERING DOWN THE MANAGERIAL INVITATION

Managing creative labor begins with an invitation, something SoniCo's owners offered as part of their three-pronged approach to management. One owner (nicknamed "the great connector") extended the invitation, seeking to make workers "feel" creative and "take ownership," as if SoniCo were their business. Another occasionally reminded workers of their duties, something employees jokingly called "the hammer." The last involved the cultivation of friendships, something discussed by Fred, one of the owners:

FRED: Here's my function here: The three of us [owners] have very different roles. Owner 1 is kind of a hard-ass sometimes and does most of the financial end of things. Owner 3 is the great connector. He knows everyone in the world and is constantly connecting us and networking us. My job is just basically to be the day-to-day guy. Most of what I do, the guys who work here, who are technically my employees, I guess. I almost never think of them like that. Those guys are my friends and they will air grievances to me that they won't necessarily air to the others.

MICHAEL: Is that because you're here all the time?

FRED: I'm also friends with them. I hang out with them outside of work, y'know? They're some of my best friends. I want to know their concerns, and I want to try to resolve any issues that we have. I feel like a lot of times they'll say, "This thing went missing and I don't want to tell the other owners because they'll freak out." So, I say, "OK, well, let's find it." I basically take on that role of like kind of like a weird dad.

In practice, the "hard-ass" seemed rather friendly, never simply barking orders and often leaving things open for conversation, not unlike the increasingly common "conversational" or "be yourself" management styles found in the customer service and technology industries.[6]

Employees often spoke of the times when the "hard-ass" had "brought the hammer down," but I never saw him intensely angry. Over time, I came to realize that these were jokes about management's laid-back approach. For instance, I sat outside with Nathan one day after he had finished a shift. We sat idly smoking cigarettes and chatting with the engineers and their musician clients. Rodolfo, the "hard-ass" owner-manager rushed out of the front door. Clearly annoyed, he asked, "Is anybody working?!" Forceful, sure, but still polite. Nathan said, "Well, I'm not on the clock, and Jason should be on the front desk." "Okay, well, I'm tired of people just walking in and out of here without someone paying any attention." Robert, the supervisor, rushed inside to check on things, and a client asked, "Did I just see the hammer come down? Was that Rodolfo bringing down the hammer?" Emmerich said, "Yeah. Actually, that was more like the rubber mallet. I've seen the hammer come down, and it ain't pretty. I've gone shooting with that guy [at a gun range], and it ain't pretty. He does a quick draw and fires right through the head of the target in seven-tenths of a second. You don't want to mess with him when he's angry." Months went by and I never saw anything more alarming than this level of intensity between owners and employees, but I often heard secondhand stories of times when the owners got "angry" or "flipped out." I worried that I must have been missing something, so I asked Jason, a front office worker, about "bringing the hammer down." He said, "It's more, so like bringing the hammer down, that talk [from the owner-manager] is like, 'Let's try not to do that ever again.' It's pretty, it's very relaxed."

"The Hammer" told me that he invited workers to take responsibility for their own supervision and to devise the best approach for completing their tasks. As he said, "It helps to have people that can make their own rules, essentially 'this is how we're going to solve that problem.' I'm not going to step in. I'm just going to acknowledge that in order to solve this we need to do two or three things, and then I'll give them a second chance in order to get to X, Y, and Z." So, rather than direct control, that is, the despotic authority commonly found in entrepreneurial firms of the nineteenth and twentieth centuries, SoniCo's owners exert power or control through invitation and, occasionally, the "soft hammer." Making work feel creative depends upon these invitations to self-manage and, as I argue throughout this book, on work's materialities—what the organizational scholar Pasquale Gagliardi calls the fourth dimension of control, or "aesthetic landscape."[7]

AN INVITING SPACE

Work's aesthetic landscape includes both décor and technology, so let's take a walk through SoniCo, from the street to the recording rooms and offices, before discussing workers' experiences vis-à-vis technology. Despite being a relative newcomer in the Los Angeles recording industry, SoniCo's interiors resembled many of the city's premier studios, such as East/West, where a receptionist greets incoming clients from behind a desk made of guitars, or Westlake Studio's large, wood-paneled recording rooms, which evoke the famous recording rooms of yesteryear. No different, SoniCo sets the tone for visitors with a brightly painted exterior. Beyond the front door, the studio's lobby resembled a retro-styled bar, with vibrant red walls and a checkered floor. A sign invited passers-by to "relax" in addition to just recording and rehearsing. Sculptures made of broken guitars and large, floor-to-ceiling paintings of ominous purple and red orchids punctuate the studio's hallways. Several leopard-print couches contrast with the main recording room's earth-toned walls, each adorned with floral and paisley tapestries concealing special foam tiles—"sound treatments" to diminish reverberations. Large, multicolored ottomans, Persian-style carpets, and ornamental lighting fixtures provide a vaguely exotic atmosphere somewhat at odds with the paintings of UFOs hanging on the walls. The studio's control room was populated by banks of audio equipment sporting countless blinking and twinkling LEDs. As musicians and engineers often said, the room had a "vibe."

In the equally "vibey" and dimly lit front office where Robert chatted with clients, a few Grammy awards hung alongside cheap dreamcatcher decorations and high-end equipment manufactured by the various high-profile brands that held sales partnerships with the studio. Though ostensibly for sale, Jack, a supervisor, said, "Most of this stuff is never sold, but it makes the space look better. Livens it up a bit." Later, I will show how these technical objects mediate the relationship between firm and employee.

Around the corner, a cacophony of overlapping performances emanated from themed rehearsal studios rooms. Norteño blended with hip-hop overlapping with "electro" dance music and the barked shouts of grindcore and punk rock. Each themed rehearsal studio contained equipment manufactured by SoniCo's partner brands. Customers and employees may choose from a variety of themed rehearsal studios, including "monster movie," "tropical," "1960s psychedelia," "urban," and "cowboy." Employees enjoyed the look of these rooms, often taking part in their design. They took pride in the spaces they had helped create, one of the seemingly few avenues for "creativity" in their otherwise routine jobs. Jeffrey, an office worker in his early thirties, said, "I like that [décor of the front office]. I like the tacky decorating. The dreamcatchers are hilarious. The pictures of people, we don't know who they are. It's hilarious. It's like a sense of humor that I think we all have to have, and I think that's why we work there." Another said, "I love the neighborhood-themed room. I like the horror room. I wish I could've been here when they did it and like, helped out with ideas." These spaces appealed to the employees because they had, in part, created them.

For example, the front office had been rather dull before I arrived at SoniCo, consisting of two computers for bookings and payments in a dark, windowless room. The owners wanted to "do something fun" with another room, and Robert suggested that they instead "consolidate the two, and it should be hourly check-in and retail." Management gave Robert free rein to design and operate the office's retail section, encouraging him to "be creative" and "take ownership"—common euphemisms for encouraging an entrepreneurial attitude toward work. In turn, Robert enjoyed that he had control over the office and expressed a sense of ownership with regard to the retail element. Excited, he told me, "Every month, rehearsals brings in the largest contingent of money. It's about 50 percent of our sales, but slowly but surely, retail moved its way up to almost 25 percent of our intake." Robert called some of the rooms "pretty cheese-dick," but he enjoyed the space he'd had a direct hand in designing, which further added to his felt ownership over his division's success.

A core argument of this book is that accepting the managerial invitation to "be creative," that is, to provide creative labor, depends upon work's aesthetic dimension. This includes décor, sure, but also technology. Technology enchants and enables creative labor, something that will become clear as I show how the creative labor process produces, on one hand, an entrepreneurial attitude characteristic of neoliberalism and, on the other, a fragile, partial consent to managerial authority, one grounded in workers' aesthetic subjectivities just as much as their economic or identity-based interests. This fragile consent hangs alongside workers' precarity, papering over but never resolving creative labor's contradictions. Work may *feel* cool, but employees remain painfully aware of their economic uncertainty. These incongruous valences form the *positive and negative poles of creative labor*. In this chapter, I focus on the positive pole, explaining how precarious work becomes desirable and illustrating what I call *aesthetic enrollment*, a process wherein interactions between workers and organizational artifacts (technology, in this case) captivate and bind workers to precarious work. As I said earlier, work's aesthetic dimension includes décor, sure, but also technology. The latter's importance appears most clearly in the working days of sound recording engineers.

THE SONIC WIZARDS AND THEIR WANDS

Engineers often used words like "passion" and "magic" when talking about their studio "wizardry" and "dark arts"—echoing the more romantic view of workers' creativities described in the previous chapter. These allusions to magic should come as no surprise to music fans. After all, recording studios have been called "temples of sound" and "shrines of mystery" since at least the 1970s, when audio engineering became both more professionalized and visible among music fans thanks to the rise of star producer/engineers.[8] As high priests in these "temples," passionate adepts fabricating mass society's aural commodities, engineers mediate the social and technical within cultural production.[9] Technologies extend engineers' capacities for creative labor and allow them to imagine future possibilities for action. Through these interactions, technology binds engineers to their work, as if the wizards' wands cast their own spells.

Engineering required the flexible use of knowledge about sound frequencies, electrical systems, and complex sonic technologies—and emotional labor. A late-night session illustrates this well. The band had been drinking beer, getting drunk while a sober engineer downplayed the musicians' increasingly poor playing in order to secure a usable performance. Around midnight, the group's singer apologized profusely after he drunkenly fumbled multiple takes. The engineer calmly said, "Nah, don't worry. Everything's cool." Likewise, another engineer described the interactional demands of work as follows: "They [the musicians] were all acting weird around me. . . . Everyone's moping the fuck around. So, this job, I had to make a really great record despite them and come up with a method to get like everyone playing and jamming. . . . This band needs momentum. That's my job in this thing: momentum!" He described how engineers must manage the affect, "vibe," or "momentum" of a session by remaining calm and reassuring and encouraging inebriated, recalcitrant, or discouraged clients.

Managing a session's emotional tenor required engineers to withhold their opinions, especially when arguments broke out between musicians or other production personnel. During a session with a British psychedelic rock band, Emmerich, SoniCo's head engineer, entered the front office to see if anyone wanted to accompany him on a cigarette break because he needed a rest from the "dick swinging contest" going on in the recording room. Apparently, the band had been arguing with an additional engineer that they had brought to the studio. Emmerich explained, "There are eight people in the studio, and it's much too crowded and heated in there for me. It's great to get paid while people are arguing, but I got two would-be producers in there right up in my face, and it sucks. I can't even fart in the studio. I've been holding it in all day." Setting aside Emmerich's digestive distress, this session and the inebriated musicians highlight the necessity of engineers' emotional labor in addition to their creative judgment and professional expertise.

More central to my point, engineers act as a nexus or crucial node in project-based work.[10] In addition to managing a session's traditionally social component, engineers mediated relations between humans and nonhumans, controlling musicians' access to the expressive technologies that shape musicians' recordings.[11] A typical fourteen-hour session begins an hour before the arrival of musicians. Engineers prep the studio by unraveling cables, tuning instruments, testing equipment, and choosing potential microphone placements. Following these tasks, engineers open a computer's digital audio workstation (DAW) software and prepare the software's virtual environment to record the signals from the microphones that he or she just set up. They then ask musicians to play their instruments or sing while carefully adjusting knobs, "faders," and other control surfaces via which they manipulate an assemblage of audio subsystems, computers, and cabling.

Musicians frequently ask to modify the timbre of their recorded sounds. For example, musicians make abstract suggestions like "make it more like a dance kick [drum]," "make it more blue," or even "make it pillowy." Engineers must quickly interpret and translate musicians' abstract commands into concrete technical adjustments and, in the process, they develop a close relationship with technology. Having become attached to his gear, a veteran engineer explained, "When I hear something, my brain formulates [technical] decisions." As "sonic wizards," engineers stand between musicians and these complex technical assemblages—the wizard's wands that enable and extend their "aesthetic agency" or power to effect changes in their sensory environment.[12]

During sessions, engineers had a high degree of autonomy, beholden only to their musician clients and with little to no managerial oversight. They tried their best to meet their clients' needs, striving to produce sounds in line with contemporary pop trends and genre conventions. Engineers' attendance to these conventions highlights the altogether more social character of conventional media production in comparison to later discussions of platform-based work. Here, an engineer explains how genre conventions informed her choices in microphone placement and the use of additional sound technologies such as reverb and echo ("delay"):

[As an engineer,] you're basically creating a lens for someone to view this song through, and the way that you frame it completely, completely dictates how the audience will perceive the song. That comes down to simple things, like if I mix the kick drum with too much top end, it'll sound like a metal record, and I can't put a kick drum that sounds like that on a folk record. So, [it's about] using your creative and artistic judgment to say for the vibe of this band and this production for what they're trying to accomplish.

That conventions inform and guide music production should come as no surprise to sociologists of culture. As Howard Becker pointed out in his book *Art Worlds*, genre conventions structure creativity in the production of culture, especially music.[13] As an engineer said, "You gotta know what trends are going on in music. Not just in terms of what's popular song-wise, but sonically. Sonically, what are the trends?" By this he meant trends in the use of effects, microphone positions, and the relative volume of instruments within a song (the "mix"). As he explained, "I mean, in the nineties drums were loud and vocals were dry [with minimal audio processing]. Now it's more about a loud kick drum and wet [heavily processed] vocals. These things, these sonic things are anchored to time, man." That these sonic trends or conventions directly inform engineers' decisions differs sharply from later chapters, in which I will show how social conventions take a back seat to the pursuit of metrics, an orientation imposed by digital platforms.

Engineers tended to desire sessions in which they could be inventive, using a wider array of equipment in the service of high-profile clients. The success of the client can reflect positively upon everyone that worked on a project, which in turn may increase engineers' earnings—what economic sociologists call a "spillover" effect, something commonly found in film and television production.[14] For this reason, studios and engineers typically provide a list of previous clients in their brochures and websites. Alongside career advancement, desirable sessions allow for the deployment of expertise in ways that suit engineers' professional interests or personal interpretations of conventions. Technology both enables and extends engineers' skill and expertise, and so desirable sessions often coincided with the availability of more elaborate equipment, or "gear." Lengthier, more complex sessions tended to generate more talk around the studio than simply working "a pop," or pop music session, which required minimal effort from an engineer. A pop typically required an engineer to set up a single microphone to capture sound from a vocalist, who would sing over top of music composed and recorded by a producer prior to the session. Pops might be easy money, but they were not particularly sought-after gigs.

The session with the psychedelic rock band highlights the desirability of longer sessions, their complexity, and the issues that arise from SoniCo's lack of full-time recording staff. SoniCo's staff buzzed excitedly when the band first scheduled two weeks' worth of sessions. Being a fan, I jumped at the chance to show the band's leader around when the group arrived, getting him coffee and chatting with him about our favorite albums. I expected the engineer for the session to be similarly excited because of the band's music, but he explained to me that he looked forward to the session because the group had booked two weeks of studio time.[15] This length of booking allowed him to more fully develop the recording. Time, coupled with a full band (guitar, bass, drums, synthesizers, and horns), enabled the engineer to more fully employ his skills, to exercise judgment in the use of a wider array of equipment, and to shape the sonic characteristics of more diverse sounds.

Even so, the session had not been without a few hiccups. While lengthier, more complex sessions provide more opportunities for problem solving and inventive use of expertise, they also increase the number of potential problems. There was the aforementioned argument among band members, but the size of the session, combined with SoniCo's lack of full-time assistants, further complicated the head engineer's job. Emmerich entered the office one day during these sessions and asked me to help him move some things in the studio. "This bass rig is too loud, and I need to partition it off from the rest of the studio," he said as we walked into the main recording room, passing the computer, racks of audio equipment, and the band's leader, who sat on a large couch in the control booth. Inside the main room, the rest of the band members were adjusting their equipment, plucking notes on their guitars, or tapping rhythms on the drums. Emmerich and I grabbed a large, portable wall (a "gobo," or go-between) from a storage closet and placed it in front of the bass player's massive amplifier rig, which consisted of several fifteen-inch speakers and a cabinet with four ten-inch speakers, all powered by a four-hundred-watt amplifier—a rig suited more for a live performance at a two-thousand-person-capacity club than for the intimacy of a recording studio. The bass player offered to turn down his volume, but Emmerich insisted that the gobo ought to be sufficient to achieve enough "separation" for recording.

Frantically, Emmerich muttered, "Man, I need some fucking interns. I need interns for this shit," as band members shared stories from their heyday in the 1970s. One of the younger members asked, "Back then, hanging out with [the anarchist punk band] Crass, did those girls really beat up that guy for singing some misogynist song?" An older member of the band launched into a lengthy explanation. "No. No, they didn't beat him up. What happened was that he had written a song about this 'orrible fella that used to always say 'Yeah, but does she suck?' about every woman, and it was this song written from this really 'orrible guy's point of view. So they thought that he was singing it in first person, like it was his opinion, and didn't get the song, that it was about some guy that always thinks about sex like that. So, that got into an argument." Later, Emmerich asked me to move the bass rig into a separate room. I asked him if things had been going well in the session. He said, "No, it's over before it's even started in there today."

This session highlights both the effects of SoniCo's limited number of on-staff engineers as well as the intermingling of technology and engineers' creative labor. Engineers mediate musicians' expression and technological potentials, requiring Emmerich to think quickly and improvise a way to make the bass player's equipment useful for recording. Generally, this required various tools, in this case, the lowly gobo, a rather simple means of blocking out unwanted sound, or "bleed," from microphones. If SoniCo had had an on-staff assistant, the implementation of the gobo might have occurred seamlessly, with Emmerich simply asking an assistant or intern to perform the task. Instead, Emmerich left the session, found me, the local sociologist, and then explained his plan. Alternatively, he might have hired an assistant or intern for the session, cutting into his own pay and inclining Emmerich toward economization. Here, Emmerich exerts his aesthetic agency, his power over sound, through technology, and the materialities upon which his creative labor depends. Though the gobo provokes little in the way of enchantment, I bring it up to highlight how the enchantments I now turn to stem not from a fetish-like perception of powers peculiar to the object itself but as powerful parts of a human/non-human assemblage.

Creative labor as an assemblage of human and nonhuman components may be readily seen in the control room during recording and mixing, when, to use engineers' words, they "enter the Matrix"[16] or "disappear" into the equipment, gaining machine limbs that extend their aesthetic agency. Immersed in the flow of work, engineers rarely paused to comment upon the studio's vibrant population of LEDs, multicolored microphones, and rack-mounted audio processing equipment. Absorbed in work, they knew what the equipment might do and exercised considerable control over the objects' affordances. Physically engaged, engineers often operated their gear with all four limbs, adjusting sound by way of knobs, sliders, and foot-switches. Further exemplifying this human/machine integration, engineers often gave visual cues to musicians through a glass window between the control and recording rooms. These cues were primed by the engineers' experience of the song as mediated by the computer display system just as much as by their familiarity with a composition. The display system depicts songs as multicolored visualizations of sound waves for each recorded signal from a microphone. Engineers "read" this sound graph as the song plays. They can "see" drumbeats, guitar strums, and singing in ways that the musicians, experiencing the sound immediately, cannot.

The material arrangement of the DAW's display can become important to individual engineers' work styles. Orlando, a freelance engineer who worked on hip-hop and electronic dance music, explained that whenever he began working on a song that he received from a band or another producer, he immediately adjusted the aesthetics of the display:

Yeah, for instance, I got this session [file] today. [Opens file on the computer]. So, I got this session today [Clicks in screen] and this is how a session looks sometimes. . . . You know, it's just not organized. So, what I would do is usually I'll just [Plays song in session file]. I'll listen to it real quick, and as I'm listening . . . this is what I do standard, make sure [the waveform size] is 99, display all display markers, adjust colors, MIDI track colors. Then I listen again. [Plays session] I'll start moving stuff and color-coordinating the stuff. [Clicks around the screen, drags, drops, and adjusts the color of the visual depictions of soundwaves].

Customized and adjusted to his particular visual sensibility, Orlando's virtual, on-screen workspace becomes conducive to his performance of creative labor. Wanda, the only female engineer with whom I spoke, also highlighted creative labor as a sociomaterial assemblage of technology and human labor, suggesting that the sensual aesthetics of her tools mediated her sense of hearing: "Like you're touching a button or control, usually many controls and how those are [designed] affect your hearing ability too. Your ability to perceive very, very minute differences. Additions and subtractions from the bassline and how that shapes what the artist wants to come through." In this illustrative quotation, Wanda describes the difference between working "in the box" or on a computer screen like Orlando and working with analog "outboard" equipment, where she adjusts sound by touching knobs ("potentiometers," or "pots") and sliding linear volume controls ("faders").

Beyond the social dynamics of recording sessions, engineers' work included extended editing and mixing sessions, which foreground the interactions between an engineer and the studio's equipment. These sessions further demonstrate technology's mediating extensions of engineers' creative labor. For example, an engineer in a mixing session might play just a few seconds of a song before stopping playback and saying "Oh that's not good" or exclaiming "Somebody fucked up!" I failed to hear these errors until he called them out verbally, something he seemed to do even in my absence. Before I could ask how he perceived these imperfections, he said, "I'm glad you're here because then I don't feel as crazy talking to myself." He explained that many of these errors would not be perceptible to him later, after leaving and returning to the studio, nodding in agreement when I asked if he thought that this had anything to do with the fact that he was seeing the sound, that is, seeing the waveforms on a screen. Pointing out these transient sounds, he said, "There's some string creak there. It's just normal string creak, but why keep it in there if I don't have to?" He explained that some engineers even remove breaths from vocal recordings, something he found unsettling. "If I listen to a whole song and don't hear a breath, I'm just like . . . [grimaces]."

The screen provided a visual trace of sounds, and, over time, one learns to "read" the screen for clear indications of a breath, a pop, or an unwanted sound. These imperfections included slightly off-time guitar strums or drum hits as well as transient sounds such as breaths between words or fingers moving along the neck of a guitar. Again, this suggests that the formal characteristics of the technology both extend and mediate engineers' capacity for creative labor as well as their sensorium, allowing them to work and *hear* more because they can *see* more. In order to fix these "errors," he pulled alternate takes of each instrumental and vocal performance and then performed microedits at the level of one hundred to two hundred sample lengths (0.002–0.004 seconds) to "smooth" the takes together—a practice called "comping," or compiling. Reminiscent of workers' romantic creativities described in chapter 2, he said, "This is the black magic. Most people don't get to see this."

Critical approaches to work often posit technology as a tool of capitalist domination, one that alienates and deskills. Liberal scholars prefer to highlight how technology might liberate us from work, heightening our satisfaction.[17] Neither interpretation really captures a sound engineer's experience. Instead, creative labor's tools appear altogether more neoliberal. Rather than freeing engineers *from* work, these technologies instead provide engineers with the freedom *to* work by extending the laboring body. As a prosthetic part of their sensorium, technology permits engineers to see the unseeable and, as with Wanda and her knobs, feel the hearable and hear the feel-able in meaningful, nonverbal ways. The music production process thus depends upon this fluid human/machine interaction, and, in a very material way, these objects provide for the engineer's aesthetic agency, a capability that remains circumscribed by client and management interests. Ralph, a forty-year veteran of the industry, made similar claims when he explained how digital technologies had changed his work practices:

> Like the music that most people listened to [in the past], it's going to change now because you know, now there's been a certain amount of time where there's been music that was recorded in ProTools and, you know, editable music. But of people of a certain age, most of the music they have listened to wasn't recorded this way. They never saw the waveforms. If they try to put the stuff on the grid, it wouldn't line up. They would have to be edited to fuck [i.e., heavily edited] to line up, and that's the music they love and that's the music they grew up with. And that's often what they're trying to emulate.

Ralph is describing changes in recording technologies over the past thirty years as the industry switched from recording on analog, magnetic tape machines to fully digital recording on a computer. In the former, songs were treated as multiple tracks running continuously across a long reel of tape. The latter presents songs as a set of "regions" or "segments" made visible and manipulable within a DAW computer program.[18] On the computer's screen, portions of recorded sound may be edited at the level of fractions of a second along a visible grid. Digital technologies often provoked anxiety and fascination among engineers. Many engineers waxed dystopic about the dark possibility of a future of rigid-rhythmed music that adheres to a merciless grid. There, Ralph was no different. At the same time, digital technologies offer new possibilities for the free and easy manipulation of sounds.

To use another example, Emmerich often worked alone in a small, dimly lit studio, producing and editing music for use in advertisements and television. He liked the lighting low because it put him in the right "mood" for compiling pieces of songs recorded by musicians located elsewhere in the city or in other parts of the United States. He used these to create modular, interchangeable song parts (i.e., chorus, verse, etc.), which he then sold to an online vendor. From that vendor, other media professionals could purchase the music for use in movies, advertisements, or online content. Emmerich's isolated editing sessions resembled what Karin Knorr-Cetina and Urs Bruegger call "post-social" relationships, wherein humans primarily orient to and interact with nonhumans.[19] Other people were not present, so he oriented himself toward the only other entities in the room: gear. Emmerich edited and "retimed" performances using a computer that enabled him to manipulate each beat and note of a recorded performance, an example of engineers' integrated dependency upon technology. These actions rendered the songs virtually free of human "error." Software analyzed each musician's performance and attempted to calculate the proper rhythm of each performance. Using the software's grid overlay, Emmerich made each note of each performance perfectly match the tempo, crafting a "perfect" performance by virtually assembling a technically perfect whole from multiple fragmented performances. Software enables quick assessments of technically specified quality and permits him to produce an objectively "perfect" song wherein each note can be made to occur on the computer-defined beat.

Not simply a slave to the grid, Emmerich exercised judgment by allowing for the occasional deviation from the grid's rationalized rhythm.

"Some real wizard shit!" he exclaimed as he went about retiming, "auto-tuning" (microadjustments to pitch), and removing sonic artifacts of the singer's body (e.g., the smacking of lips, breaths in between syllables). Software and its accompanying materialities enabled and extended engineers' abilities—allowing them to manipulate the technical and affective qualities of a performance. These firm-owned technologies mediated and co-constituted engineers' aesthetic agency. By using these technologies, engineers could exercise their creativity, producing objects used by consumers in their daily lives or by other cultural producers farther downstream in the production of music.

THE "PORN SIDE OF THE JOB"

Engineers merged with the machinery, their everyday experiences of gear grounding the ideology of "creativity," enabling their acceptance of the managerial invitation. As one engineer said, "We truly love that stuff. The gear is the fun part. It's the porn side of the job. I'm for real about that," echoing the feeling of being "turned on," which Edward Kealy found in his 1970s study of recording engineers in Chicago.[20] At first glance, one might want to point out the historically specific, gendered relationship between men and machines, a point that certainly resonates with other studies of creative labor wherein technical tools afford the possibility of enacting a masculine identity.[21] Still, making such a hasty connection risks overlooking the centrality of technology to this particular occupation, often cutting across gender lines. As much may be seen in Wanda's expressed desire for gear. As she said, "I'm interested in equipment. I definitely lust [pause] *lust* after gear [laughing], yeah, I definitely want pieces of equipment, only because for me the satisfaction they provide me is the fidelity and the warmth. It's more for me from an artful standpoint. When you listen to [the British rock band] Queen, for example, and I've researched like what components and what mixing consoles [they used]." Even though she expressed interest with some reservation—her laughter, which suggests a subtle nod to the more general, historically specific gendering of technology as male[22]—Wanda shared male engineers' intense fascination with technology.

The studio's gear exerts a certain power over engineers, luring them back to the studio. When asked whether the equipment affected his desire to work at SoniCo, one engineer said, "Yeah, it does actually. Like I love the possibilities of what something can bring me." Engineers working at other studios and live music venues would describe their desire to work in specific locations as being inspired by a combination of the staff's friendliness and the quality of the studio's equipment—often highlighting the "beauty" of the mixing console, a central component of any studio. When we hung out between sessions, engineers frequently pointed out specific items that they were excited about, such as a gold-plated microphone, "symphony quality" microphone stands, various analog and digital synthesizers, and computer programs that perform a variety of sound manipulation tasks, such as adding reverberation or performing dynamic volume adjustments (compression). Only once did an engineer deny his interest in gear—and he then proceeded to spend three hours recounting each piece of equipment he had used in every session in his ten-year career, along with the lore associated with each object.

More technically complex, obscure, or expensive technologies elicited the most excitement. Playing back a recording at the end of a lengthy session, one engineer said, "I had like $60,000 worth of microphones rigged up during this session. It sounds great!" He then isolated the song's lead vocals and said, "That's what a $20,000 microphone in front of your face sounds like. Beautiful." Beyond dollar value, the same engineer explained that he enjoyed the session because the musicians took direction well, allowing him to exercise judgment in selecting microphones and microphone placements. The experience of these tools entails fluid interaction and integration with the equipment, and so the engineer develops an attachment to these objects (e.g., "I love them" or "they're beautiful"). Engineers saw their aesthetic agency and creativity as bound up in these objects, and so these tools came to be seen as fun, enjoyable, or, more often, ineffably "cool." In that the firm owns this technology, engineers lacked ownership over their technologically mediated means of expression but were no less affectively attached.

As I noted earlier, engineers had a lot of control in sessions, beholden to their clients rather than to management. Rather than directing engineers, management appeared more concerned with retaining them as regular freelancers. Securing freelance engineers as studio clients revolves around the studio's gear and "vibe." In general, engineers at SoniCo and other studios emphasized the desire for "vibey" studios. Typically, this refers to a certain "gritty" or "funky" décor—something SoniCo certainly had—but also having great gear enabled SoniCo to provide the feel of "being creative"—what Erving Goffman[23] might have called the studio's "expressive equipment" or objects needed to materially enact a "creative" organization. Gear also fit into management's secondary strategies of revenue generation, such as renting the studio for film and video shoots. As one owner explained, SoniCo lost several opportunities to rent the space for film shoots because it lacked an analog mixing console, a piece of gear that most music fans might recognize as the large, visually striking device that stands behind musicians or engineers in documentaries and TV shows. In addition to being technically important, large analog mixing consoles form part of the studio's aesthetic landscape. The descriptions of engineers' working days suggest that along with the more social aspects of control, a studio's "vibe" provides a sort of glue, binding engineers to their work. This attachment elicits a partial consent to work's precarious conditions. Interactions with technology constitute the sensorial "feel" or aesthetics of the job, providing what Gilbert Simondon called "a motoric pleasure, a certain instrumentalized joy, a communication—mediated by the tool . . . a very particular pleasure of sensation."[24] This aesthetic subjectivity—developed through work in an expressive occupation—serves as a precondition for management's strategy of creative control among the studio's office staff.

Before moving on to discuss office staff, I want to discuss how the studio attempts to attract and retain freelance engineers. To put this in context, one needs to understand engineers' typical career paths. They start as unpaid interns sweeping floors and cleaning up after recording sessions. From there, they might become runners, more commonly called "go-fors." Runners move on to become assistant engineers, then house engineer, and, finally, freelance engineers. SoniCo only has one house engineer; the rest are freelancers. From management's point of view, house engineers should eventually go freelance in order to bring more clients to the studio. As the studio supervisor stated, "The mentality toward interns and assistant engineers at every studio is you cultivate an intern to become an assistant [engineer] to become [house] engineer to then go freelance and them bring clients back to you. That's the end goal of any studio."

As with other aspects of their approach to managing employees, SoniCo aims to cultivate social relationships, thus blurring the lines between employer and employee, hoping that freelancers might bring their projects to SoniCo rather than going elsewhere. As the supervisor said, "I know some studios that treat their employees like dog shit, and they will never go back to that studio." Treating people well was, he said, "a business thing," insofar as relationships developed over the course of an engineer's early career may create business opportunities for the studio. Echoing the supervisor at SoniCo, an owner-manager at another studio said,

> You know I've been in this business for seventeen years, and when people approach me, my first questions are what can you bring to this business? . . . If you really want to get in [to the industry] you got to bring value to an existing organization. Like, you can bring clients to an existing organization, you can increase revenue. . . . The young people coming out of audio schools are looking for a job. There are no jobs.

Skilled competency as a recording engineer does not in and of itself justify employment. Instead, budding engineers need to be able to "add value" by bringing in new clients and, as he went on to say, need "supporting skills like video development, web development, social media execution. Those are valuable assets and skills that you can bring to an existing business and show that you have value." In other words, engineers must be capable of deploying their creative labor across a variety of generic technological systems beyond strictly audio recording gear.

As suggested by SoniCo's studio supervisor, studios aim to shift the burden of client procurement onto workers by pushing engineers to go freelance, thus converting employees into customers who bring their gigs to the studio. While there may be "no jobs," plenty of work existed,[25] so long as engineers found it themselves. At SoniCo, aspiring engineers either take up work in the studio's office in the hope of getting occasional sessions or exit the formal boundaries of the organization in search of more desirable projects to bring back to the studio. Desirable gigs occur quite frequently but tend to be brought to the studio by freelance engineers or Emmerich, the supervisor. Assistant gigs were often given to office staff, but only sporadically and unpredictably.

For example, an engineer named Thomas had been working in the office when Emmerich, the studio supervisor, called to ask him to work a session later that day. Thomas, having already committed to working from 9 a.m. to 7 p.m. in the front office, would then work from 10 p.m. to 6 a.m.

in the studio. In total, this added up to an eighteen-hour workday. Thomas became concerned with complications arising from such a long working day and started thinking out loud to himself. "Fuck, I have obligations from nine to seven. I have obligations from nine to seven, then he wants me in for a session." Cheering him on, a woman who ran a small business nearby and frequently stopped by the office said, "You can do it Thomas! You can do it!" Pacing now, Thomas said, "That'd be thirty-six hours without sleep." Given moments such as these, where work comes intermittently and often conflicts with the "day job" that supplemented the meager wages provided by part-time engineering, going freelance seemed logical. Pursuing freelance work appeared economically rational insofar as it seemed to offer greater economic opportunities and more control over the rhythms of work.

Engineers then became clients of the firm, with the engineer renting the studio and charging musicians a fee to cover both the studio time and the engineer's hourly rate. As such, the goal of management is no longer to "manage" engineers per se but to secure engineers as frequent clients by providing a "vibey" studio space, the requisite technologies, and a pleasant social atmosphere. Management also engages in gift giving with the more notable freelance engineers ("hook-ups"). Common gifts included free microphones and the sundry small, disposable items used in recording, such as cabling or foam microphone windscreens. Still, the social aspect of SoniCo's interactions with freelance engineers appeared just as important as getting "hooked up" with microphones. An engineer's description of another studio highlights SoniCo's strategy: "[At the other studio,] I would get the shitty rap gig where they knew it was going to go all night. Like, certain people that would come in, clients that nobody wanted because they knew it was going to suck. So, I had that, like and it just got like really, because it was a bigger studio and it wasn't the more mom and pop thing where it's kind of like you're in control." SoniCo falls into the "mom and pop" category, where engineers experience a density of social relationships and more control over sessions. Though SoniCo's engineers generally work long, twelve-to-fourteen-hour days, some end up working a more grueling twenty-to-twenty-four-hour day at larger studios. As one engineer explained to me, "Once you're on your own, it's just whatever." As I discuss in chapter 4, this "just whatever" varies quite a bit. Engineers must perform additional, unpaid work as they hope to mitigate their precarity and secure the possibility of paid employment. One of their tactics for mitigating precarity included working in SoniCo's office, a job to which I now turn.

FEELING "CREATIVE" IN ROUTINE OFFICE WORK

"Cupid, draw back your bow, and let your arrow go, straight through my lover's heart, for me," sang Sam Cooke over the office PA system while Jack plunked away at a computer's keyboard and Robert chatted with some musicians. A bearded, blonde Australian rocker walked in to ask for quarters so he could play a vintage arcade game set up in the lobby—imagine the Norse god Thor with a beer belly, thinning hair, and a penchant for one particular submarine-themed game. "Man, you're obsessed with that game! You even sink any ships yet?" asked Robert. "Yeah, I have," said Thor. Robert shot back, jokingly, "You're not practicing at all are you? Not doing any work on your music. Just playing games in here?" He handed some quarters to the paunchy thunder god before calling in an order for office supplies and studio equipment.

Jack, along with nearly everyone with whom I spoke while researching this book, said, "There's no typical day around here," when I asked about their workplaces, but this moment certainly echoes the one with which I began this chapter. Were these typical, mundane moments illustrative of workers' "creativity"? Recall that managers claimed to invite "creativity" in the form of self-management and solving predefined organizational problems. Robert and Jack seem to be doing just that, inventively performing service work alongside administrative tasks, free to work, often with minimal supervision save for the gentle prods of a rather soft "Hammer."

Still, this instrumental pragmatism differed from the more romantic versions espoused by workers, and so there remains a gap, one that management attempted to close by managing how work *feels*. As an owner-manager said, "We just really have to encourage creativity in the work environment." This strategy included "managing people in a way that they *feel* empowered and are empowered on some level but still things get done that need to get done." SoniCo called itself a "creative space that feels creative," a claim that supposedly extended to office staff as well as clients and engineers. Now, Robert described his job as front office supervisor as "basically dealing with a lot of menial stuff," but there was also "the

Christmas everyday aspect of the job where I get to order all the gear" and "the actual getting to play with all the fun stuff that we get."

The earlier discussion of engineers' technological desires ought to give some inkling of what might make for SoniCo's 365 days of Christmas, but what about the "menial stuff"? Office work consisted of four main tasks: checking in clients, equipment troubleshooting, cleaning or "resetting" rehearsal studios, and downtime, during which office employees performed clerical and sales duties such as answering phones and taking studio reservations as well as selling and maintaining the inventory of items for sale (e.g., guitar picks and drumsticks). Managers often cited the gear-centered benefits offered by the studio—using the facilities and equipment at no charge—as an alternative form of compensation. In contrast, staff bemoaned the rarity of these "benefits," given their busy work schedules and because managers or supervisors often removed or moved their scheduled use of facilities without their knowledge. Supervisors—rather than lower-level employees—tended to be the majority users of these "benefits."

Absent those perks, work objectively consisted of clerical tasks, customer service, and light manual labor. They would greet musicians with a smile, a brief "hello," and a question: "What can I do for you?," "Whatcha need?," or, when speaking with female musicians, "What can I do ya for, *darling*?," then inquire about recent events in the musicians' careers: "How's the record coming along?," "How many rehearsals do you have coming up?," or "When's the next gig?" As a manager explained to me, these interactions were crucial for "creating a creative space" with a "creative vibe." Another manager reiterated this sentiment, adding that he hired "affable" people who would not be "bitter about being a musician serving other musicians." As Jack, a supervisor, explained,

We can't be stressed. We can't make our stress visibly or tangibly known, because our customers don't want to be in that environment. Larger studios, everyone who works there is very on edge and it's operated in a hierarchical, assembly-line fashion. There's not a very strong bond between the customers and the guys behind the desk. First and foremost, when a guy comes in, there needs to be a personal connection. Some of that's joking around before you collect their money or asking them about their next show, just treating them like a human being and a friend.

Notably, SoniCo hired struggling musicians and audio engineers for these jobs because they were "used to being paid nothing," and so, while this hiring practice resulted in a socially cohesive workplace made up of people attuned to the practices, rhythms, and problems specific to cultural work, office work required staff to conceal their stress and often to suppress their identities as musicians or engineers.

Despite these everyday indignities, employees saw a congruity between their aspirations and their working lives. As an attendant named Thomas said to me, "Even if I'm up front answering phones, adjusting the PA, wrapping cables, or trying to fix a guitar amp, at the end of the day, I'm still doing something musical. I don't know. This place is just, well, the easy answer would be to just say that I like the people, but really, it's just a cool place." Thomas and the rest of the guys in the office seemed equally likely to cite friendships and social interactions as crucial to their satisfaction as they were to suggest an assemblage of ineffable qualities of the workplace that seemed to exceed a strictly social explanation, at least if we take social as referring to interactions between humans. In stating "it's just a cool place," Thomas suggests as much. Perhaps if the workplace could speak, it might borrow a line from the funk singer Morris Day and say, "You wonder how I do it? There's just one simple rule: I'm just cool!" Rather than accept such a "simple rule," we need to ask what made SoniCo "cool" and how exactly could such routine work *feel* creative? To begin to answer this question, we first need to know what the office staff found enjoyable about their work.

THE "DISAPPEARING" OFFICE STAFF

Jeff sat behind the desk in the office as distorted guitars, trumpets, and thumping drums escaped from the rehearsal studios, providing a cacophonous score to another boring shift. Wearing a T-shirt that revealed his tattoo-covered arms, he walked over to some nearby synthesizers and assorted music equipment provided by management. Turning them on, he tapped out a melody on the synth and then a furious solo on a nearby guitar. Customers came in and asked Jeff about the gear, and he happily explained how each piece worked. Sometimes they purchased the items, but more often they did not. Regardless, Jeff's drift away from the desk and toward the gear served an organizational purpose. Alleviating his boredom, he *learned* about and, indirectly, demonstrated products to potential buyers. Jeff's escape from boredom is, to borrow from the owner-managers, "creative" and indirectly beneficial to SoniCo's bottom line. The technology affords Jeff an escape from the dead time of the working day and, potentially, increases sales.

Acknowledging the link between technology (gear) and managerial strategy, one of the owners said, "Yeah, yeah. For better or for worse, my managerial style is to provide guidelines and encourage creativity in work." As the staff often said, these objects made work more "fun," forming part of management's invitation to "be creative." Put differently, Soni-Co's managerial invitation included opportunities to assert agency by shaping work's aesthetic dimension through music selection, room design, and producing sounds through and within gear. These experiences facilitate acceptance of management's invitation and thus ground the ideology of creativity in the mundanity of the labor process. In more concrete terms, the front office's gear replicated the feel, if not the content, of more expressive work. By illustrating this process, I develop the concept of *aesthetic enrollment*,[26] that is, object-mediated immersive experiences that loosely bind workers to the organization while eliciting desired behavior. In quite a different sense than is usually employed, part of the constellation of factors that enroll employees in managerial or organizational projects is the relationship between workers and working machines, that is, labor and the instruments of labor.

At SoniCo, management attempted to make downtime more productive by providing workers with technologies, often ones that afforded pleasurably immersive, aesthetic experiences. For employees, this made SoniCo a "cool" place—one that did not *feel* like work. While stocking a vending machine in the studio, Arnold described the tasks of procuring gear as follows: "I'm ordering all this gear, some input/output Symphony boxes, new compressors, and then we've got these pre[amp]'s, you know EQ[ualizers], preamp strips for microphones. I mean putting in orders for this stuff and getting it all set up, that's not work to me. It's great. Some kid here was like 'yeah you've got a cool job,' and I'm thinking, like, 'Yeah, well I'm restocking a vending machine right now.'" Arnold suggests a certain distance from his work. He found restocking unpleasant, yet ordering gear did not seem like work. Even an employee who left SoniCo stated that, despite hating the job because of low wages, SoniCo did not "feel" like work. This "cool" part that does not "feel" like work tended to be linked to gear in the office. In conjunction with the workplace's social context, these objects provide for pleasure in what amounted to a low-paying job.

Interactions between office staff and clients usually ran smoothly, so eliciting appropriate customer service was less of a pressing concern for managers when compared to employees' use of downtime. Bear in mind that SoniCo's office work included a fair amount of downtime. Marcus, one of the office workers, said, "It's pretty predictable. I don't like predictability in my life, but in my time that I sell to someone else I like as little stress as possible. I prefer to use my body [rather] than head because my head is reserved for more important and expensive endeavors [like art and music]." Staff often filled downtime by surfing the internet on their cell phones or the office computer—something frowned upon by management—or by playing creative games and taking time to work on songs or prepare for auditions. As a supervisor explained, "There's only been three to four people that I worked with that I wouldn't have back, and I can say that all of them were comfortable with watching movies on their computers while on the job."

When staff expanded their leisure activities to include watching You-Tube videos, sports games, or movies on the internet, they were fired, but management tended to tolerate music-related pursuits. For instance, workers played a game similar to the artistic composition technique called "exquisite corpse," where one person begins a creative project and several people finish the process without input from the first. Workers on one shift would compose a portion of a song using the office computer and leave the unfinished song for a coworker to complete on the next shift, cooperatively creating a song over the course of a day. Not unlike other workplace games described by sociologists, collaborative composition at SoniCo provided a chance for meaning making and offered a moderately challenging activity that alleviated boredom.[27] Still, workers' games typically involve a clear economic incentive. For example, factory workers attempt to increase their pay by playing a game of outpacing their coworkers, and call-center employees endeavor to increase their earnings by treating each call as part of a "learning game" through which they might accumulate skill and finesse.[28] SoniCo's game lacked such clear economic incentives. Instead, staff played to create, to demonstrate skill, inventiveness, and ingenuity, but no one could boost their earnings by participating in the game. Suggestive of an attempt to focus these creative efforts, a manager removed the collaborative songs from the office computer. Though it seemed to contradict management's stated goal of "encouraging creativity at work," the deletion of these songs redirected their employees' game toward the use of gear that the company displayed for sale. Thereby management more closely linked any on-the-job creativity to profit.

The arrival at the studio of high-end Moog synthesizers clearly illustrates how these managerial gifts provided SoniCo's obscure patina, the "cool" that made the job "not feel like work." On the day management informed us that some Moog equipment would be returning from being on loan to an art gallery, Thomas and Robert got excited, even giddy. The office buzzed with anticipation for the remainder of the day as Robert began to play songs featuring Moog synthesizers on the office stereo. As a supervisor and thus somewhat closer to management, he repeatedly emphasized the exchange value of these items. Regular employees, on the other hand, emphasized how they would be able to use these devices in the studio and play with them while at work. "Oh man! That's going to be so cool to play around with later. There's a Theremin in there. You know what those are?" asked Thomas, turning toward me. I nodded.

"Here's your toys, guys!" said the manager as he unveiled a box full of sleek, white Moog devices—an echo of the same manager's unveiling of equipment during my first day of fieldwork, which I recounted in chapter 1. The affective tenor of the office shifted to that of Christmas morning. Staff explained to me that these white effect boxes, or "pedals," were limited editions. The standard models only came in black. Everyone dropped whatever it was they were doing, rushing to assemble the Moog equipment for display and use in the office and studio. Thomas said the Moog equipment had "beautiful knobs that are so cool." The better part of an hour passed as we put together a display for the Moog pedals. As we neared completion, Robert said, "I know just the guitar to test these babies out!" He then left the room to find the instrument, leaving Thomas and I to assemble the Theremin—an instrument that generates sound through bodily manipulation of invisible electromagnetic fields. Once assembled, the Theremin emitted high-pitched squeals and low-frequency wobbles as we gestured frantically above its metal poles, our manual wizardry conjuring sounds from thin air. "This is so cool!" Thomas exclaimed.

What was I to make of this situation? Was this simply an emergent form of play, or did the "cool" of the working day stem from management? Was this their way of fostering "creativity" at work? I asked the gear-bearing Moog Santa manager, and he said, "That Moog deal was just as much about everyone at the company being like 'this is cool' as it was about a [sales] partnership. In the work environment we have to encourage creativity. To me it's all about making sure people are lined up with what they're doing." "Lining up" organizational demands with workers' creativity came in two forms: supervisors were encouraged to take ownership of their divisions, and lower-level employees were encouraged to play with the equipment that SoniCo rents and sells to clients. "Cool" as the Moog equipment might have been for staff, they were also potential sources of revenue, so long as employees could demonstrate the Moog hardware to customers. Above and beyond requisite office tasks, employees had to learn to operate the items, generating surplus knowledge for the firm and potential sales revenue.

Play in the office had been encouraged by management and reinforced by supervisors. For example, Robert sent out a company-wide email asking employees to tinker with the equipment, with a half-joking but mostly serious conclusion, "If you don't already want to [play with this stuff] you have no soul." The objects provided a source of "cool," focusing workers' attention as they use and develop tacit skills. This "cool," grounded in the objects' materialities, served as a control mechanism, enrolling workers through the reproduction of expressive work's sensuality. They *felt* creative, and that feeling served as a delicate, precariously placed bandage, enrolling employees by focusing knowledge accumulation.

In the months that followed, employees frequently took breaks to diddle the keys of the synthesizers or play their favorite instruments through the limited-edition effect pedals, most often during the slowest shifts, when few clients appeared on the rehearsal schedule and thus when there was little administrative/clerical work. One evening, an employee brought a homemade cigar-box guitar to the office. He intended to play this homemade instrument through the office's impressive array of timbre-altering devices. When things were slow, he approached the Moog display in the corner of the office, but the guitar amplifier had been removed, potentially bringing to a premature end his intention to noodle. "Where'd the [amplifier] head go to?" he asked. "Hmm, they must've sold it." Though he shook this off in a way that suggests that the absence of his distraction held little importance to him, he appeared noticeably curt with clients and visibly distressed for the rest of the shift. He repeatedly looked around for the missing amplifier and restated to coworkers that he had planned to play his homemade guitar through the equipment. Later, we found out that it had only been removed for repair. Recall that in the context of engineer work, equipment such as this appeared inseparable from workers' skill and the pleasures of creativity. If the firm's objects enable aesthetic agency, then the denial of these objects denies what Theodor Adorno claimed to be the promise of aesthetic objects: "dispensation from a life that is always too little."[29]

During another quiet shift, a Moog Voyager XL synthesizer arrived, an expensive piece of equipment retailing for upward of $5,000. Intended to replicate the look and feel of vintage instruments from the 1970s, the large, wood-paneled Voyager possessed nearly limitless sound-generating capabilities—a tagline used in the promotion of the device, sure, but also a feature of its design. Beyond the object's retro exterior, the device's design provided an abundance of visible, potential uses, many of which were suggested by Voyager's multiple control interfaces and patchbay, which allows users to manually route electrical signals via an array of cables. Marcus, an attendant, was working in the front office that evening. He said, "I'm working up here, but [the managers] want me to figure out how that thing works, so I got a bunch of patch cables for the patch bay. [That synth] makes you want to smoke some weed and disappear into that thing." Earlier, Thomas and another attendant named Arnold had made similar comments about how they had spent a lunch hour "lost inside" a similar device.

Similar to the engineers' enjoyment of technologies with seemingly infinite expressive possibilities, office staff tended more to be captivated by equipment when they were only partially familiar with the object's capabilities or by its seemingly innumerable expressive possibilities. To become captivated, they must first imaginatively infer their potential aesthetic agency. These enchanting technologies captivate employees by way of their perceived beauty and uncertain uses, a marked difference from the economic uncertainty that once compelled factory workers to engage in the shop floor's competitive, economically rational games.[30] In other words, they may know about the brand name (e.g., "oh, it's a Fender model" or "Oh, dude! Moog!") but not the precise limits of the object's functionality (e.g., "I don't even know all the kinds of stuff you can do with it"). In contrast, employees found equipment with clearly delineated functions to be less enchanting or unremarkable (e.g., "This amplifier will be used by a bass player during tonight's session" or "This microphone is best used for quiet singing under specific conditions"). The former appears as a bundle of imagined potential uses, while the latter appears as a specific, technical function. The enchanting object, perceived as a bundle of imagined uses, captivates the employee, offering real, imagined avenues for aesthetic agency. More simply put, they disappear into the object.

Phrases like "disappearing" or "getting lost" inside an object gesture toward the same subjective absence as found in an engineer's earlier comment about "entering the Matrix." When pressed for explanation, Marcus explained disappearing as "hyper-focus where time is irrelevant and hunger or going to the bathroom are [irrelevant] too," like "reading a novel and not wanting to put it down, that kind of immersion." Another employee called this "being in the zone," which "does not feel like work." Days after I spoke with Marcus, I heard strange electronic sounds emanating from the front room. Through the doorway I saw Marcus in front of the synthesizer, though not touching it. Marcus had inserted cables into the patchbay's numerous holes and had found the "hold" function that he had been searching for previously. This allowed for the manipulation of tonal parameters without pressing any of the device's keys. He pointed to a button and said, "Yeah man, it's right here. Man, this is fun." When I left the studio several hours later, Marcus was in the same place, making even more bizarre sounds. He flashed me a mischievous smile while having a bit of fun at work.

These objects reproduce a commonly found experience among workers in media's more expressive occupations: pleasurable absorption, or "flow" states.[31] Coined by the psychologist Mikhail Csikszentmihalyi, "flow" refers to subjective states wherein workers "stop being aware of themselves as separate from the activity they are performing."[32] However, this definition ignores the materiality of these experiences and thus the extent to which "flow" depends upon particular felt experiences vis-à-vis objects. For this reason, I prefer the term "aesthetic experience," which highlights how these moments depend not simply upon individual psychology but upon the social relations made durable by material objects' design and function.[33]

Immersion and disappearance are common features of aesthetic experiences in diverse theoretical traditions ranging from the more pragmatic approaches of Alfred Gell and John Dewey to Theodor Adorno's critical approach.[34] In each of the examples in this chapter, workers' interactions with technology bear a remarkable similarity to Alfred Gell's theorization of power and art objects.[35] Gell theorized that aesthetic objects—emically defined as beautiful—serve as technologies that constitute social relationships and groups.[36] He refers to this as "enchantment," which depends upon the inability of some viewers to fully understand the means by which beautiful objects come into existence (e.g., marveling at the production of a painting). In eliciting aesthetic experiences, objects act as indexical signs of human agency[37]—the "magic" of creative labor. Thus, the interaction between objects and individuals constitutes a social relationship between human agency embodied in objects and a sensing subject. As Gell wrote, the aesthetic object "is inherently social in a way in which the merely beautiful or mysterious object is not: it is a physical entity which mediates between two beings, and therefore creates a social relation between them, which in turn provides a channel for further social relations and influences."[38] The interaction results in captivation, which consists of being confronted with an object that displays a "spectacle of unimaginable virtuosity," eliciting deep fascination or "becoming *trapped within*."[39] To explain relations between technical artifacts and creative labor, Gell's captivation requires modification. In considering workers or spectators with some degree of artistic inclination or training, I take Gell to mean that aesthetic objects invite observers to imagine processes that produced the object. While aesthetic objects may contain "unimaginable" actions for untrained observers, those possessing a degree of knowledge regarding their production or use may infer creative processes congealed in or afforded by the object. Observers may not, however, have imagined these processes before the encounter.

SoniCo's "beautiful" pieces of gear index processes that they also enable, and so these objects also index the agency of the observer or user. Because the observer had not previously imagined these processes, the object captivates, constituting a social relation between actors (management and workers) mediated by the object. These objects appear to workers as subjectively beautiful while also enabling aesthetic agency or their human capacity to be expressive, exerting control over the sounds and sights encountered in daily life.[40] Rather than abducing another's expressive activity (the process that produced an aesthetic object), SoniCo's gear invites employees to imagine their potential aesthetic agency or processes of producing *with* the beautiful technology. In that the firm owns these objects, this constitutes a relationship between firm and employee mediated by the objects, which facilitate the production of culture (music, in this case) as well as knowledge and other products of cognitive capitalism and the information economy. The imagined, potential, and indeterminate expressivity afforded by these technical artifacts provides for what I have been calling aesthetic enrollment. Returning to Gell's aesthetic theory, the employees appear captivated by the potentials for aesthetic agency perceived as immanent to gear. In these moments of captivation, they gain a moment of dispensation from work. This contributes to the "love" for the job. As a source of pleasure, "gear" distracts workers from the wounds of low wages and minor skirmishes between customers and employees.

Gear also provided a basis for more traditionally social moments. Two years after the Moog incident, Clyde and Jeff were setting up a Boss Electronics pedalboard display containing fifteen timbre-altering effect boxes, or "pedals," arranged in three rows on a board. Jeff plugged a Fender Jazzmaster guitar that regularly hung on the office wall into the pedalboard and started turning random pedals on and off—an "auto-wah" envelope filter, a flanger, a phase shifter—before focusing on three pedals that add "gain" to a guitar's tone, producing the loud, gritty sound typical of various strains of rock music. "Oh, that's like a Marshall [amplifier]," he said as he clicked on one pedal with his hand and unleashed a bluesy run of notes. Jeff said, "Man, Frank [another employee] is not allowed to play through this. I don't want to hear [him play] Eric Clapton." "Endless fun," said Clyde with a laugh. Jeff continued to play, soloing atop looping chord progressions by using a pedal called "Loop Station." After about fifteen minutes, Clyde said, "Okay, your five minutes are up," and Jeff hung up the guitar and shut off the amplifier. "Man, that made work a whole lot more fun." Jeff and Clyde form a bond while filling their downtime, and, in doing so, they learn how to operate and explain the gear.

Technology may facilitate social interactions and aesthetically enroll workers, but this process is far from seamless or certain. Instead, control over creative labor appears highly tentative, always on the cusp of slippage. Aesthetic enrollment temporarily stabilizes labor relations, binding workers to the organization's project of profit making, but only for a relatively short time. Even then, workers withdrew from their tasks or left the job because of overwhelming economic insecurity, which I will describe in chapter 4. Before exiting, they chose to disappear into their smartphones instead of into SoniCo's gear, or, like Melville's Bartleby,[41] they "preferred not to," engaging in atomized resistance or exit rather than collective mobilization—a situation typical of media industries in North America.[42] Even unhappy workers like the one quoted earlier in this chapter still understood SoniCo as "cool," a situation that presents a conundrum for those interested in potential labor resistance. How, after all, does one mobilize against that which one desires?

CONCLUSION

Before turning to workers' alienation and economic precarity in the next chapter, I want to round out this chapter by contextualizing SoniCo's positive pole within labor studies and conclude by situating this case within my larger argument about cognitive capitalism. SoniCo may seem idiosyncratic, but management's invitation to be creative bears a striking similarity to more widespread, contemporary managerial strategies for controlling labor. For example, tech firms invite employees to express themselves, opening up a "conversation" between managers and staff, and management in call centers and other customer service jobs encourage "authenticity" or "being yourself" in order to enchant the workplace and mask more rigid, technical control mechanisms.[43] Still, SoniCo differs from these contexts insofar as SoniCo's invitation to be creative depends upon a particular structure of feeling rather than by allowing workers to enact an "authentic" identity. Controlling creative labor depends upon sensual engagement, whether it be through the much-publicized opulence of tech-sector workplaces or the low-voltage excitements found in every potentially productive, postsocial interaction between workers and technology. The observations presented earlier as well as research from other scholars concerned with creative labor suggest the importance of managing how work *feels*.[44]

My observations run rough against explanations that focus too closely on ideological belief or economic rationality—the *illusio*, ideology, or discourse so often highlighted as key explanans in studies of creative work or the more squarely economic approach typical of conventional labor studies. Both would point us toward an economic explanation focused on the pursuit of interests while ignoring the sensual experience of creative labor. Focusing on how a complex assemblage of humans and nonhumans produced a particular feeling provides a more grounded explanation of how creative workers come to enjoy and thus consent to precarious employment. At SoniCo, objects aid management in making workers feel "creative." *Things* help reproduce the subjective experience of work in another, expressive context (i.e., as musicians or engineers), which is then leveraged by management as a form of control, one that secures cheap labor with requisite forms of tacit knowledge. To borrow from Paul Willis, office employees work for little money "amid provided commodities"—the instruments of cultural production—and in addition to their small wages they receive management's "essential, rare, irreverent gift: creativity."[45]

In sum, this chapter illustrated three components of a theory of creative labor. First, creative labor is managed and subject to control. This may strike some as unsurprising, but it runs contrary to both common-sense understandings of creativity as a "free" activity and portrayals of creative labor as unmanaged.[46] Engineers and office workers both possessed autonomy with minimal direct managerial oversight, but they remained subject both to managerial control and the professional conventions of music production. At SoniCo, control depended upon social relations between management and workers—often mediated by technology—and upon social conventions specific to the field of music. Likewise, the valorization or valuation of creative labor tended to depend upon social ties and social qualities (e.g., reputation, status, etc.), and so SoniCo might best be described as a *social* regime of creative labor. This appears fundamentally different from the firm to be discussed in part 3, wherein the valuation of creative labor tends toward the impersonal and quantified. Second, SoniCo's expressive and routine jobs both required creative labor, or the interpretation, manipulation, and production of signs and symbols, as well as emotional labor. Thus, the distinction between routine and expressive work in the culture industries appears empirically salient but not theoretically important insofar as both required creative labor.

Third, performing creative labor at SoniCo required the use of technologies that engaged workers aesthetically or sensually. Embodied pleasures vis-à-vis technology constituted a part of creative labor's positive pole, and so I argue that "creativity"—as ideology or *dispositif*—depends upon distinct workplace materialities in order to secure consent to precarious employment. Explanations leaning too heavily upon the crutch of ideology or discourse miss this material dimension of supposedly "immaterial" or cognitive labor. Experiences elicited by work's distinct materialities aesthetically enroll workers in organizational processes and thus bind workers to the ideology, discourse, or what Brooke Duffy and Elizabeth Wissinger call "mythologies" of creativity.[47] Aesthetic enrollment elicits a partial, tentative consent as workers experience attachment alongside intense dissatisfaction caused by low pay and precarious employment. This is what I mean when I say that these aesthetic experiences paper over conflict, loosely binding workers to work like cheap adhesive tape on a wound in need of stitches—functional for a time, sure, but ultimately unstable and never resolving creative labor's conflicted polarities.

Management engaged in soft forms of direct control, encouraged responsible autonomy or self-management, and altered the employer/employee relationship by encouraging freelancing among engineers. This strategy "businesses" workers,[48] shifting the costs of finding gigs in a system of project-based employment onto workers and reproducing neoliberalism's entrepreneurial subject. Project-based employment incentivizes engineers to engage in the professional networking and entrepreneurial practices described in the next chapter. Engineers develop an aesthetic subjectivity prone to finding sensorial pleasure in technology. Technology appears desirable, magical, or beautiful thanks to its ability to extend engineers' techniques of expression and control over sound. Their desire to create and express—to exert aesthetic agency—tends always to be bound up in technology. As such, they desire to know and understand technology in order to "be creative," and they "disappear" into these objects as they labor, losing themselves in work.[49]

Among office staff, management structured work's aesthetic landscape, populating the office with similarly pleasurable or "beautiful" objects that afford creative explorations—"disappearances"—in the context of otherwise routine work. These fleeting moments were similar to the "pleasurable absorption" or "flow" experiences found in other studies of workers in cultural and information industries.[50] By disappearing into the object, staff experienced otherwise mundane, tedious, or exploitative work as pleasurable, in part because of these objects' enabling of creativity. Through their promise of real (potential) aesthetic agency, these objects align workers' desire for expression with management's desire for instrumentally pragmatic problem solving, a process by which workers become affectively bound to their tasks, what I call *aesthetic enrollment*.

At SoniCo's positive pole, objects provided a basis for articulating sensual, embodied meanings with the *managerial invitation*, propelling workers forward in their daily tasks. As part of work's aesthetic dimension, technology enchants workers and forms part of the control mechanism by which capital secures creative labor. Creative labor comes to be activated and deployed through technological systems that act upon while also mediating a worker's sensorium, and so a worker's desire to accept the managerial invitation bears a similarity to what Boutang theorizes as cognitive capitalism's distinctive mode of desire: *libido sciendi*, or the desire to know.[51] The positive pole illustrated in this chapter may partially satisfy workers' *libido sciendi*, but what of their entrepreneurial aims and economic precarity? SoniCo's positive pole blurs distinctions between work and leisure, employer and employee, precarity and pleasure. These blurred boundaries suggest potential obstacles for collective labor mobilization insofar as workers do not recognize their activities as made up of a common, "immaterial," or creative *labor*[52] but, instead, as creative *entrepreneurs*. With this entrepreneurialism in mind, I turn to creative labor's negative pole.

Chapter Four

SONICO'S NEGATIVE POLE

Mitigating Precarity and Alienated Judgment

In 2016, I met Sam, SoniCo's youngest office worker and an aspiring recording engineer. His hair greasy and disheveled, jeans fashionably torn from wear, he spent a lot of downtime in the office with his headphones on working on recordings on his laptop. He came to Los Angeles from the Southwest, where his life had been "really crazy." "I was exposed to like, heroin and drugs at fourteen. I was homeless for a while—still going to high school. And then I was living in an apartment, some drug dealer above us got robbed and killed with a shotgun. We heard it downstairs and were just like, 'What the fuck is happening?!' And then a week later, the cops found a decaying body below us in another apartment." He left after that, making his way to LA with no job prospects and no safety net. He had attended the same trade school as Emmerich, SoniCo's head engineer, and used that lucky connection to find work. "I started as his intern and then found work here after that. I was living for three months on credit, not working." He now earned around ten dollars per hour, without benefits, aside from free access to SoniCo's equipment, rooms, and any potential networking opportunities offered by the job.

One night, I sat outside the studio with Sam as he smoked a cigarette. Thomas passed by, and Sam asked him for advice on a project and when he might be able to use the recording room—one of the "benefits" of the job.

Like so many other conversations at SoniCo, this one revolved around gear and audio processing, specifically their favorite microphones and a program, or "plug-in," which digitally simulates the sonic qualities of recording to analog audio tape. Sam rattled off some microphone model numbers, noting which ones he liked best. Thomas liked his choices. "Yeah that's great! If I just had two mics, it'd be the M400 and MU-45." Happy to see me back at SoniCo after some time away, Thomas laughed and said, "Well, that was some nerdy conversation. *That* hasn't changed around here. We're nerds." Likewise, he still enjoyed his work, especially more complex sessions like the one he had just finished—fourteen songs with a band whose style mimicked the well-known speedfreak rock band Mötör-head. As he said, "It's not hard, well, it's sort of hard with the layers, but it's fun. It's really fun."

Sam finished his cigarette and walked inside to finish his shift, only to return to the benches outside the studio after he clocked out to wait for prices on Lyft, a ride-sharing app, to go down. His car had recently stopped working, so he relied on ride-sharing services to make the long commute from the San Fernando Valley. This cost him thirteen dollars for a one-way trip. It was one of the busy times of day, when Lyft's prices doubled, so he decided to hang around to chat with more experienced recording engineers and smoke a joint before requesting a ride. This networking opportunity would, with any luck, provide future recording gigs. Back inside, Jeff ordered food from a nearby taqueria and asked Clyde, another recent hire, if he wanted anything. Clyde declined, in part given Jeff's preference for the cheapest, least palate-pleasing restaurants, but also from thrift. Clyde relied on his girlfriend to bring him food from the restaurant where she worked. Like Sam, Clyde used ride-service apps such as Uber and Lyft to commute from the Valley to SoniCo. Luckily, the couple had found an affordable apartment closer to the studio, and now he would only have to pay five dollars each way, and nothing when she could pick him up.

Cheap food was a perennial topic of conversation, and tonight was no different. Like many Angelenos, they frequented taquerias and taco trucks for cheap eats. Jeff preferred the dollar tacos available around the corner from the studio, but most of the guys opted to pay a little more, as much as $1.75, for better-tasting food. Emmerich preferred a truck located just around the corner. "Really, burritos are kind of hard to fuck up. It's rice, beans, meat. Okay, you can fuck up the meat, I guess, but really, it's just these basic staples of food put in a tortilla. So, it's all about the salsa. The truck around the corner, to me, has the best salsa." Clyde preferred Poquito Más, a regional chain mostly located in the San Fernando Valley, a choice politely dismissed by Emmerich. Clyde backpedaled, "I like it, but their salsa sucks. I don't like the local truck. They use whole beans instead of mashed-up [refried] beans. What's up with that?" Angling for the last word, Emmerich offered some solid advice on combining salsas: "I don't know. I like the local truck. Better salsas. You put that green avocado kind with the red kind. It's great!" When the food arrived, Jeff ate his burrito while Clyde waited for his partner to deliver his meal.

Some months earlier, Marcus, one of the previous chapter's disappearing workers, had stood on the rear gate of a U-Haul truck and exclaimed, with more than a touch of sarcasm, "Just think! All this for indie rock!" The other workers and I laughed as we finished packing two trucks full of gear for a concert sponsored by the studio. No one liked the performers on the schedule, least of all Marcus, who saw the concert's lineup and immediately said, "Wow, this looks like a boring indie festival!" His taste veered toward the experimental and avant-garde, a preference illustrated by his hobby of tinkering with uncommon technologies, such as his homemade "hydrophone," or underwater microphone. Likewise, he did not enjoy much of the music made by SoniCo's clients. It ran rough against his taste—yet here he was, clad in his tattered leather jacket and black jeans, loading pieces of a stage, guitar and bass amplifiers, mixers, turntables, and microphone stands in the trucks. Just imagine, all that for indie rock.

These moments lay bare some of the wounds that are often bandaged by the immersive disappearances and friendships described in the previous chapter. I call these experiences the *negative pole of creative labor*. To begin, here are two young men, new to LA and struggling to make ends meet. They make entrepreneurial use of their time while waiting for food and transport, using these moments as opportunities to network with senior staff, potential clients, and high-status freelancers. Like so many working men of yesteryear, they rely upon the hidden labor of women to aid in the provision of care and sustenance. Like so many of today's working people, they rely upon apps for transportation because they cannot afford to own property, not even a functioning car, let alone a home. Some things change and some things stay the same: they use apps but still depend upon the unpaid carework of women to survive. The example of Marcus shows workers' distaste for the very music that depends upon their labor. In conceptual terms, these workers struggle to reproduce themselves despite low wages and precarity, and, ultimately, to reconcile matters of taste or judgment. Creative labor's positive pole may ease these tensions but fails to resolve them. Management's invitation to "be creative" and employees' disappearance into technology may bind and bandage, but they provide no sustenance, no reconciliation.[1]

This chapter is organized around two questions that move toward a theory of creative labor. First, how do these people survive on such paltry wages? Second, how do workers relate to their products? The first calls attention to the labor of reproduction—an answer to which the vignettes just described provide a beginning—while the latter calls forth alienation, a fraught[2] specter whose relevance to creative labor remains hauntingly undertheorized by even those most attentive to labor under cognitive capitalism. In addressing these questions, I trace the valences of creative labor's negative pole, which include the uncertainty of employment, a cruel orientation to the future, and a distinctive form of self-estrangement that I call *alienated judgment*. The positive pole portrayed in the previous chapter called to mind the biggest fear of critical labor scholars: subjectivity molded to production's demands and capital's full subsumption of the social. This fear arises again and again, starting with Lukács's discussion of reification and the dark prognostications of the early Frankfurt School and continuing on to the "social factory" hypothesis taken up by theorists of cognitive capitalism.[3] The sounds of workers diddling the keys of a synthesizer, enchanted and aesthetically enrolled, certainly resonate with this fear, but should we be so afraid? I think not. Workers' subjectivity may be ever more subsumed by capital as the working day provides for their enjoyment, but that same working day alienates judgment, providing the conditions of possibility for the collective mobilization of disparate occupations requiring creative labor.

PRECARIOUS EMPLOYMENT, CLASS, AND EXPLOITATION

Precarious employment broadly refers to nonstandard work arrangements, often mediated by markets rather than "standard" employment within a firm. This includes a wide variety of jobs from high-paid tech contractors, to day laborers hired out of Home Depot parking lots, to the sort of platform-based work I will describe in later chapters. Precarity is on the rise in all sectors of the U.S. economy, and labor protections and unionization[4] continue to decline. While some forms of precarious work offer high wages and autonomy, many others tend to be what the labor sociologist Arne Kalleberg calls "bad" jobs. In these "bad" jobs, employees lack control over their hours and tasks, receive no health or retirement benefits, and gain no opportunities for regular, predictable wage increases. Both "good" and "bad" forms of precarious employment share nonstandard or irregular patterns of work. Instead of confining everyone to "standard" employment (e.g., a forty-hour work week within the stable confines of a single employer), capitalism now leaves everyone free to become a temp or a contractor, an "enterprise of the self" selling services to other businesses.

If this sounds a bit like SoniCo's recording engineers, that is because irregular patterns of work have been the norm for decades in the culture industries.[5] In music, much like film and television, work tends to be precarious and project based, with workers drawn together into teams for set periods of time and then thrown back into the labor market. Most exert little control over the employment situation and over the quality of their products beyond their specific labor inputs.[6] Thus, creative jobs tend also to be "bad" jobs by Kalleberg's definition. While some claim that the experiences I describe as creative labor's positive pole balance out the fiscal deficits, cognitive burdens, and emotional wounds produced by bad jobs, others highlight workers' oscillation between freedom and deep-seated anxiety.[7] The latter stems from "existential, financial, and social insecurity" associated with heightened demands for worker flexibility.[8] Rather than view workers' experience as a ledger perfectly balanced by deposits of autonomy, community, and sensual enjoyment and the debits of economic insecurity, we might do better to think this tension as irresolvable—held loosely together by work's engagements or aesthetic enrollments.

As precarious employment grows, scholars and activists have tried to expand definitions of "working class" to include the struggling self-employed and creative professionals alongside those in less formal careers who lack professional identities.[9] Expanding the definition of exploited workers forces sociologists of labor to consider those that might appear to be entrepreneurs as *workers*. This is, of course, not an entirely new idea. Nearly sixty years ago, the Situationist International, a left-wing art collective, commented on knowledge workers and artists by saying that "they are identifying themselves with a category separate from the workers (artists for example)—in which case we will fight this illusion by showing them that *the new proletariat is tending to encompass almost everybody*."[10] The "new proletariat" of 1962 reappears today in the form of the free and anxious "precariat," or the "multitude," groups that capital wants "to work for free whenever it has possibility."[11]

This expanded definition of "worker" requires a reconsideration of exploitation, an often emotionally charged term most clearly defined by Erik Olin Wright as any unequal exchange relationship wherein the dominant actor's position depends upon the subordinate position of the dominated actor.[12] This definition does much to move beyond the more limited view of exploitation as coterminous with excessively harsh or unsafe conditions, especially when considered in tandem with what the economist Yan Moulier Boutang defines as second-degree exploitation.[13] While first-degree exploitation depends upon physical labor power consumed during the working day, second-degree exploitation depends upon capturing the inventive, improvisatory potential of creative labor. Creative labor tends to be expelled in the labor process but remains "living labor," forever inhered in workers' cognitive processes and thus not easily separated from workers and incorporated into machinery as in automation. In later chapters, I show how platforms alter this process. Regardless of exploitative degree, Christian Fuchs argues that precarious work under cognitive capitalism constitutes "over-exploitation," wherein exploitation "approaches infinity" because of underpayment or pushing workers toward self-employment.[14] Fuchs argues that in order to maintain economic solvency, businesses in the information and culture industries depend upon low or no wages. If these businesses were unable to evade payment or push workers outside the bounds of the firm as SoniCo does, the organizations would fail to profit.

This produces a potential crisis of reproduction. Despite being largely dependent upon the mind, creative labor requires a body, and that body requires housing and sustenance. Even cheap tacos require money, something in short supply despite long hours of work. The constant need to improvise, develop, and maintain multiple sources of income results in an entrepreneurial disposition in line with what Paul duGay calls the broader "businessing" of labor.[15] Rather than organize collectively as a class, they engage in work that *may* yield income later—what Gina Neff calls "venture labor"—as a way of "managing" their precarity and maximizing "freedom" in the labor market.[16] Though they may resemble precarious workers in what Kalleberg calls "bad jobs" or the "precariat," they interpret their situation positively, as entrepreneurs and empowered individuals, rather than as an oppressed collectivity. In what follows, I focus on how underpayment and the push toward self-employment force workers to perform additional work-to-labor in their efforts to shore up economic gaps and temporarily solve the crisis of reproduction.

THE CREATIVE PRECARITY OF
THE ENTREPRENEURIAL ENGINEER

Engineers may work *at* SoniCo, but they rarely work *for* SoniCo, and so they tend to depend upon referrals from within their professional networks for securing steady flows of work. All my interviewees expressed an equal amount of fear caused by job insecurity, often recounting promised gigs that never materialized, though they also described finding work as "easy" or "not a problem." Even successful, midcareer engineers like Toby, a producer of Latin dance music, said as much. When we met, Toby was a sought-after recording engineer and producer in LA, but his career had begun in New York. He had worked his way up from lowly assistant to "first call" engineer after some chart-topping successes. Still, he felt no more secure in his future than others. He was "hot right now" but worried what might happen if his career turned a more wintry temperature:

> I'm hotter than I ever could've been as a producer right now and I'm making the bills, but what does that mean if I'm warm? [If I'm just warm] I'm going to be fucking a little broke 'cause hot is just paying the bills. [Laughing] You know what I'm saying? I could use a haircut. You know what I mean? [Laughing] So, what I don't like about the job is the uncertainty. Are you good [at your job]? We all need the lucky break. We all need breaks. What a terrifying concept. Like, it's not about how good you are. Do you know what I mean?

Orlando, an early-career engineer who earned anywhere from fifty to one thousand dollars per song, said, "Nine out of ten people you meet will be full of it. Even people you're cool with. You know, dude, I lost track of how many people I just stopped talking to because I just saw they were shady." Orlando and his wife both work, and the couple receives nonmonetary support from their immediate and extended families in the form of child-care and other domestic assistance. A father in a precarious career, he said, "Yeah, it is stressful. When you have a kid, you're going to worry. Where's the next check coming from? So yeah, I worry. Even to the point where I want to give up and get a regular job. I was at that point last year and then got a call from my buddy, got a good project." Despite the stress of precarity, engineers stay in the field, something partially explained by work's engagements and aesthetic enrollments.

Understanding *how* they persist requires that we understand their perception of possible career trajectories. One well-known way of explaining how people imagine their career trajectory and thus their persistence in a risky career path goes something like this: workers imagine exponentially large returns on investments of their "human capital"—what I would call selling their labor power—and this imagined future propels them forward, despite uncertain outcomes. This runs through both the sort of Bourdieuian explanations discussed in chapter 1 and more squarely economic explanations such as those found in Venkatesh and Levitt's study of street gangs.[17] In the latter, they argue that potential long-term rewards derived from moving from the bottom to the top of a hierarchy motivate people to pursue high-risk work (e.g., the drug trade, academics, the arts, etc.) despite more stable options available in other occupations (e.g., fast-food or clerical work). A midcareer engineer named Dean who works out of SoniCo suggested a similar orientation to the future:

> My main focus is just trying to mix the best songs ever because when I mix an awesome song, I'm associated with really good artistry, and that's the goal for right now. I'm not thinking of this part of my career as that time of my career where I'm going to make a lot of money. That's going to ideally come like five or six years from now when I break into the major-label scene or I'm doing more high-end production and stuff like that.

For engineers, however, there exists no clear hierarchy within which engineers would or could rise, and, as Dean explained, engineers' relative invisibility compared to musicians diminished his ability to develop a reputation and benefit from his accomplishments. Dean suggested as much when he described the recording process for popular R&B and hip-hop songs:

> If I mix a song and it becomes a digital single on iTunes, you'll never see my credit. It won't show up on the Internet.... For example, I was the main engineer for a Grammy award–winning record, however the way that things work out in the music industry is like if you spend three years making an album, and let's say you send a song to Andre 3000[18] [to add a single vocal track] and his engineer records his vocal and they send it back. Well, that's, now there's two engineers that are credited on the album.... So, you end up having an album where you did most of the work, but there is like six people credited for [the album].

Engineers like Toby and Dean may orient toward future rewards, but the rewards tend to be unevenly distributed and never fully settled. Toby may turn cold, and, as Dean said, "I'll go from like, having assistants and being like, flown all over the world and million-dollar studios every day with food budgets and stuff and then like, then the next project will be in someone's living room or whatever."

So how do engineers deal with unstable employment? Orlando glossed over the subject and said he just kept "trusting god and having faith," but most engineers described concrete, entrepreneurial tactics. These tactics are examples of "creative precarity," or the development of diverse entrepreneurial ventures intended to manage risk by expanding sources of income derived from the few assets possessed by workers (i.e., their labor power and equipment).[19] Uncertainty in the labor market leads to tactics of creative precarity, an increasingly common finding in studies of creative labor in both the United States and United Kingdom.[20] For engineers, creative precarity consisted of developing and maintaining diverse networks of peers and clients in order to avoid dependence and secure continuous work opportunities (diversification), taking up work adjacent or related to their professional skillset (skill flexibility), and becoming a microbusiness. Engaging in these tactics obscured SoniCo's dependence upon engineers by changing what might have been an employer/employee relationship thirty years ago into a business to microbusiness relationship.

Diversification and Skill Flexibility

Engineers' first tactic for managing precarity involved diversifying sources of income, or, to use the language of neoliberal economics, their human capital investments. We saw an example of this tactic in the previous chapter, where Emmerich, SoniCo's house engineer, sat alone editing and arranging songs that he had created for use as royalty-free music in the production of film, television, and digital media content. He even hoped to expand his range of services beyond music production by making use of SoniCo's "dark magic" technologies for additional work as a forensic audio analyst. Others engaged in similar tactics, and so, even alone in the studio, he and other engineers held practices in common in reaction to their precarity.

For instance, Dean, an award-winning recording engineer, diversified by offering consultations to aspiring engineers. For a fee, he would review others' work via the website Audio U. Dean also diversified and expanded his professional network by procuring gigs through Soundbetter.com, a website through which potential clients offer work to engineers via an online bidding system. Crucially different from the digital creators who appear in later chapters, Dean does not depend solely upon these platforms for work even if they are becoming more common. Among those with whom I spoke, gigs obtained through internet referrals and online labor market intermediaries such as Soundbetter.com were described as highly undesirable, low-status gigs. For example, Orlando said,

> I got hit up by a guy on Twitter from London. I'll show you some. It's terrible. He hit me up and was like, "yeah, the song doesn't sound right." I did it because I'm going to get some money. Let me help him out because maybe he has potential. He could maybe potentially have some potential. [Laughing] Some people are just delusional, straight up. The music they produce, the content they produce is draining. . . . My mentor hits me up to work on a big artist's record, but then I'm hitting Ls [making lots of money] with these scrubs. [Laughing] It's crazy. It's absurd man. You get to a point where I think you don't like what you're doing.

Orlando's colorful statement requires a bit of unpacking. Always in search of work, he took a referral via Twitter despite misgivings. In his words, it could "potentially have some potential" but was ultimately "draining" because the artists were "scrubs" (losers). Despite the easy money ("hitting Ls," or "hitting licks," slang for robbing liquor stores), the low-quality, low-status project results in alienation. High-pay, low-status work may seem to balance out, but just as often engineers take on low-pay, low-status work. Many simply cannot afford to be inactive—or even be perceived to be—for long periods of time. As Emmerich said, "If it's a low amount of money and I have the time, I'll do it. I can't really turn down work when it comes."

Dean started to produce social media content as a promotional strategy, interviewing his clients after recording sessions and producing short comedy sketches intended for YouTube. Between sessions, Dean roamed the hallways with a cameraman discussing possible shots and concepts for videos. For one series of videos, Dean decided to use what he called a "Bob Barker microphone"—a reference to the distinctive slim microphone with telescoping handle favored by the deceased host of the American television game show *The Price Is Right*. Dean obtained one of these microphones by asking SoniCo's management to purchase one for the studio. He claimed that the purchase was a wise investment given the microphone's ability to retain value. As he said, "Yeah, well, they don't go down in value so you can just buy one for $400 and sell it for $450 . . . some go for $1,000." In the video, he planned to record a drum kit using the Bob Barker microphone. Developing dialogue for the video, Dean said, "[The Bob Barker microphone] really gets that tone, that zany tone." A studio intern chimed in, adding, "You know they have such a unique frequency range." Dean riffed a bit more, "Yeah, you know for when you want some zane [sic] on the snare drum."

Dean imagined this promotional work as a springboard for an additional income stream and thus a way to diversify his labor investments further. He intended to use the novelty microphone to build a "sample pack," or library of prerecorded drum sounds, for use in digital drum programming—another potential source of income derived from human and fixed capital investments in his brand-building YouTube venture. Dean said,

I know my [social] network is still not big enough to where I would be just crushing it So, that's one of the reasons why I'm starting my YouTube channel and this and that. Because gone are the days where I think it's really smart to be just a mixer, right? I love mixing, it's my passion, but part of what I want to do going into the future is like build up a brand, it could be anything from like, or for example we already have our first sponsor. So, we're going to do all these crazy videos, but we're going to package advertisements in the videos, and there is—all sorts of consulting you can do, and then if I build up the show, then I can get ad[vertising] revenue from that. And this is how I'm just trying to diversify and do a lot of things.

Notably, Dean's entrepreneurial venture depended upon an assemblage of technology and labor power or human capital (the body and knowledge).

Skill flexibility is another tactic for managing precarity; this consists of constant learning and tailoring of one's presentation of skill in order to further diversify income sources. Engineers called this being "flexible" with their skillset, a tactic that management scholars call being an "amoeba," a metaphor suggestive of how capitalism understands workers as shapeless, minuscule, intensely versatile entities.[21] This increasingly common approach to job hunting coincided with and supported the engineers' broader diversification tactics.[22] Dean developed new skills, acquired new technologies, and assembled a small team in order to accomplish the tasks of video production that will, in his view, promote his engineering career. Wanda also flexed her skills in the labor market. In addition to daily gigs as an engineer, she designed and installed sound systems for use in corporate boardrooms and school classrooms "all over LA." As she said, "I've done some IT/AV [information technology/audiovisual] stuff as related to computer networking a little bit and audio." In addition to being flexible in terms of time, one must be, according to Wanda, "flexible with the description of your work. [Laughing] A lot of times it can work in your favor, and you can put yourself out there to do more than one task." Like Wanda, Emmerich also earns "a fair amount of money doing studio building and consulting work. Those are rare, but they're a nice paycheck." While different from their core skillset, these extensions help them "diversify" their "portfolio," spreading risk across multiple sources of income—a rather neat fit with descriptions of neoliberalism's entrepreneurial subjectivity. According to Foucault, neoliberalism views workers not as labor but as "human capital," or entrepreneurs of themselves, something echoed in critiques of cognitive capitalism in which theorists describe workers as "virtuosos" who provide creative labor, improvising upon and acting through signs, symbols, and technology.[23]

Theorists of cognitive capitalism often refer to creative labor as "immaterial," which can have the effect of denying materiality and embodiment when discussing creative labor. Creativity and cognition, as parts of workers' "human capital" or labor power, always appear coterminous with the body. No one exists as a brain in a jar, and even if they did, that brain would require its jar, some means of connection to external stimuli, and some means of acting upon that external stimuli. If the neoliberal, entrepreneurial body exists as a "machine that produces an earnings stream,"[24] then Wanda, the ever-eloquent engineer, provided the most clear articulation of her machine's temporal and physiological limits:

> I think you can be really good at your job, but I also feel like you're also working against time. Our listening abilities are skills that we develop over time, but our bodies age, and we can't always perform the same way that we did years before. Even a man that thinks it's very manly to be in the music industry as a touring engineer, like I'm going to lift all the equipment and I'm going to haul all this heavy gear, what happens when you're seventy and you have a herniated disc and you can't do it?

While acknowledging creative labor's embodiment, Wanda suggests a hard limit to skill diversification. Creative labor requires maintenance of the body, something not often afforded by the tactics of creative precarity in which engineers engage. Whereas assets such as tools and technologies may be replaced, fixed, or augmented, workers' primary assets cannot be so easily restored. There comes a point where skill cannot be expanded upon or as flexibly deployed because the ears, the hands, the eyes, and all the other parts of the body-as-earning-machine wear out—something minimized by those who insist on calling creative labor "immaterial." Alongside this gesture, Wanda's reflection also reminds us that music production, like other culture industries, tends to be dominated by men.[25] That no woman won a Grammy for record engineering until 2019 suggests as much.[26] Returning to engineers' entrepreneurial tactics, Wanda and Emmerich both used the language of diversification and investment, and Dean discussed his personal brand. Their discussion of their tactics illustrate how entrepreneurial discourse has become a common tongue, one distinct from "creativity" but spoken by workers in many industries.

Becoming Studios

Further illustrating the entrepreneurial orientation developed within creative labor processes, engineers become microstudios, quite literally small enterprises servicing clients and other small businesses. This process begins after years spent accumulating enough equipment so as to offer services as either small studios housed at SoniCo or as mobile studios capable of recording at performance venues, nightclubs, rehearsal rooms, and other, less conventional production spaces such as basements and garages. Engineers also rented their equipment to other engineers as an additional revenue stream. For example, Toby, the engineer who feared the day when he might turn cold, rented his microphones and other pieces of gear to musicians and other engineers in order to gain more revenue. Avoiding studios altogether, Jeremy, a freelancer in his early twenties, worked out of his garage. Echoing SoniCo's owners, Jeremy described the importance of equipment in enchanting and attracting clients. His gear gave him a "weird credibility." As he explained, "Literally just having something that's a centerpiece to the studio and is big and pretty and lots of lights. People are sold by that."

Renting a small space at SoniCo, engineers become something not unlike a barber, hairstylist, or tattoo artist who rents a chair within a brick-and-mortar business while retaining their autonomy as an independent microbusiness. Producers such as Dean and Toby or "mix" engineers tend to become studios-within-a-studio.[27] Locating their microbusinesses within SoniCo reduces costs associated with renting or owning a building while offering increased networking opportunities thanks to the sheer number of musicians that pass through SoniCo's doors every week. Remember, management touts these networking opportunities as a perk.

In this context, everyone is a potential client or potential source of cheap or free labor for a project. While taking a break, Toby, the "hot" producer, and I sat outside chatting with some musicians, one of whom played ukulele. Toby asked him to "lay down" some ukulele on a few songs, or "tracks." We made our way to Toby's studio, where he quickly set up a microphone to record some ukulele. Toby played a song a few times and then, after a few trial runs through the tune, asked the ukulelist to record a few takes. All of this occurred inside of twenty minutes. Neither party discussed payment. Taking up residence within SoniCo affords Toby the potential to capture free labor by way of the networking opportunities available to him from the thousands of musicians that pass through Soni-Co's doors every month.

THE CRUELTY OF "STANDARD" EMPLOYMENT

In another tactic for mitigating precarity, engineers sought safety in "standard" employment by joining SoniCo's office staff, yet they continued to struggle to meet their basic needs. Several employees, like Sam, hoped to stretch their paychecks by living ten to twenty miles away from work—sometimes with relatives or parents—to offset LA's ever-rising cost of living. Even by LA standards, their commutes were lengthy. Those who lived nearby could walk or bicycle to work, but then their higher rent accounted for 40 to 60 percent of their monthly earnings. Those living farther away, like Sam, made use of platform-based transportation services such as Lyft or Uber. Paying $10 to $26 per day for transportation ($200 to $520 per month) may still be cheaper than car payments, insurance, and maintenance, but the working week and its lengthy commute left little time for the work of reproduction. Without time to shop for and prepare meals, they dined on LA's panoply of cheap food options or, like Clyde, relied upon friends, family, or romantic partners for culinary and, sometimes, pecuniary support.

Even with social support and extreme frugality, office staff still struggled to make ends meet. Gabriel, one of the few employees who quit during fieldwork, explained this quite clearly:

GABRIEL: Yeah, they're working more and just getting the allotted sum [salary] no matter what. It was literally unsustainable for me. I was barely scraping by.
MICHAEL: Yeah, I don't understand how some of you all do it.
GABRIEL: Yeah, even living on the East Side is hard. Even if you pay $750 a month, that's still not a lot of money left.
MICHAEL: That's maybe $1,600 a month before taxes and then, maybe $1,200 after taxes?
GABRIEL: Yeah.

Gabriel's salary came from a forty-to-sixty-hour workweek. Based on his estimate, rent accounts for 62 percent of his net wages, leaving roughly

$450 for utility bills, debt payments (e.g., credit card, car, or student loan payments, etc.), and groceries. Gabriel likened the situation to "slavery." He eventually quit eight months later and took up more lucrative work as an art handler, a comparably routine, creative job focused on transporting and installing fine art.

Initially, Gabriel took the job at SoniCo because he thought it might offer opportunities for work as a recording engineer—just the sort of future orientation that supposedly explains persistence in risky careers. Having trained in music production and composition, Gabriel possessed the necessary skills, and, of course, management presented the job as offering just these sorts of opportunities. As a supervisor explained, "So, [networking is] sort of seen as a—it's presented as a bit of a cachet. Like, oh you're interested in music, this can be a step up in terms of connections." Gabriel never managed to obtain session work, and even those that did struggled to fit sessions into their already full-time work schedules. This could be seen clearly in the previous chapter, in my recounting of Thomas's struggle to balance office and recording work.

The demands of office work stymied the very opportunities that initially led many engineers to work at the studio, an example of what Lauren Berlant calls *cruel optimism*.[28] In Berlant's usage, optimism refers to a future orientation, an openness to emergent possibility. Optimism becomes *cruel* when a situation that allows a person to imagine a possible, desirable future—here, the apparent promise and anticipation of desirable work—thwarts a person's ability to flourish. The social interactions described here, combined with creative labor's positive pole, comprise a situation wherein attachments both to humans and nonhumans (people and gear) bind workers to the organization. These attachments that sensually excite and give hope also block employees' path to the work they so desire and keep them locked in a groove of precarious, "standard" employment.

Some moments I shared with Nathan, an office worker in his late twenties, illustrate this point. I often sat with him while he took breaks. We sat outside the studio's front door discussing music, life in Los Angeles, and, of course, work as we chatted with musicians and engineers coming in and out of the studio. One day, Nathan told me that his career as an engineer was going well. "I gotta get my own music together though. Gotta try to get that going too. You know, I got solid recording gigs lined up, but now,

now I have to really get my own stuff. I figure now that I'm set up pretty good, I can get that going. Man, I just wish I had a day that I wasn't here." In one of his more lucrative recent gigs, he had earned a day rate of $125 for a twelve-hour day, just barely more than the ten dollars per hour he earned in SoniCo's office. For the rest of the day, he kept watching the clock and said that he could not wait until the end of his shift rolled around. Perhaps he hoped to work on the music he had been producing rather than schlepping amplifiers in and out of rooms or "disappearing" into SoniCo's gear. Either way, the job taken in order to solve Nathan's problem of spotty employment offered only a moderate amelioration of precarity and even seemed to obstruct his career progression. Still, Nathan remained hopeful and optimistic. "Whenever something good is happening for someone else, I just figure it'll be my turn soon enough."

While waiting for their turns, office employees worked full-time at the studio in addition to second, third, or even fourth jobs that included manual labor at live music events; working at local bars as bouncers, doormen, or bartenders; serving coffee; selling bodily fluids; and part-time office work elsewhere. Since many were also aspiring engineers, these jobs were in addition to the time spent engaging in many of the entrepreneurial tactics described in this chapter. For example, Sam claimed always to be ready to record by carrying a small digital audio recorder and several microphones with him in his backpack wherever he may roam.

The studio seemed at the very least to offer possibilities for what Guy Standing calls "work-to-labor," that is, the often unpaid and unrecognized work needed to obtain employment.[29] Work-to-labor includes skill building and networking, something that SoniCo, potentially, allows. As Miles, a thirty-something office worker, said, just after he explained his fondness for the studio's "vibe": "So, how lucky am I that like I get to be in a place that's not going to stress me out, where I can make connections, where I can learn, where I can practice, where I can execute, where I can keep going? Dude, like man, you know what I mean? I feel really lucky, man, from like having—not having shit to like having somewhere to go where you're good. Man, that is priceless right there, dude."

He started at SoniCo after a long stint as a supervisor at a media distribution firm. Though somewhat atypical among SoniCo's office staff, his trajectory reveals the widespread instability and nonlinearity of creative careers, even for routine workers. His previous employer fired him when he demanded a raise after his workload increased. After being fired, Miles moved back in with his family before finding work at SoniCo several months later. Like Sam and Clyde, he commuted about twenty miles to work the night shifts that no one else wanted. These began at 5:00 p.m., during the middle of the evening rush hour, and so the commute could take well over an hour. Still, Miles liked the "vibe," something he said more than a few times, often gesturing at parts of the studio's décor, such as a Buddha-shaped light. Above all, he was happy to be working again, and, with any luck, he thought he might soon be able to move out of his parents' home.

Miles saw SoniCo as pregnant with possibilities for acquiring skills and networking, forms of work-to-labor that often occur informally through the technological interactions described in the previous chapter and through interactions between office staff and more advanced, freelance engineers in residence at SoniCo. Interactions between novices such as Sam and more established engineers occur quite frequently, leading office workers to claim that working at SoniCo affords the possibility of continued learning and networking. As Sam said, "I can continue to learn, man. Like I was sitting around with dudes that have engineered and mixed and like produced for some of the biggest people you could think of, man," and then added, "So, that is my other goal right now is to learn from like Emmerich and like even—not even the dudes that—like not even the dudes working for SoniCo, but the people [freelance engineers] that have rooms here like Toby and Dean." For Sam, SoniCo offered the possibility of reproducing and enlarging his skillset in order to become a better engineer and, potentially, more employable. Having these opportunities available within the workplace solves, in part, the problem of performing work-to-labor outside of working hours and the need for constant learning on the job—an increasingly common feature of work in a variety of fields.[30] Combined with the aesthetic enrollment processes described in the previous chapter, these social interactions make for a workplace full of dense sociotechnical relationships perceived to be replete with possibility.

These possibilities feel real through interactions like those that began this chapter. Recall that Sam explained to Thomas, a more experienced engineer, how he had been working on a track using a software "plug-in" that simulated the sonic effects of analog, magnetic tape. The plug-in caused an undesirable shift in sound frequencies ("phasing problems").

Offering advice, Thomas said, "Oh you shouldn't get that with [the plug-in]. You just using one microphone?" "Yeah," said Sam. "Yeah, that shouldn't happen," said Thomas before asking Sam what microphones he had been using. Though Sam received less than helpful advice, moments like these certainly made the possibility of skill-sharing palpable.

Another example shows how the imagined possibility of acquiring work feels real. One day, Toby asked Sam to build a sound library for him. Wages were not discussed, but it seemed to be implied that Sam could use the sound library for free upon completion and that this would serve as a sort of compensation. As Toby said, "I was thinking of having you open up my sessions sometime and just go through and make a sound library from my sessions. Congas, timbales, there's great sounds in there, but I need someone with a brain to do it. You can't get an intern to do that. Right?" Toby could easily perform this work himself; however, he and Sam frequently took cigarette breaks together, so Toby knew that Sam had been trained as an engineer. As he said, "You need a brain for this." In these interactions, workers network with higher-status professionals, seemingly building their professional network. In this case, Sam also (potentially) gained another crucial resource: sounds to use in his production work. A library such as this could be used to produce new music using elements from Toby's recordings. As Toby said, "Congas, timbales, there's great sounds in there." This reuse of recorded material is another means by which engineers attempt to make their time more economically productive. In a similar situation, Jeff and Clyde were on the clock up at the front desk while they played with some gear and talked about Jeff's new songs. Clyde liked the new tunes, so Jeff asked if he wanted to produce and engineer them, so long as they could find time in the studio.

Even after ten months at SoniCo, the degree to which workers benefited from the supposed opportunities remained rather unclear to me. Were they moving forward, standing in place, or falling behind? I cannot say for certain, but the types of social ties being built at SoniCo tended to be dense, strong ties among similar people with regard to class and status. The studio certainly provides real opportunities for skill development and networking but offers fewer chances to form the weak ties that tend to bolster careers by bridging gaps between different groups of people of varying status.[31] In contrast, owner-managers and supervisors clearly benefited from this situation, with the benefits for the owners being quite obvious.

Supervisors developed ties with other local businesses, which facilitated SoniCo's larger organizational project of becoming a major, global recording destination for musicians.[32] One of the supervisors, for example, became a very visible person within the local ecology of live music thanks in part to his association with SoniCo and his ability to provide small favors to local businesses and musicians, such as discounted rates on equipment and rehearsal rentals. These practices, shared by owner-managers, built their reputations and spread SoniCo's name through these frequent interactions and exchanges.

While SoniCo grew and some supervisors flourished, office staff stood still, immobile, save for their ability to exit.[33] A year after fieldwork, Clyde told me that he had not worked on any new recording projects in some time and was considering moving back East. Marcus, the microphone-building hater of indie rock, left LA altogether, as did Jack, another supervisor. Thomas also left LA after four years, which had included a year-long stint as a supervisor. Strapped for cash and sleeping on his brother's couch, Jeff returned to where he grew up. He still writes and records music and seems happier. "Standard" employment neither solved the problem of precarity nor advanced their careers, at least not in a clear, direct way. I do not mean to imply that workers had perceived their situation incorrectly but instead to claim that they became affectively attached to "a bad life that wears out the subjects who nonetheless, and at the same time, find their conditions of possibility within it."[34] If aesthetic enrollment and dense social ties comprise the valences of creative labor's positive pole, then precarity, the unfulfilled promises of opportunity, and alienation comprise creative labor's negative pole.

ALIENATED JUDGMENT

While I was researching and writing this book, more than a few colleagues told me, "It's simple! They love their work because it's entertainment," "It's music," or "It's culture." A naïve observer might expect to find cultural commodities—the totems of mass culture—plying their magic, enchanting work, obscuring exploitation. As with most aspects of social life, examining what people do and say complicates naïve interpretations. As one engineer said, "When I go home, if I spend an entire day here, I don't listen to a damned thing. It's silence. I'm reading. I don't want to hear anything. Don't want to hear music. I feel as though, yeah. It does take a lot out of me actually. That constant bombardment of different bands and hearing them all combined into one noxious sound." So much for those common-sense explanations.

The engineer claims to be both overwhelmed by the unrelenting abundance of music (too much of a good thing, perhaps) and unable to exercise judgment over the music that he helps produce. Sound does not become music so much as it becomes a sort of flatulent cacophony. At the end of the working day, he regained his ability to exercise *his* choice over what he heard and chose silence. Engineers exercise their agency upon and through sound, shaping popular music while also alienated from music. His body may be engaged, aesthetically enrolled, but the creative labor process subordinates his cognition, in particular his taste, and taste, of course, is a matter of judgment.

While talking about "precarity" seems all the rage these days, "alienation" comes off as a bit old-fashioned. Creative jobs, after all, reunite the planning and execution of tasks that Taylorism divided in the twentieth century—what Braverman called deskilling. Thus, capitalism would seem to have resolved at least one of its many contradictions, something suggested by scholars who claim overabsorption as a key problem for creative labor.[35] After all, how can one be alienated from engaging work when management invites "creativity?" In contrast, critical theorists claim that alienation takes on a renewed relevance with the rise of service and information economies, in which "immaterial" or emotional and creative labor appear most central.[36] Even so, they do little to identify the alienation distinct to creative labor, and more empirically minded scholars abandon the concept altogether, giving little in the way of theoretical hooks to apprehend alienated creativity.[37]

A turn backward to the twentieth century provides a better means of apprehending creative labor's alienation. In *White Collar*, C. Wright Mills claimed that the aims of creative or "information" workers "must, of course, be set by the decisions of others rather than [their] own integrity."[38] "Integrity" seems a bit vague, but creative labor certainly requires some of workers' most integral parts (the body and knowledge; cognition or rational intellect; and intuition, feeling, or affect).[39] Creative labor's positive pole attends to workers' affective needs, enrolling them in organizational projects of profit making, but what of "reason" or, in less loaded terms, reflective thought? If we live in an era of *cognitive* capitalism, in which creative labor provides a key source of value for capital, then what does cognitive capitalism alienate?

As I argue in the remainder of this chapter, providing creative labor requires workers to exercise judgment, but their judgment tends always to be only the means for another's ends—what I call alienated judgment,[40] the third valence of the negative pole. For all the autonomy management afforded to instrumentally pragmatic employees, the managerial invitation denies autonomous judgment. Reflective thought required for judgment remains alienated, put toward another's ends despite all the affectively engaging, aesthetic enrollments described in chapter 3. Work may *feel* interesting, exciting, or engaging, but workers' judgment remains subordinated to the demands of the organization and clients.

This much may be seen in how engineers classify gigs. Recall that in the last chapter, engineers divided gigs or sessions into two types: desirable projects, wherein they were allowed to freely deploy their expertise and professional judgment, and undesirable, "easy money" projects in which they used very little expertise and lacked control over the final product. The latter required simple technical setups that offered little in the way of exercising skill. Most gigs available to engineers fell into the second classification (simple, undesirable, "easy money"). Superficially, this might seem to fit the classic Bourdieuian opposition between heteronymous production (other oriented or, often, market oriented) and autonomous production (oriented toward formal innovation and status specific to the field), insofar as the more desirable gigs allow engineers to take more chances, chances that may increase their status or symbolic capital.[41] Though relevant, focusing solely on the accumulation of status leaves little room for work's enchantments and workers' equally intense distaste for their products.

This creative labor process requires that workers subordinate their autonomous judgment to others. As one engineer said, "That's what the money's for. Unless they're trying to haggle me into doing something for next to nothing, it's like, people are paying to not be told that they suck and not be told to take a hike." Despite finding immersion and engagement in their interactions with studios' complex technological systems, engineers' judgment tends to be subordinated to clients and thus alienated. This stands in contrast to Blauner's influential theorization of alienation and technology in *Alienation and Freedom*, which drove debates in the sociological investigation of technology and work up through the 1980s.[42] Though Marx touched upon workers' relationship to technology, Blauner provided a more rigorous, social-psychological examination of technology's relation to alienation, describing four major components: powerlessness, meaninglessness, integration in industrial communities, and self-estrangement. Insofar as creative labor requires dispositions and capacities for acting through and upon symbols, self-estrangement seems most relevant to creative labor (not unlike emotional or aesthetic labor). Blauner defined self-estrangement at work as "a heightened awareness of time, as a split between present activity and future considerations."[43] He contrasted this with nonalienated work's "immersion in the present."[44] The moments that I term aesthetic experiences are, in fact, just this. Blauner claimed that new technological developments often directly increase self-estrangement unless the technology increases workers' autonomy by freeing them *from* work, as in his classic example of workers who ate lunch while monitoring machines in automated factories.

The technologically mediated immersion shown in the previous chapter suggests the opposite. Technology makes work sensually exciting and viscerally engaging, essentially making work feel "creative" and making the managerial invitation *to* work all the more enticing. Rather than being alienated from their immediate tasks, workers tend to be alienated from their capacities to decide, to render a judgment upon an object (e.g., sound or music). Alongside status concerns, workers' distinction between good and bad gigs hinges upon control over the ends to which others put their creative means. In other words, someone else's decisions direct their creative contributions to the product rather than what Mills might have called their "integrity."

The final product (music) often results from conflicts between musicians and engineers as each attempt to establish authority over sound. Each conflict between musician and engineer is simultaneously a conflict of status and judgment, as shown quite clearly at the beginning of this book when we met Jerry, the lead engineer at a concert in a small gallery. As he said, "Yeah doing these events is usually a big pain in the ass, but this one, this one here really takes the cake." Recall that Jerry had set the sound levels for the performance as best he could but then musicians had contested his decisions. The musician's choices caused ear-piercing feedback that they could not fix. They then repeatedly asked Jerry to fix the situation. In asserting their agency, the musicians contested Jerry's judgment, which led him to disavow his contribution to the performance. As he said, "I let him do his thing, and if he makes it sound crappy, what do I care? It's not my name on this bullshit." Similarly, Thomas the engineer-turned-office-employee explained to SoniCo's head engineer that a musician might want to sit in the room while he mixed and edited her songs. Thomas said, "I told her to trust us, that you're really good." Emmerich quickly quipped, "Oh you're making me blush." The two engineers then discussed the problems of having clients in the room when they edited and mixed recordings. Emmerich forcefully said, "I hate that! It's just like, let me do my work. Let me do what works. Oh, this part isn't adding anything to the song? Well, delete." He mimed pushing a button.

In other cases, engineers' judgment appeared wholly circumscribed by decisions made by clients or their employing organization. Here, an engineer describes leaving a job at a larger, more regimented studio to work at SoniCo: "You edit it, auto-tune it, and send it on its way. Like, it was just no fun. I just really didn't want anything to do with it. If I wanted a boring job like that, I would've stuck with what I was doing before that, so I went for something more enjoyable. And make much less money!" He explained that SoniCo differed insofar as it was a smaller, flatter organization that offered "a little more variety. I actually get to point microphones at sources. There [at the larger studio], they only ever do vocals, so there's just a vocal mic up." Likewise, Orlando described working on a simple, "tedious" project in equally negative tones: "This record [that I'm working on right now] is not that big of a production, but [my job is] just getting certain elements to stand out in the mix. Like this is how it sounded before [plays song]. That's how it sounds now [plays new mix]. That's a lot different. That's the difference, you know. You remove the blanket from the speaker." In the previous chapter, I quoted Orlando when I mentioned some of the metaphors used by engineers to describe their immersive experiences vis-à-vis technology. He likened some tasks to "entering the Matrix," but here he simply removes the "blanket," adding clarity or "crispness" to an otherwise unremarkable or "muddy" recording. He used his expertise in only the most limited of ways. In most cases, engineers also lacked control over the type of music being produced. In both, engineers acted as mere appendages of another's creative decisions, a form of self-estrangement.

One of SoniCo's front office employees described this quite clearly when he said that he did not actively pursue engineering work at SoniCo because "I don't like the clients [SoniCo] chooses, and that can be torture . . . if it was ideal for them [the company] it would just be country and indie type stuff, which is fine, but not really [my thing]."

If engineers felt alienated from their judgment, how did SoniCo's office staff feel about all the music they endured every day at work? As should be abundantly clear, engineers and office staff differ little with regard to requisite labor, training, their relationship to technology, and conditions of employment. The same may be said of alienated judgment, and, again, workers' relation to music illustrates their alienation. Music constantly played over the office stereo and boomed out from behind the doors of the rehearsal and recording rooms at nearly 100 decibels, the equivalent of a garbage truck driving by or a machinist's shop floor. The staffmembers also filled their downtime with sounds of their own creation. While making their own music or just noodling on instruments helped bind the workers to their jobs, office staff repeatedly claimed that, overall, work had made them enjoy music *less*. Work alienated them from pleasures most people associate with leisure—an aspect of social life generally understood to require a great deal of creativity.[45] As Jason said, "It's like if you work at a hot dog restaurant, you don't want to eat hot dogs when you're at home. When you're surrounded by a product all day long, it's nice to get a break from that product including, in my case, music. It's nice to just not hear it or think about it when I'm at home." Echoing the engineer that began this section, another claimed that the abundant, relentlessly loud music at work altered his taste, lessening his interest in rock music and increasing his preference for silence.

In the previous chapter, I argued that the creative labor process elicits a fragile consent. Now I want to show how the bandage provided by aesthetic enrollment comes undone, allowing alienation and precarity to push workers toward refusal and, often, exit. The staff and I often joked about the racket being made by rehearsing musicians. While on a shift with Jeff and Sam, a band began performing "Wish You Were Here," a song by the British rock group Pink Floyd. Jeff offered his expert opinion: "Do you hear that? That band is playing the Pink Floyd song. How fucking lame!" He said it drove him "nuts" to see all the musicians coming in, working on "shitty music," and added, "I like listening to [sports] because listening to music is hard for me because I hear so much of it. So much of it is so bad that it's broken my spirit kind of. So I just listen or I watch sports." Suggestive of what I am calling positive and negative poles, he said, "It's hard, because I know their future. Working here, it's manic [depressive]. I can be up one day and down the next. You know, I'm in my thirties and I just think maybe I should give up [being a musician] and get a real job."

Jeff hated the music at work despite being a musician in his free time and having been previously trained as an engineer. On especially slow days, he occupied his downtime by watching football on his smartphone, though management preferred employees to use their downtime to play the instruments in the front office or perform administrative and clerical duties. On one of these slow days, some electronic dance music came on over the office stereo system. Jeff said, "This music sucks. That's why I don't play the company's internet radio station. One of the owners said that I could do my own radio show and play whatever I wanted, but you need all the MP3s for that, and I don't have an extensive music collection. I just use Spotify. No one listens to this shit anyway!" Jeff's nonexistent music collection prohibited him from accepting management's invitation to exercise his taste; here again, management's creative control depended upon objects' accessibility and on sensibilities developed before entering (and reproduced within) the workplace.

Lacking the necessary materials to accept the managerial invitation, combined with his distaste for the music that *is* available at work and his financial difficulties, Jeff exerted agency through simple refusal. Just as he finished complaining, one of the owners walked in and politely asked, "Hey, why isn't the internet radio on in the lobby?" Jeff tapped at the iPad that controlled the stereo and said, "It's on. [It] should be on." The owner said he could not hear it. Jeff adjusted the volume and asked, "Is it on now?" After the manager left, Jeff explained that he already had to hear enough music he did not like and so sometimes forgot to turn on the stereo. Perhaps he just forgot, but his forgetting suggests an act of passive resistance. Jeff prefers silence to music and exerts agency in refusing to add to the studio's already overabundant congeries of sounds.

Preferring not to, Jeff asserted his taste, which is, after all, a matter of judgment.[46] As noted by the sociologist of music Tia DeNora, the ability to exercise control and judgment over one's everyday sense experience constitutes a key mode by which individuals exert what she calls "aesthetic agency."[47] Making a similar statement, Lauren Berlant claims that personal expression through listening "is powerful because [music] accompanies one as a portable hoard that expresses one's true inner taste. . . . Your soundtrack is one place where you can be in love with yourself and express your fidelity to your own trueness."[48] In expressing one's "true inner taste," listeners render a judgment, most often known only to themselves. Jeff's demand for silence when faced with undesirable music suggests this much.

SoniCo's workers used their judgment to help produce another's ends, cultural commodities for which they have no use. To follow "common sense" and claim that these people "love" their work because "it's entertainment" or "it's culture" would be inaccurate. The music being produced plays a marginal and sometimes negative role in explaining their enjoyment. The positive pole described in chapter 3 provides a better explanation, one grounded in the working day. SoniCo's creative labor processes alienate judgment, creating a situation not unlike that described by Theodor Adorno when he wrote, "Ask a musician if music is a pleasure, the reply is likely to be 'I just hate music.' For him who has a genuine relation to art, *in which he himself vanishes*, art is not an object, deprivation of art would be unbearable."[49] We might best understand Adorno to be describing musical creativity as a process that workers enjoy and strongly desire to participate in, and so while they "disappear" or "vanish" in this process (e.g., manipulating sound or filling downtime by playing music), they find music produced in accordance with others' judgment, music as an object, to be unbearable. Self-estrangement stands side by side with the immersion that Blauner associated with "freedom" and the experiential unification of task and worker that many call "flow." The latter processes may engage or aesthetically enroll workers, but workers still lack control over the final product, and so creative labor processes objectively alienate judgment, leaving workers feeling unhappy upon reflection.

I want to conclude this section on a hopeful note. As I said earlier, office employees often choose to exit the music industry altogether rather than pursue work at another studio. Jack, a musician-turned-supervisor whom I met during my first six months in the field in 2013, illustrated this well. Like others, he took the job because of the opportunities it seemed to provide, and, like others, his interest in music waned from being surrounded by music all day. In his early thirties, he had been a musician most of his adult life, but after several years in the studio, he had mostly laid down his guitar. Two years later, Jack had left the company to pursue work outside the music industry. Despite exiting the industry, he had begun to perform and write music again as a hobby and regularly rehearsed with a band at SoniCo. I asked, "What changed? I thought you didn't want to perform anymore." Now a customer rather than an employee, he explained that he felt a renewed desire to write, record, and perform after he quit. No longer subject to an endless stream of music over which he had no control, Jack decided to put his creative labor toward ends of his choosing. Any *déformation professionnelle* appeared rather impermanent.

LEAVING THE SOCIAL REGIME

At SoniCo, management exerted power through invitation, inviting workers to express themselves, to "be creative," and to lose themselves in aesthetic experiences, temporarily eluding all that might grind them down. Social ties were framed as business opportunities, as wise investments for their next entrepreneurial venture. This bleeds over into the negative pole. Power operates by what it allows, and the creative labor process certainly allows much, but it still denies economic security and autonomous judgment. The pleasures of creative work never balance the ledger; creativity always remains the means to someone else's ends regardless of how "entrepreneurial" a worker may be.

These opposing valences leave workers fractured, simultaneously enthralled and alienated. They enjoy their jobs, experiencing genuine pleasures when they are allowed to "be creative," but their working lives never come out all one color, their subjectivities never fully submerged in the demands of work. This contrasts with both Marxist scholars, for whom a workforce whose critical capacities have been diminished, defanged, or deflected remains a perennial concern,[50] and the arguments of affect theorists, for whom embodied experiences exceed all attempts at control. Diverging from both, I find that work may at times satisfy an affective or aesthetic rationality, but just as frequently work fails to satisfy workers' economic needs and values. SoniCo illustrates multiple, conflicting rationalities within creative, working subjects. This presents a serious challenge to any presupposition of a single, unified actor—rational or practical—in both economics and economic sociology. Though I draw primarily upon affect theory and empirical research in aesthetics, one might do equally well in harking back to Max Weber's typology of social action. Weber claimed four ideal-typical modes of rational action. These are the instrumental, value, affectual, and traditional rationalities. In this chapter, I highlighted creative workers' instrumental and value rationalities, while the preceding chapter focused on an affective, or aesthetic, rationality—what Weber defined as actions "determined by the actor's specific affects or feeling states."[51] These three forms of rationality (instrumental, value, and aesthetic/affective) appear co-present but not necessarily unified. In other words, work may feel good while being detrimental to economic stability. Simultaneously, work may seem to offer economic potential despite actually thwarting workers' ability to flourish—what Berlant calls "cruel optimism." Though Weber, of course, argued that multiple modes of rationality may be co-present in any given situation, his writing suggests a certain unity that I did not find at SoniCo. The economic and aesthetic subjectivities described in the preceding chapters never quite resolve to a unified whole and instead appear held in permanent tension. For the sociology of work and labor, part 2 highlights what remains obscured when focusing too closely on identity, ideology, or classificatory struggles as the most salient objects of analysis in the move toward reinstating a "full subject" into critical theories of work.[52]

SoniCo may "fix how they feel," but the creative labor process subordinates workers' judgment, leaving them both engaged and alienated. This tension between aesthetic or affective feelings and reflective thought involved in making a judgment provides a condition of possibility for collective resistance.[53] Conflicting rationalities (economic, aesthetic, instrumental, value, etc.) inform workers' interpretation of their common situation. As we have seen, technology provides an aesthetic (i.e., material, sensible in relation to an object) modulation of work's felt experience as it impinges upon the body while mediating and engaging the senses. Concurrently, technology extends and enables the deployment of skill and expertise. Kant's division between reason (conceptual, reflective thought, the faculty of judgment) and the nonconceptual faculties of intuition and imagination further highlights this tension. Though fraught, Kant's separation of feeling and thinking echoes claims about affect's "autonomy" from ideology or discourse and the political potential therein.[54] In *Critique of Pure Reason*, an experience that "immediately satisfies the senses" may be "mediately displeasing" upon reflection, the mediation of sense experience by the "faculty of reason," or, to use a less loaded term, judgment.[55] This separation between sensual satisfaction (the "porn side of the job" that does not "feel" like work) and reflective judgment leaves room for workers' critique, not burning in blood and sinew as affect theory would have it but smoldering in the body nonetheless. If power operates by ensnaring our prereflective, embodied experience, then potential resistance lies in our reflective thought or cognition, the part of our bodies most required for us to provide capital with creative labor. This points toward a labor politics of judgment, a topic to which I return in the conclusion.

In this and the previous chapter, I focused on what I call a *social* regime of creative labor. Under the social regime, creative labor's value depends upon *social qualities* such as reputation, status, and social ties or the ability to maintain or develop these qualities for others. Both SoniCo and its workers develop these social qualities to attract people to the studio and acquire clients. Though work's pleasures stem from the human/machine interactions discussed in chapter 3, work still tends to be structured by social relationships between people, for example, in a recording session or rehearsal check-in. In a social regime, organizations control creative labor by inviting expression while framing the workplace as full of opportunities to develop the *social* qualities needed to find work, to make their labor valuable. Likewise, social relationships between clients or the employing organization structure the alienation and precarity experienced by workers. With each day, work becomes more embedded within the global capitalist infrastructures commonly called platforms. In part 3, I show how these infrastructures alter the creative labor process by imposing a *quantitative* regime and thus how capital exerts power at the level of infrastructure.

PART III

The Future's Quantified Regime

Chapter Five

THE FUTURE'S POSITIVE POLE

Platform Discipline, Transience, and Immersion

At a Hollywood coffee shop, I met Tammy, a twenty-something woman who posts her vlogs (video blogs) on YouTube. They cover topics such as makeup or the dynamic awkwardness of app-based dating. Her vlog brought in a few thousand dollars a year, a second income on top of her day job in a corporate marketing department. No simple hobbyist, she continually invested her money and time, buying production equipment and developing new skills as she attempted to hone her brand and grow her YouTube channel. Despite differences in gender, age, and nationality, Tammy had a lot in common with Dennis, a YouTube creator and part-time factory worker in Western Europe. He spent four days a week working in a converted barn, creating stop-motion animations with an elaborate, homemade computer-controlled camera system. He found the production process fascinating, a pleasure dovetailing almost too perfectly with his passion for learning new skills and building new equipment. His videos often went "viral," garnering millions of views, but his labor-intensive content required months, sometimes years to complete and so he tried to keep his audience engaged with behind-the-scenes videos, revealing his production process to fans as it unfolded, gaining views and earning money each week.

This chapter returns to creative labor's positive pole, now embedded within YouTube, a digital media infrastructure, or "platform." Embedding work within this platform quantifies creative labor, a point made in my earlier discussion of creativities. If workers accept capital's invitation because of how their jobs feel "creative," as in part 2, then how does this quantified creativity feel? How does it feel to chase after views? In Texas, I sat down for some barbecue with Frank, a former comedian turned YouTube creator in his late thirties. Like Tammy and Dennis, Frank earned his living by drawing massive amounts of viewers to his YouTube channel. For each view, Frank earned a few cents. These few cents arrived after both YouTube and The Future, a multichannel network, took their portions of the advertising revenues (30 to 60 percent) that pay for the majority of platform-based media. Like many YouTube creators with whom I spoke, metrics and data guided Frank's decision making. When I asked Frank how he felt when he looked at his data on a version of the interface pictured in Figure 5.4 later in this chapter, he said, "I'm obsessed with it. It's a video game. It's the best video game I've ever played in my entire life. You think [the video game] Rollercoaster Tycoon is fun? That's dog shit compared to playing my channel, where it's real life Rollercoaster Tycoon with real money and real consequences. It's electric and a blast. It's awesome." "Obsessed" with data, Frank had been caught up in the "electric" thrill of entrepreneurial accumulation. Again, technology played an important part in a process of binding, one generative of desire and passion for precarious work. But how does one acquire this obsessive curiosity, and who sets the rules of this game? Answering that question requires a swim upward through the video streams to The Future, a type of media management company called a "multichannel network," and then farther upstream to YouTube, the platform around which The Future is built.

In The Future's Los Angeles headquarters, a young, college-educated woman dressed in black sat at a receptionist's desk answering phones. A small, white projector emitted a ray of blue light, throwing YouTube videos upon the wall behind her back. Whenever she leaned into her work, the projector's beam hit her full in the face, exposing her eyes to the flash-bang virtual murders of online video games and impeccably made-up young women giving cosmetics tutorials. While she sat quite literally blinded by media, the British indie singer Morrissey crooned "I'm so sorry" over the office PA system—part of a soundtrack of soul, indie rock, and reggae curated by her fellow employees and the Workplace Experience team, a gloss on "human resources." She claimed not to notice the projector's light but guessed that it might be the cause of her new need for glasses.

Down the hall, Cooper and Desmond, whom I introduced in this book's introduction, sat with two other men, each at a brightly colored IKEA table in a dimly lit office affectionately dubbed the "Men's Room." Music from the PA system continued to play, now the Who warning us against being "fooled again." Posters of superheroes and pop singers adorned the walls. Against this backdrop, The Future's full-time staff earned between $32,000 and $45,000 per year, with people like Cooper and Desmond at the upper end, thanks to bonuses for meeting weekly quotas and monthly growth goals tied to the same metrics that govern creators' earnings. Meeting those goals required extensive searching for and reaching out to creators.

One morning during my first few months of fieldwork at The Future, I woke to an email from Cooper, my supervisor, telling me to come directly to his desk when I got to work. He sat atop an exercise ball in the "Men's Room," talking on the phone with a creator whom he wished to sign to a management contract. He gestured for me to wait a moment, so I sat in a chair beside Desmond, also chatting on the phone with a potential creator/client. They both gave the company's standard pitch while rapidly cycling through YouTube videos on their company-issued MacBook Pro laptops. The pitch included mention of The Future's "hands-on" approach and the firm's ability to increase creators' earnings by "optimizing" content.[1]

Desmond and Cooper's advice came straight from YouTube's official training programs. Both were certified by YouTube in "Audience Growth," a six-hour-long training program that included a segment in which a young, white American man in oxford cloth shirt and khaki pants encouraged creators and other downstream professionals to self-invest in technology and develop a brand through on-screen "rituals." In another segment, an Asian American woman explained the importance of metrics and data analytics before inviting viewers to take a short quiz on what they learned. Like all multichannel networks (MCNs), The Future depended upon YouTube's infrastructure to earn money through advertising revenue generated by views of videos made by thousands of content creators located around the world. In exchange, The Future provided a minimal suite of services, not wholly unlike a traditional talent management company, except at a much larger scale and with a global range. YouTube, as an infrastructure, enables this global range while imposing a primarily quantitative mode of valuing creative labor.

QUANTIFIED CREATIVE LABOR

This chapter continues the work of building a theory of creative labor by extending concepts developed in part 2 to a new context, asking how platforms reconfigure creative labor processes by examining The Future's "creators" and office staff. Unlike SoniCo, The Future, its staff, and its creators depend upon Google's YouTube. This structural dependence, I argue, shapes their working days and approaches to producing cultural products. This is most clearly seen when examining how the platform's metrics, as opposed to professional conventions, shape the work processes of creators and office staff. So, alongside my broader emphasis on work's aesthetic dimension, this chapter shows how YouTube shapes creative labor processes located downstream and, by extension, cultural production. The platform does so by imposing a quantitative mode of valuation that reconfigures key cultural distinctions between art/nonart that supposedly structure and control creative work processes.[2]

I begin by describing YouTube's efforts to discipline a geographically distributed workforce before following the flow of streaming video to the working days of creators and office staff. In doing so, I explain how platforms owned by global capital and mediating firms such as The Future coordinate production and thus control a globally distributed workforce. Similar to management in previous chapters, The Future and YouTube control labor through a combination of managing how work feels and encouraging an entrepreneurial disposition. This differs from the social regime insofar as these strategies appear secondary to metrics. Thus, control over production tends to be more closely linked to the platform: its interface, training materials, and algorithmic content moderation. Both the interface and training materials emphasize the importance of metrics and entrepreneurialism, serving as vectors for platform discipline by educating and orienting creators to the platform's production demands. Additionally, the platform algorithmically manages creators through its content moderation systems, often enforcing economic penalties for creators and thus serving as another vector for platform discipline. The Future reinforces platform discipline by setting quotas for staff and by having staff advise creators to tailor content to YouTube's guidelines while also encouraging entrepreneurial strategies such as self-branding.

Returning to the aesthetics of creative labor processes, I again examine the felt experience of technology. Under SoniCo's social regime, technology afforded deep, sensuous attachments that tenuously bound workers to work. That process depended upon dispositions formed earlier and then reproduced within the workplace. How does this change when creative labor comes to be embedded within a global digital infrastructure? In the context of platform-based media production examined here, capital (i.e., The Future and Google/YouTube) depends upon a highly diverse, global workforce with wide variation in terms of workers' professionalization and social positions, while work requires both the platform and more common technologies (e.g., screens, computers, the internet) alongside more rarefied production equipment. If, as the technology scholar Sherry Turkle claims, artists and musicians develop "close, sensuous" relationships with their tools,[3] then what of The Future's creators and office staff, who spend their working lives on screens? Turkle claimed that the dominance of technologies designed to facilitate ease and smooth interaction upon surfaces (i.e., the "mimetic aesthetic" of Apple and Windows operating systems) engendered a "new 'musical' culture of computing."[4] In this "musical" computing, the screen supposedly provides for sensuous attachments much like those found among the studio workers. Before investigating these issues ethnographically, I provide a brief history of YouTube and the industry that emerged around the platform during the 2010s.

FROM PARTICIPATORY MEDIA TO PLATFORM LABOR

YouTube initially provoked serious attention given its supposed democratization of media production and distribution. Media scholars waxed utopian during YouTube's early years as the platform supposedly extended the participatory joys of media production to all.[5] Just a few years later, those utopian visions faded. Scholars began to describe users of social media platforms such as YouTube, Twitter, and Facebook as "hyper exploited" digital labor.[6] Around the same time, in 2011 MCNs like The Future rose to prominence as management and production companies, capturing value from thousands of professional and amateur media producers around the world. By 2012, media conglomerates began to purchase MCNs for nine-figure sums.[7] This wave of mergers included purchases by major global conglomerates such as AT&T, Disney, and

Bertelsmann along with smaller global companies such as RTL, Chernin, and Pro.Sieben.[8] In 2015, an investment banker at VidCon, an annual industry conference held in Southern California, encouraged these mergers, showing a video of himself parodying the then popular "World's Most Interesting Man" advertisements from Dos Equis beer. While the beer company's mascot encourages consumers to "Stay thirsty, my friends," the banker said, "Keep merging, my friends!" Disney's 2014 purchase of Maker Studios less than a year before marked a high-water point, valued at $750 to $900 million, but most sales hovered near $100 million. Journalists began to call YouTube and its growing industry the new digital Hollywood, or "HollyTube."[9]

So how did we get here? YouTube's shift to advertising-generated revenue and the development of the "partnered" program mark key turning points. Just after its acquisition by Google in 2007, YouTube introduced the "partner" program, which enabled users to earn money directly from the platform. Early on, creators had to apply for "partner" status. Successful applicants demonstrated a record of previous success based on metrics. By 2011 YouTube relaxed criteria for entry into the partner program, extending the opportunity to earn money through advertising to all creators. YouTube gained potential access to a globally distributed workforce that now hovers around one billion users strong. Now, more people than ever may participate in the production of digital media as waged workers, leisurely "prosumers," or advanced hobbyists. Though YouTube currently claims a 50 percent annual increase in partnered creators earning six-figure incomes,[10] the platform pays all media producers by piece rate. A six-figure income requires quite a lot of pieces.

Similar to any other form of advertising-supported media (i.e., broadcast TV, commercial radio, and print periodicals), YouTube creators produce a dual commodity: media content and audiences, or, more specifically, saleable estimates of audience exposure to advertisements.[11] When YouTube creators "partner" or allow YouTube to "sell ads against content," the platform pays creators for each view generated by their content. Creators receive a piece rate per thousand views (CPM, or "cost-per-mille") that usually ranges from $0.50 to $7.00, though some creators have reported receiving up to $13. CPM fluctuates from minute to minute and from video to video. Notably, YouTube's user agreement prohibits creators from discussing their CPM rates with each other or anyone else.[12] Likewise, most MCNs

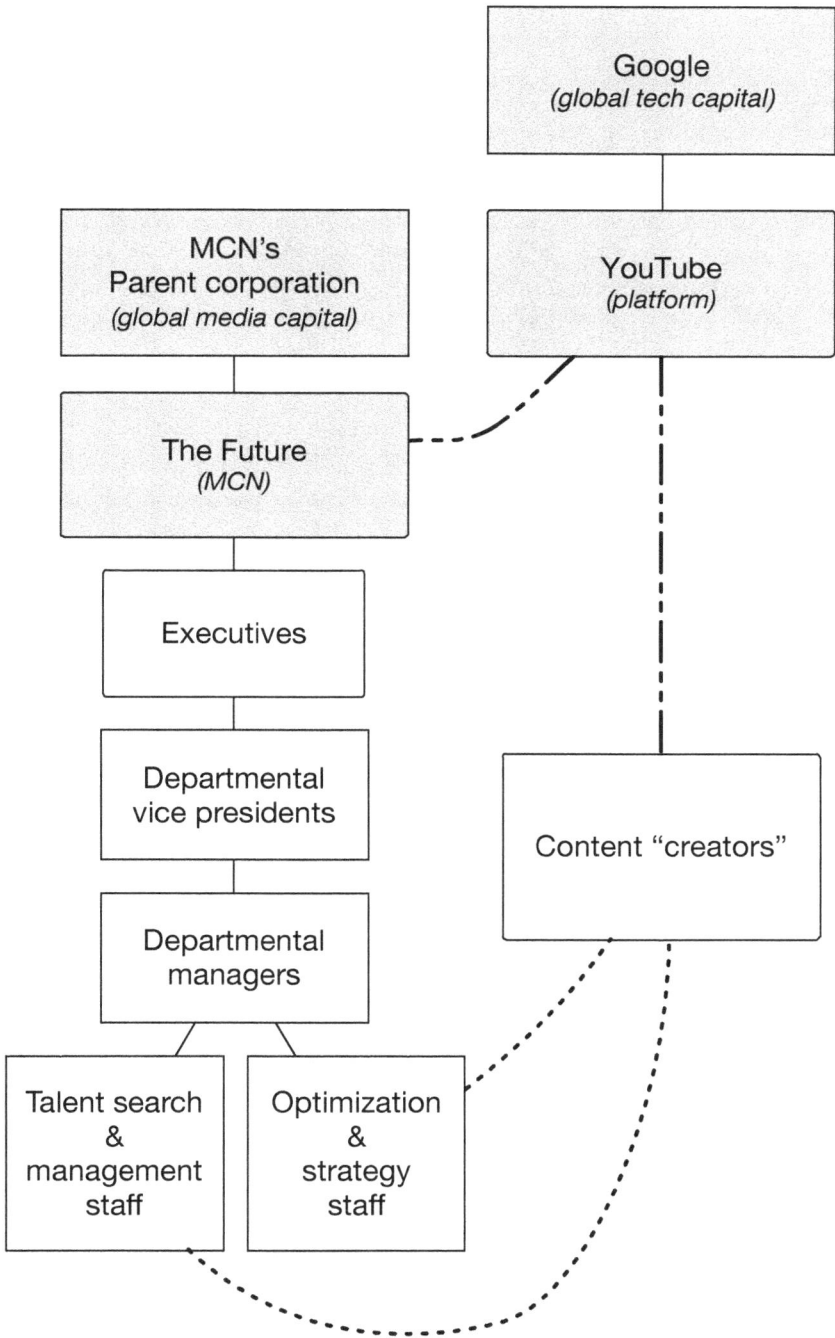

FIGURE 5.1 The Future and platform-based production. Solid lines indicate relations within the firm; small dashes indicate contractual ties to The Future; long dashes indicate infrastructural ties via the platform.

required creators to sign a nondisclosure agreement, ostensibly shutting down workers' discussion of wages.

From 2011 to 2017, MCNs like The Future flourished, managing thousands of creators, capturing value from a heterogeneous media workforce. This platformed organization of production can be seen in figure 5.1. MCNs earn revenue by taking a percentage of their thousands of creators' YouTube earnings. In exchange, the MCNs offer access to "royalty-free" music, better piece rates ("monetization," CPM), and career guidance ("optimization"). To explain this in terms familiar to most casual consumers of media, creators' YouTube channels are to MCNs as a particular television show is to ABC, NBC, or HBO, but unlike television or radio networks, MCNs do not employ production teams and rarely pay anyone beyond the advertising monies paid out by YouTube.

CREATORS' INFRASTRUCTURAL, INSTITUTIONAL, AND ECONOMIC CONTEXT

Creators differ from conventional media workers in at least three ways. First, creators primarily rely upon a single platform for distribution and remuneration. This infrastructural difference directly affects creators' economic situation insofar as creators develop a connection with the platform before their contract with The Future or any other production company. The Future simply reinforces and mediates the platform's disciplinary practices. Despite creators' infrastructural and economic dependence, the platform is neither an employer nor a media company, at least not according to Google.

Second, creators' institutional context differs from most modern fields of cultural production insofar as there exist no awards or institutionalized sources of valuation for pursuing nonmarket goals. Current sociological theories of cultural production suggest that workers pursue precarious jobs because they buy into an "art for art's sake" ideology with salient cultural distinctions between producing for the market and producing in order to advance the field—what Bourdieu called heteronymous (market-oriented) and autonomous (field-specific orientation) production. The field of YouTube production lacks this sort of distinction. Rather than evaluations based on professionally determined "quality," as in other fields of cultural production, YouTube bestows awards upon creators when they reach growth goals. This begins with the Silver Play Button Award at one hundred thousand subscribers and continues up through to the Ruby Play Button at fifty million subscribers. The industry trade web magazine *TubeFilter* celebrates these creators as "YouTube millionaires"—a term referring to their number of "subscribers," not earnings. Rather than "art," "music," or even "video," creators produce "content," and no one I met while conducting research for this book produced "content for content's sake." Content denotes a roughly interchangeable commodity rather than a singular cultural object. The term refers to nothing in particular, just some *thing*. Content is common, or, as I often heard during fieldwork, "Content is everything." Ostensibly, the platform considers all content equal so long as it conforms to certain formal features—not unlike "normal" commodities such as coffee, oranges, or pork bellies, all of which must be made to conform to formal standards so as to be considered valid for their category.[13] Platforms differ from other markets insofar as the platform maintains a monopoly over the right to enforce these standards, and the platform changes these formal standards often, usually without warning.

Third, there exist few barriers to entry, and so the labor market appears remarkable in its sociological heterogeneity. Unlike SoniCo's recording engineers, creators required no formal training and little specialized equipment. Anyone with internet access and some form of video recording device may create content for the platform. Given that many, if not all, cell phones and computers now possess a camera capable of high-definition (HD) video, many people become or can become creators. Despite their demographic heterogeneity and geographic dispersion, all creators and their products occupy a structurally subordinate position vis-à-vis the platform and management firms such as The Future.

No publicly available data exist for creators' wages, job tenure, demographics, or other information typically used to sketch the terrain of an occupation.[14] In place of wage data, figure 5.2 displays channel subscriber data ("channel size") as a rough proxy for economic success. Subscriber counts tend to be strongly correlated, if not synonymous, with audience size and thus income because the metric represents the number of people who actively choose to subscribe to a YouTube channel. Subscriber counts tend to follow a negative binomial, or "superstar," distribution, with many people at the bottom and a few wildly successful people at the top. Along

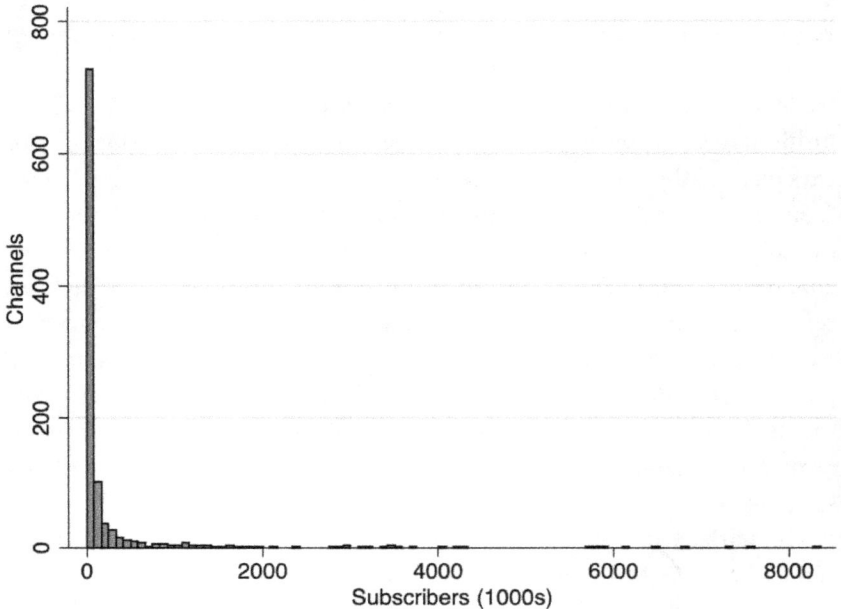

FIGURE 5.2 Subscribers per channel at The Future.

with being common to all creative industries,[15] this distribution's many near-zero earners and a slim number of middle earners also appears in many other kinds of platform-based work, for example, in transportation (Uber and Lyft) and hospitality (Airbnb).[16] Half of all of The Future's creators fall below thirty thousand subscribers.[17] Creators with whom I spoke reported a range of earnings, from $0 to $100,000 per year, with a median of roughly $19,000. Monthly earnings varied wildly, with creators sometimes earning $4,000 one month, $500 the next, and $1,500 the month afterward.

For example, Hank, the Midwest father and survivalist introduced at the beginning of this book, ran a channel with 75,000 subscribers—a "small" channel, but still more than twice the median number of subscribers for channels managed by The Future. In 2016, he earned roughly $9,000 from YouTube after both the platform and The Future took their cuts. His channel's views ranged from 150,000 to 300,000 per month, for which Hank earned a piece rate of $3 to $5 per thousand views. Hank calculated his budget for each video based on these estimates, thinking in cents per view rather than dollars per hour. Through an abundance of additional work, which I will discuss in chapter 6, he earned an additional $26,000, for a total of $35,000. Combining his YouTube income with his full-time salary from a job in an unrelated industry, Hank provided what he considered a "comfortable" life for his wife and children.

Norman, another Midwestern creator, ran a channel with over 80,000 subscribers, from which he earned roughly $1,200 a month. YouTube is Norman's main source of income. Painting a rather grim portrait of class in the United States, Norman said, "The YouTube community is just like the overall economy. There are a few people at the top and the rest of us, we're scratching for scraps really." Three years after I met Norman, more than two dozen creators publicly released their CPM pay rates in April 2020, claiming to have suffered a median 27 percent decline in revenue as advertisers scaled back their budgets at the beginning of the global COVID-19 pandemic.[18] Though by no means a representative sample, creators' pre-COVID pay rates shed light on just how little they earn despite relatively large audience sizes. Pay rates ranged from $3.70 to $10.43 per thousand views for channels with a median of $7.36 and a median subscriber count of 334,000. The subscriber counts for these channels ranged from 9,500 to 2 million. Assuming at least one view each month from each subscriber, the annual income for a median-sized channel earning the median pay rate would be around $29,500, just over five thousand dollars shy of the median income for a single person in the United States. Despite these relatively low wages, creators—even Norman—frequently claimed to enjoy their work and described the platform as liberating or empowering. As Becky—a "lifestyle" vlogger in Los Angeles said, "I can just put [content] out into the universe, put it on to the internet and nobody's censoring me. I can do whatever it is that I want to do. I mean, other than like being naked or doing drugs or, I don't know."

TABLE 5.1
Years producing content for YouTube by gender

	Average time on platform (years)	Number of respondents
Male	7.7	21
Female	6.4	5

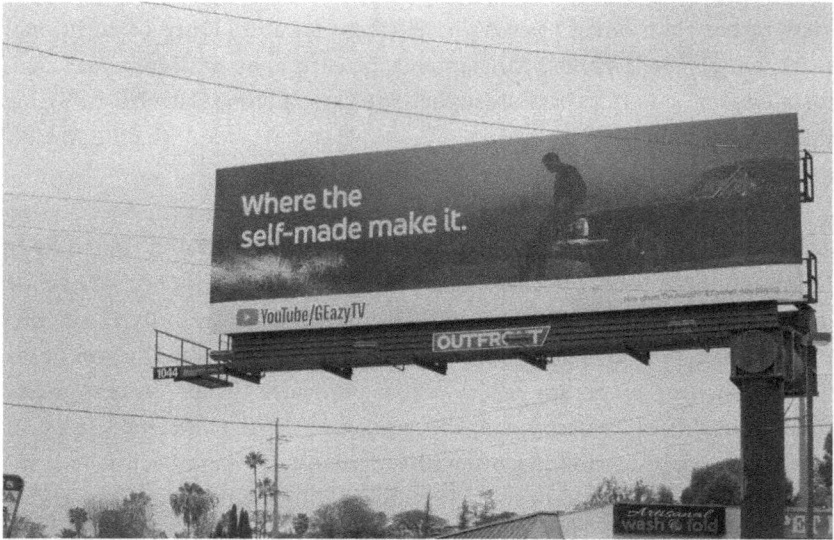

FIGURE 5.3 A YouTube billboard in Los Angeles presents the platform as a space for entrepreneurship.

The creators with whom I spoke ranged from twenty-two to forty years of age, and, on average, they had produced YouTube content for close to eight years, often signing with The Future or another MCN quite early in their careers. Younger creators claimed to have "grown up" with the platform—first as viewers and, shortly thereafter, as active content producers. Older creators tended to be more instrumental, using YouTube as one tactic to gain entry into the film and television industries in Los Angeles or, for those outside major media hubs, an escape from diminished economic possibilities. For instance, Hank and another male vlogger both began to produce online content after suffering layoffs in other, unrelated industries during the "Great Recession" of 2008. They imagined YouTube as providing a livable future beyond work, a future wherein they might become creative *entrepreneurs*. Echoes of this entrepreneurial sentiment appear common among platform workers, such as the Uber drivers in Alex Rosenblat's *Uberland* and the online sex workers described in Angela Jones's *Camming*, who use video platforms to earn money from live broadcasts of their performances.[19] Creators with whom I spoke were quite heterogeneous in terms of class, ethnicity, gender, and sexuality, yet all shared a structural relation vis-à-vis global capital, providing Google with a diverse, contingent, globally distributed media-production workforce.[20]

PLATFORM DISCIPLINE

As I argued in part 2, control over creative labor begins with an invitation. YouTube invites users to produce, to create and express, to "be yourself." The platform's sociologically heterogenous users generally accept this enticing offer, becoming creators when they begin uploading their content. YouTube's seemingly open invitation, however, contains attempts to control or discipline creators in three distinct ways. First, the platform's interface orients them to particular kinds of information, which shapes their decision making. To use terms drawn from science and technology studies, the interface "configures" or disciplines creators by indicating "appropriate" or "correct" behaviors and orientations through instructions, guidelines, and design.[21] Second, YouTube provides educational materials that inform creators of "best practices," advice reinforced by The Future's staff. Third, the platform regulates creators through the uneven application of copyright law and, to a lesser extent, YouTube's "community" standards.

Engagements of the Interface

Accepting YouTube's invitation to create, to "Dare to Be You," as one of YouTube's LA billboards said, starts with the platform's interface, where users first upload content, beginning their transition from media consumer to content creator. While the specifics of this interface change and evolve almost daily, most users' engagement with the platform begins there, and so their relationship to the interface remains pertinent even if the specific details of that relationship change with time. As of this writing, the Creator's Studio (CS) is located in the upper-right-hand corner of YouTube's landing page. There, creators upload videos and, once audiences begin watching the videos, gain access to data visualizations as part of YouTube's "analytics." These form what Karin Knorr-Cetina calls "scopes," or dynamic displays of situation-specific information to which users orient, thus shaping their actions as they react to "scoped" information.[22] Seen in figure 5.4, CS first displays "watch-time" data—the most

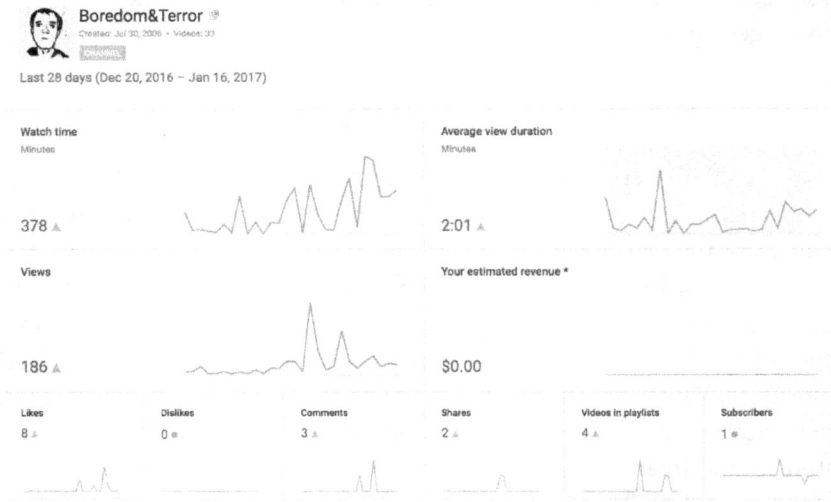

Boredom&Terror ⚙
Created: Jul 30, 2006 • Videos: 33

Last 28 days (Dec 20, 2016 – Jan 16, 2017)

Watch time	Average view duration
Minutes	Minutes
378 ▲	2:01 ▲

Views	Your estimated revenue *
186 ▲	$0.00

Likes	Dislikes	Comments	Shares	Videos in playlists	Subscribers
8 ▲	0 ▬	3 ▲	2 ▲	4 ▲	1 ▬

FIGURE 5.4 YouTube Creator Studio's Analytics Interface, January 2017.

important metric according to the platform—followed by a red or green arrow that indicates decline or growth and a line chart that displays changes during the previous twenty-eight days. This basic structure repeats for each relevant metric, descending in level of importance within YouTube's algorithm and ascending in granularity (e.g., from "average view duration" to a series of engagement metrics and demographic information). Each visualization may be clicked on by a creator in order to view more detailed information (to "deep dive"). The interface's dynamic screen environment provides for embodied engagement and, for some, intense fun—what a creator called the "best video game," one that provides palpable excitement, the sort of low-voltage, electric "blast" of effervescence that binds individuals to meaningful, collective projects.[23]

Along with these effervescent sparks, the interface suggests the possibility of a sovereign, self-interested economic actor. Implying an all-knowing, all-seeing YouTube creator, these scopes provide just the sort of god's-eye view so often associated with individual sovereignty—an ideology made material in the design of the interface.[24] While creators may be structurally subordinate to the platform, the design of the interface (which is also the interface of Google Analytics, the most-used cloud-based analytics service worldwide) suggests a sovereign, creative entrepreneur by providing the means to navigate a complex, highly uncertain world—media production, in this case. It does so by rendering visible the invisible actions of audiences. At the same time, the precise calculative mechanisms and procedures that make the creator's view from nowhere possible remain obscured, making the entrepreneurial creator appear structurally subordinate to the platform.

Educational Programs

If working within and through the interface provides one disciplinary vector by structuring information to which creators orient, then YouTube's training programs provide another.[25] These training materials intend to educate, disciplining creators by explaining "best practices" for increasing the aforementioned metrics. Training courses ranged from three-minute videos to multihour online certification programs. In both, YouTube's employees and star users explain how to "grow" a personal "brand" through a variety of practices aimed not just at increasing audience size but at creating obsessed fans. Strategies included creating shared meanings through group names, symbols, words, and rituals (see chapter 2)—a bit like classical sociology and anthropology by way of an airport newsstand's books on pop psychology and marketing.

Courses provided concrete strategies for implementing these rather vague suggestions. For instance, YouTube recommended that content appeal to the widest possible audience in order to be "accessible," advising that creators include "enough backstory so new viewers who stumble upon that video can enjoy it without needing to see any of the past episodes." YouTube also recommended that creators fabricate rituals for their "brand community." A course in "Audience Growth" recommended repetitive phrases and on-screen actions as practices that created a "consistent brand":

> YouTube is a place where you can interact with your fans in a way you never could before. You can build in games, annotations (click here, choose your own adventure), or even let your audience submit ideas for your next video. By giving your viewers something to *do* during or after watching your video, you are setting up your fans for a really "sticky" experience—they have fun watching, participating, and interacting with you and your community—and these actions will make them want to come back to your channel for more.

This particular strategy (a "call to action") arose early on in the history of YouTube, with vlogs—a genre wherein a single person addresses a camera directly through a monologue. As early as 2009, the vlogger Marina Orlova encouraged fan participation, addressing viewers as "my dear students" and asking audiences to engage with her through comments.[26] Eight years later, the platform encouraged "calls to action" as a "best practice." Notably, the platform's "tips" never suggested particular themes for content. Instead, YouTube focused on form and structure (e.g., well-lit, clear videos with calls-to-action at the end of the video). An easy summarization might read, "Do what you wish shall be the whole of the law (so long as you wish to maximize your metrics)."

The platform also emphasizes form in training modules on video titles, descriptions, and preview images ("thumbnails"); literary scholars call these "paratexts." Closer to home, in economic sociology, Lucien Karpik calls them "judgment devices," or objects that enable audiences to judge whether they may enjoy a particular cultural commodity (e.g., book reviews on the back of a dust jacket, album covers or other images used in marketing music, notes from the editor, etc.).[27] Judgment devices, according to Karpik, enable audiences to decide to consume some particular object rather than another. For example, if presented with two books on the same topic by unknown authors online or at a bookstore, an exciting front cover and glowing back-cover praise from the *New York Times* or notable authors may lead to purchasing one book over the other. The cover and the praise enable people to judge the potential quality of a book. Absent these judgment devices, consumers may be unable to make a decision and make no purchase at all. Such indecision may, in the aggregate, result in market failure.

Rather than focus on the subject matter of any particular video, YouTube's training programs attempt to secure stable production of useful judgment devices. This includes practices for increasing a video's likelihood of being "surfaced" or found by a viewer in a search. One training module shows several potential titles for a video alongside several thumbnail or preview images and then asks which pairing works best. The "best" image/title pairing is highlighted, and a narrator explains that the "best" thumbnails should look "good at multiple sizes, including close up, be in-focus, of high resolution and high contrast, descriptive, visually compelling, and, most importantly, match what's in the video." The course's study guide adds, "Audience engagement during the first ten to fifteen seconds of your video can tell you how well your title, thumbnail, and description are matching the expectations of viewers." The guide then suggests: "Go to YouTube Analytics and look at Audience Retention. If you see a steep decline in the first few seconds of your video, experiment with a new title/thumbnail combination and check back to measure the impact." The guide concludes with an easily referenced table wherein each judgment device (title, description, thumbnail) can be seen beside its associated metric. These included click-through rate (CTR) and the method by which a viewer discovered the video (e.g., direct search or algorithmic recommendation). A quiz that concluded the training module asked which of three potential thumbnails for a video entitled "Fun with Shadow Puppets" best fit YouTube's guidelines. Possible thumbnails included a brightly lit photo of a clean-shaven, bespectacled man's face with a shadow puppet projected onto a white wall behind his head, a poorly lit and obscured face of a teenage male, and a stock image of a person wearing a gasmask.

Perusing YouTube, you still find wildly diverse and, sometimes, inexplicably strange content. Sometimes videos resemble "normal" or "professional" media, and sometimes they do not. Many people cherish this formal diversity, from celebrated creators to amateurish inventiveness, but corporations looking to sell eyeballs to advertisers do not. During fieldwork, a major problem at The Future stemmed from creators using cell phone cameras to record their videos. Rather than the traditional landscape orientation associated with film and television production, creators often held their cameras vertically. Unlike film or video cameras, cell phone cameras afford this possibility for vertical recording and playbook that yields a vertical, "portrait"-oriented video. At the time, this aspect ratio connoted unprofessionalism among media professionals (notably advertisers), an undesirable quality from the perspective of the platform and the MCNs. Of course, this changed in the time between my fieldwork and the writing of this book. "Vertical video" has become more widely accepted; this, of course, will also change.

What is crucially important here is that YouTube attempted to discipline or structure the formal aspects of creators' videos and the judgment devices that accompany them. Beyond that, creators were free to create whatever they wish. Before YouTube became a global seller of advertising space, the media scholars Jean Burgess and Joshua Green argued that

"YouTube's value as a *cultural* resource is actually a direct result of its unfiltered, disordered, vernacular, and extremely heterogeneous characteristics."[28] The diversity of YouTube's global, largely untrained media workforce may be culturally valuable if one considers YouTube to be an archive of human creativity, but as a source of economic value, creators' heterogeneity represents a key economic problem, one that the platform attempts to solve in order to secure the smooth production of views and accumulation of advertising revenues. Platform discipline attempts to attenuate, if not wholly eliminate, content's heterogeneity at the level of form or structure while leaving the subject matter up to the creator.

Algorithmic Management

So far, the platform's disciplinary vectors illustrate a positive mode of power, allowing and inviting creativity within boundaries, but what of the platform's negative power to sanction and punish? This sort of governance comes in two interrelated forms of algorithmic management: automated copyright enforcement and content moderation. Both appear indifferent and opaque to creators and others downstream, not unlike Franz Kafka's fictional bureaucracies. YouTube's ContentID system (CID) keeps a database of copyrighted video and music ("assets"). The CID system scans all content uploaded to the platform, looking for elements that match content in the CID database. YouTube then flags potential copyright law violators and notifies the registered copyright owners, who may then choose to sanction the potential violators. Choosing to pursue this action results in a "strike" against alleged violators. The copyright owner may then choose to have YouTube take down the violating video or allow CID to siphon a portion of advertising revenue from the violating video. Strikes diminish the alleged violator's ability to earn income through advertising revenue and, in some cases, result in the deletion of an offending creator's channel.

Some of YouTube's most innovative content brings into focus the problems that arise from CID's algorithmic governance. As mentioned earlier, YouTube content tends to be wildly diverse, often failing to resemble what many define as "professional" media production. One could call YouTube content "amateurish," but that would ignore creators' many innovations. Aside from vlogging, the most distinctly YouTube-ian content adds novelty to preexisting media elements—often other YouTube videos, movies, TV news, music, and other mass media. This description applies very clearly to some of the most popular YouTube creators, such as PewDiePie, who had 105 million subscribers and over 25 billion views as of spring 2020. Like almost all gaming channels, PewDiePie posts videos of himself playing videogames while he criticizes the game or comically narrates the action. Content such as his appears quite innovative and did not exist before the rise of YouTube and, later, Twitch, a gaming-only platform. Still, gaming creators do not produce the games they play. They buy the games, and these consumer purchases form a key part of creators' original content. In this way, the gaming channels are similar to other channels that offer commentary and analysis of popular films. These channels use preexisting film footage and reedit the footage into a review, critical description, or even new "cuts" of trailers and popular scenes. For YouTube's CID system, gamers and reviewers exist in a gray area wherein creators add novel elements to preexisting material. In the language of YouTube's training modules, these represent new "creative" works. PewDiePie plays the game and adds his voice and face to the video. The movie channels edit and add commentary to preexisting films. Others simply take preexisting YouTube content and repackage it under a different name.

In the eyes of the platform, only the last example formally counts as piracy, but even so, many creators with whom I spoke claimed to have received strikes against content that fit YouTube's fair-use guidelines. They felt powerless, describing a silence and inscrutability similar to other users of Google's infrastructures and recounting lengthy appeal processes that often failed.[29] As Dennis, the European animator explained,

> Yeah, you know you can't, like, get connected to YouTube and ask YouTube a question when you are in the position we are [in]. It's like impossible to get answers from them because—I understand that they get a billion questions a day and they can't handle answering them. So, their answer is "ask in the forum"—how do you say? Forum? But there are a lot of answers that no one knows in the forum, just "YouTube [laughing] knows the answer." So, that is probably the main reason that we are connected to an MCN.

Aside from unanswered emails, creators lacked a way to contact YouTube directly. Many of my informants claimed that YouTube's stonewall tactics drove them to sign with an MCN. The blackboxed platform dominates and disciplines creators located downstream, appearing inscrutable from below. MCNs provided protection from unpredictable punishment, yet MCNs also acted as a vector for the platform's positive, disciplinary governance.

THE CONTENT REFINERY?

While working with The Future's network and talent acquisition team, I came to call the company's reinforcement of platform discipline "formatting"—a term most associated with the sociological study of markets for more standardized commodities (e.g., fruit, coffee, iron, etc.). As described by Michel Callon, formatting begins with the selective exclusion of certain aspects of some thing (framing) in order to define the boundaries of what constitutes a saleable, commodified version of that thing.[30] Defining the frame or boundary of a commodity—often performed by regulatory bodies or, in this case, the platform—shapes the actions of producers downstream as they adjust production to conform to the frame or format.

YouTube performed the first part of formatting through the disciplinary vectors just described, and The Future reinforced this process by further educating creators, solidifying their metrics orientation. This runs somewhat counter to The Future's employees, who saw themselves as resource extractors or content refiners. Recounting a conversation with her boss, an employee said, "I refer to The Future as the YouTube Factory, and my boss said, 'No, factory implies [that] we're making stuff.' I was like, 'Oh, it's the content mines,' because we're mining the content. Then, I was like, 'No, it's not that either.' So we decided it was the YouTube Processing Plant. Like, we take the content and we put it through the content sharpener, the refinery. [We're] the content refinery." This employee's refinery metaphor dovetailed neatly with executives' statements on The Future's goal to "extract value" from creators. However, the refinery metaphor ignores how the platform and The Future shape content. Rather than simply extracting value from some ready-made resource, the platform and The Future capture value produced by a globally distributed workforce, one whose content had first been tamed and disciplined.

The Future's initial conversations with creators further reinforced the platform's disciplinary efforts, offering strategy recommendations and, eventually, itemized "optimization reports." On calls I observed in the

"Men's Room," Desmond and Cooper advised creators to include strategic keywords, or "tags," in their videos' metadata and gave guidelines on the best times to release new videos (Tuesdays and Thursdays, between 11 a.m. and 3 p.m.). Before wrapping up, they told creators that The Future also handled "brand integrations" or bespoke brand-sponsored content. Whether they mentioned this service varied by channel type. For instance, they would mention this to makeup tutorial channels but not prank channels (which feature creators playing practical jokes or staging elaborate pranks). Prank channels garner large audiences but often rely on crude, often sexist and racist humor, which many brands find undesirable. As Desmond said on the phone, "You have a brand-appealing channel, unlike pranks. Brands don't really want to be part of the prank world." He then said The Future could also help set up collaborations ("collabs") between creators. Creators were also advised to self-invest in production equipment— not unlike advice from YouTube's training materials. Here, staff framed technology as being bound up in financial potential, if not success. This inviting attempt to shift the burden of investment in fixed capital (production equipment) onto creators focused on advising creators to increase their "production value." Creators were told that increased production value might increase their visibility and attractiveness to brands, and, again, this follows from, if not exactly mimics, the platform's training materials.

Strategy recommendations and "optimization" reports followed many, if not all, of the platform's prescriptions. Each report reminded creators that "YouTube's algorithm stresses two important factors: session time [watch time] and audience engagement." Reports also evaluated how well channels conformed to guidelines from YouTube's training modules and The Future's proprietary ten-point checklist. Except for certain high-profile creators for whom The Future took an active role, optimization took the form of suggestions. As a male vlogger explained,

[My manager] was like, you've got to figure out something with the channel to make it boost the numbers. It's just not viable right now. He was totally right because I let my channel fall by the wayside. For me, I appreciate that sort of no-bullshit business thing. "You gotta do better." Ok, you're right, but, nothing where it's like, "this is the direction we're going to creatively take your channel in." It's like, "you figure it out," but just know that you've got to figure it out.

Reinforcing platform discipline, The Future's office staff invited creators to be subordinate entrepreneurs, prizing quantitative success above other concerns.

Downstream, creators claimed that The Future did "nothing" or "very little" to help further their careers. For instance, a prank creator said, "They kind of just leave me be and give me the I guess the benefits of it and let me go." A "fashion/lifestyle" vlogger with hundreds of thousands of subscribers said,

> My first [MCN] was not, they didn't really help me out at all. I signed with them for some nerdy business reasons. The first was they said they had a patent to create, basically someone could scroll over me while I'm in a video and if they liked my shirt, they could click on it and go right to buying the shirt. I was interested in that because I was starting out as fashion, "Oh this is cool and maybe I could get some brand deals," or whatever. They ended up not being able to do that, so [I left]. That was my first network. Now, I'm with [The Future] and it's basically the same thing.

Not unlike The Future's pitch to creators, the vlogger describes another MCN that attempted to link creators' future prosperity to technological innovation while promising support and services. Illustrating the imagined possibilities linked to these promises, a male vlogger from Los Angeles said, "They do a lot of production work. So, with them, I have packaged a number of projects and tried to pitch them to various outlets. If it was just the brands and they were consistently bringing me brands [deals], I would still be with them. But, the fact that I can meet with them [The Future], have an idea, and they can take that idea to knock on doors that I can't knock on is very valuable, so I enjoy the production aspect of stuff."

Having seen that the vlogger primarily produced content in his home, I asked if he made use of The Future's production opportunities. He claimed to be self-sufficient, "so there's no point—but for other people, great. It's one of those things where they say all of these things where they can make it seem like they're giving you things, but none of its necessary." His response illustrates both creators' entrepreneurial disposition and The Future's rather hands-off approach. The Future's pitch attempts to attract creators by promising "hands-on" services, but once signed to a contract, these services never materialize, leaving only gentle prods from management intended to reinforce platform discipline. But despite The Future's seemingly deliberate attempts to minimize the provision of these services, creators stayed with the firm because, alongside creators' contractual obligation, The Future offered protection from YouTube's algorithmic governance.

The relationship between creators and The Future ought to appear familiar. Much like the engineers at SoniCo, creators thought of themselves not as workers but as entrepreneurial microbusinesses to which the MCN provided services. In cultivating this relation, The Future businessed creators, linking the possibility of future economic prosperity to self-management. Similar to management's presentation of the working day as full of potential at SoniCo, the materiality of YouTube's interface, the platform's training materials, and The Future's advice invite an entrepreneurial disposition, one subordinate to metrics and algorithms.

I want to highlight briefly how this affects cultural production to draw out differences between this work process and those discussed in part 2. Recall that in chapter 2, I showed how YouTube invited a sort of subordinate or heteronymous entrepreneurialism, one oriented toward meeting preexisting demand as defined by a dominant actor, a key point ignored by celebrants of social media entrepreneurship.[31] For YouTube's creators, this meant producing content to meet the needs of an audience as defined by the platform. YouTube's interface and training modules, along with The Future's recommendations, invite creators to become subordinate entrepreneurs who engage in what sociologists of art such as Pierre Bourdieu and Theodor Adorno termed "heteronymous" cultural production. Heteronymous cultural production tends to be oriented toward market demand rather than demands of other, semiautonomous forms of valuation (awards, prestige, honor, etc.). For creators, there presently exists no other source of institutionalized validation—what Bourdieu called "consecration"[32]—and the platform and The Future's staff encourage creators to orient to algorithms and the audience. Their primary orientation toward metrics highlights the effects of the platform upon creative labor when considered against the social regime. There, expressive workers tended to orient toward the social conventions of music production (e.g., genre). Those conventions possessed a degree of autonomy vis-à-vis market demand, even if engineers were most definitely informed by current market trends in popular music. Under the quantified regime, workers primarily orient to metrics that determine earnings, which, in turn, shaped production processes as workers aim to increase output, maximizing views while minimizing costs.

OUT ON THE PLATFORM

Creators produce content under conditions that vary just as much as their social positions and geographic locations. Unlike workers on an oil platform out at sea, creators maintain a semblance of homey domesticity in the middle of the internet's digital ocean, as do some users of other digital labor platforms.[33] Creators work in living rooms, basements, bedrooms, and advanced home studios, like the one where I met Hank, the suburban dad who made content focused on surviving in the wilderness and prepping for various apocalyptic scenarios. To be honest, I was nervous when we met. He loved Alex Jones, a well-known radical right-wing media personality and Donald Trump supporter who trades in conspiracy theories, and it was the winter of 2017, just a month after Trump's inauguration. I was following a conspiracy-inspired prepper as he entered a code into a lock on a reinforced steel door that led down into his basement studio, complete with green screens, professional lights, sophisticated cameras, audio equipment, and his gun collection. I relaxed a bit when his wife brought us coffee and cookies.

Not everyone produces content in a hardened bunker. Eileen, a young Black woman whom I also met in the Midwest, used her grandmother's living room as production studio for her beauty- and makeup-related content. She started off with a point-and-shoot Kodak camera, recording herself in her bathroom in high school during what she called her "emo" phase. Her favored style had made her feel a bit askew in her neighborhood, or, as she said, "That's what I was into, and being in a predominantly Black school, that wasn't the mood," but by the time we spoke, she had found a community of fans on YouTube; she had over 500,000 subscribers. Her grandmother had always supported her in this, giving Eileen a slightly better camera and, eventually, use of the living room as a makeshift production studio. The expanded space allowed Eileen to set up professional lights, a higher-quality DSLR camera, and green screen, all of which she purchased with her YouTube earnings. Her earnings from YouTube had helped pay her college tuition, and so even though she had initially thought of You-Tube as an avenue for personal expression and community building, she now thought of the platform as a means of paying for a degree, something she saw as crucial to a desired career in marketing.

Carl, a middle-aged, stay-at-home, white dad in the Southwest, converted a spare room into a production studio, complete with a high-resolution camera, professional lighting kit, and high-quality microphones. Over donuts and coffee in his living room, Carl explained how his wife's job in the tech sector paid most of the bills while he had worked part time and taken care of the kids. He and his children made videos in which they unboxed toys and evaluated products they used around the house. He seemed to cherish the time spent with his kids, and their YouTube earnings allowed him to quit his part-time job. Still, the kids were growing older, becoming teenagers, and so, like a lot of parents, he worried that they might lose interest in their dad and the YouTube channel.

Others used public spaces as their soundstage. From 2013 to 2019, I saw the latter almost daily in downtown Los Angeles and Echo Park near where I lived in Historic Filipinotown. There, young men and women frequently film themselves in public parks or on city streets. This sort of guerilla production occurs alongside more elaborate film shoots all across the city, so creators rarely drew attention from passersby. Some channels operated as small production companies with several employees or as promotional strategies for off-YouTube businesses. For instance, a professional pianist began by making piano lesson videos for YouTube that served as promotion for subscription-based, online piano lessons. Others set up online shops for merchandise associated with their channels.

Much of the scholarly writing on social media producers focuses on the interactions between creators and fans—a supposed joyous affordance of platformed "entrepreneurship."[34] Rather than belabor this well-rehearsed argument, I wish to focus on creators' production routines and their relationship to technology. Despite wide variation in social positions, working conditions, and intentions, creators shared much in terms of production practices and the affective valences of the working day. Work on the platform was dynamic and engaging but also isolating and precarious. The platform's interface certainly provided dynamic, engaging data displays and facilitated communication with audiences through direct messages and users' comments, but creators seemed happy to spend hours talking to me about their work just to have a break from otherwise isolated days spent at home. For example, I met an animator for an interview at his home where he worked in LA. His apartment, though large, seemed empty, with few decorations or pieces of furniture save for his dual-screen computer setup. He stopped working when I arrived and then spent three hours talking to me, showing no signs of wanting to stop until I announced that I had to leave to meet someone for another interview.

Bobby, a comical "news" vlogger, converted his bedroom into a small, makeshift production studio each day, picking up his dirty laundry and tidying up before pulling down a green screen to cover a closet door. The screen allowed Bobby to call forth "something from nothing," one of workers' rather romantic ways of discussing creativity. The green screen provided something of a gateway to another world, allowing him to add any background he wished later by removing the solid color with an editing program such as Adobe Premiere, Apple's ubiquitous iMovie, or free software such as DaVinci Resolve. Lacking space in his small, shared apartment in suburban LA, he placed a small, point-and-shoot camera capable of recording HD video atop a tripod that stood precariously on his bed. He readied an iPad for use as a teleprompter by loading his freshly written script and got ready to shoot.

Across town, Nadine—a lifestyle vlogger—made content about sexuality, makeup, hairstyling, and music fandom. She started off shooting videos in a small part of her bedroom using the webcam on her sister's laptop. By the time we spoke, she had built herself into a successful "brand" and moved into her dining room, shooting her videos with a digital single-lens reflex camera (DSLR) and a professional lighting system. She hoped to upgrade to an LED ring light in the near future. "That's the newest thing that everybody's doing. It looks really good." Mirroring the platform's advice, she and other creators understood technology as coterminous with improvements in audiovisual quality and, hopefully, economic success.

Despite their diverse circumstances, creators' video-making styles followed a few patterns, which they generally described as involving a combination of brainstorming, careful scripting, and improvisation. Bobby's process illustrates a common style of production focused on discrete, one-off videos. Around 8:00 a.m., Bobby starts perusing Reddit and Facebook for news stories that he might craft into jokes. "My rule for comedy is that if there's a victim in the situation or if someone's dead, you can't make fun of it." When nothing useful comes up, he calls a friend on the phone or makes a video call to "brainstorm a little bit." He finishes his script by 11:00 a.m. Other vloggers described a similar process that began with deciding on a topic followed by, as one said, "Maybe a minimal amount of research and [then] depending on how confident I feel about it, sometimes I'll just go off the top of my head." From setup to teardown, Bobby's shoot takes a little over an hour. After he gets a few good takes of his daily mono-logue and any additional shots ("pickups" or "inserts"), he removes the memory card from his camera and places it into his computer, transfer-ring the files into his editing software. While editing, he takes a ten-minute break every fifty minutes to "shake my body out, dance a little bit just to keep me from getting cabin fever." Back at his desk, he finishes editing, uploads the video, and creates a thumbnail or preview image—one of the processes that the platform and The Future attempt to discipline. After that, he sends out emails to casting companies and corporate sponsors in search of auditions and brand deals.

Illustrative of another common production style, Kevin and Becky organized their production in batches despite operating within very dif-ferent genres. Kevin interviews touring musicians at their gigs in several major Midwestern cities. On any given night, he may be attending two to five concerts in order to shoot the interviews by himself. When we met, Kevin was in the middle of a fifteen-hour day and about to start shooting one of the three interviews on his schedule for the night. He said he needed a steady flow of content for his smaller, mid-size channel (eighty thousand subscribers), and so he posted three videos per day, seven days a week, despite only earning about $1,000 per month. Since he traveled across the Midwest to gather footage, Kevin had to be mobile, carrying his entire video production apparatus in a medium-sized black backpack, not unlike the mobile recording engineers in the previous chapter. His kit included a shoulder-mounted camera stand, an HD camcorder, a small LED array for illumination, and a "shotgun" microphone. After shooting, he broke down each interview into three to seven smaller clips, releasing them separately to meet his rigorous production schedule of twenty-one videos per week.

Back in Los Angeles, Becky reported on and reviewed alcoholic bever-ages, offering advice on styles of wine within particular price ranges and suggesting food pairings. She also worked full time as a waitress. Like Kevin, she batched production, shooting six weeks' worth of videos in a single day. Unlike Kevin the one-man production team, Becky regularly hired a cameraperson for these marathon shoots to speed her production schedule and stretch her modest budget. As she said, "It's cheaper to have just one production day that I'm having to pay my camera guy. I'm not a typical YouTuber that like films everything myself and edits everything myself. I don't have time for that." Highlighting Becky's attempt to manage her resources efficiently, her statement also contains a uniformly-made assertion of atypicality, an assertion I found common among creators. As Becky said, "I'm not a typical YouTuber," echoing all the office workers in this book who claimed to have no "typical day" to describe. Maybe there was not a single "typical" creator, but these two production styles demonstrate some common, shared production practices among producers running small-to-medium-sized channels. These exist alongside and often in tandem with more elaborate production situations that more closely resemble professional TV and film shoots. In each, creative labor depends upon a bevy of media production technologies.

THE DESIRED POTENTIAL OF PRODUCTION TECHNOLOGIES

If the platform provides a way to imagine a future through its interface and advice, then production technologies provide a means to enact that future. Creators often enjoyed acquiring and using tools, getting lost in their creative process, developing a feel for machines—and, in some cases, developing machine-like feelings. Some, like Fred, a product reviewer and vlogger, actively desired equipment and dedicated himself to demonstrating and reviewing production technologies. Equipment, he said, was "the only way to keep things interesting." Fred might seem extreme, but his statement reveals something about other aesthetically enrolled workers. Like Fred, they perceived potentials for agency as immanent to objects, usually technology. "The tools don't make the artist," he conceded, but he wanted to make his content "look the best that it can be," which, he often thought, required technological upgrades. Several DSLRs and a "fantastic" microphone helped. Likewise, Bobby described a process of learning to improve image quality and color as an effort "to just try, to just be better." After some simple Google searches, he downloaded some presets for correcting color in his videos, hoping to improve visual quality and, with any luck, earnings.

Fred and Bobby linked creativity—their most enjoyed part of work—to equipment, which both afforded the deployment of new skills and improved their control over image and sound quality. Like the recording engineers in earlier chapters, creators were excited about technology because it extended their aesthetic agency, an embodied capacity of living labor. In doing so, technology augmented the body, further highlighting creative labor as an assemblage of humans and nonhumans. As Bobby said,

> I get so excited. I am so excited about this GoPro [camera]. I have no idea how to use it! I'm excited to figure it out. What it's going to do, it will allow. You know what it is? We have five senses. Imagine that there's a sixth sense out there. If you could acquire it, you wouldn't necessarily know how to use it, but once you learned about it, it would give you a whole new dimension to work in that other people don't have or that you didn't have before. So, it's like, I don't know what impact the GoPro will have on my content, but once I learn about it, I know it's going to make my content better. All of these tricks, coloring, whatever it is, once I learn it, it's going to make everything better.

In Marx's discussion of the "general intellect," he claimed that "the science which compels the inanimate limbs of the machinery . . . acts upon [workers] through the machine as an alien power."[35] This seems distant from Bobby's experience. His GoPro camera was not "alien" at all, seeming instead like a new sense organ, extending his capacity for creative labor, a hybrid of technology (dead labor, fixed capital) and living, embodied labor. To borrow again from the anthropologist Alfred Gell, technology appears as a "prosthesis, a bodily organ acquired via manufacture and exchange rather than by biological growth."[36] Clearly linked by creators to distinct yet indeterminate affordances of technological objects, creators' desire for new potentials suggests an interactional basis within the labor process that leads them to accept capital's invitations to be creative. Remember, YouTube and The Future both encouraged creators' investments in production technologies.

Production technologies become desirable as sources of generalized potential—what Lazzarato terms the "deterritorialized desire" of cognitive capitalism.[37] Bobby said as much when he spoke of technology's potential, nonspecific uses. Similarly, Ed linked technology to indeterminate, desired possibilities, claiming that technology "feels good" and that "it's exciting to see what the new things can do." He just knew that "the video from my new Nikon DSLR is going to be a lot better" and excitedly described the potential of a new microphone. Not unlike SoniCo's workers, creators understood technologies as bundles of imagined, indeterminate, potential uses. A microphone *may* improve sound, and cameras *will* "be a lot better," even providing a "sixth sense."

This excitement for technology could be interpreted as purely ideological; their statements, after all, bore more than a passing resemblance to the language of advertisements. Still, to write this off as merely ideological ignores how these objects' distinct materialities offer equally distinct possibilities. The GoPro—a small, water-resistant, HD camera—afforded certain possibilities not offered by a smartphone camera or a webcam. Likewise, certain microphones afforded improved sound quality given their different sensitivities to sound frequencies. As bundles of potentials, technologies excited and activated creators' desire, and so technology, alongside platform discipline, points toward a more material understanding of control or power over creative labor. Again, this diverges from common portrayals of creative labor as unmanaged or ideologically duped, caught up in the pursuit of symbolic rewards.[38] In effect, the material affordances of technology exert power over work, linking the ideological invitation to "be creative" to workers' everyday experiences.

Even those who expressed ambivalence toward technology still acknowledged it as a desirable, potential extension of their agency. Nadine did not love technology or express excitement, but she still acknowledged the prevalence of this sentiment among creators. When I asked her if technology fascinated or excited her, she said, "No! Not at all! Maybe I wish I had a little bit of this because people are like 'Oh my god! The new camera's coming out!' Like, my other YouTube friends [say that] and I'm like, 'So? Who wants to pay $3,000 for that?' It doesn't excite me at all, but I know that I need good stuff. I'm not into that." Nadine reaffirmed technology as potential, as a desirable extension of her capacity for creative labor.[39] Audrey, a sketch comedy creator and aspiring actress, echoed Nadine's ambivalence when she described editing software. She said, "I definitely probably enjoy it a lot more than most of my friends do. I get really fired up having that creative control—like I said, the timing and choosing the shots. I love it!" She linked her positive feelings to the "creative control" or potential agency afforded by the software, but her "love" seemed bitter-sweet. As she elaborated, "It's just, when you run into technical snags, it can be stressful or—what's the word—deflating. It kind of deflates your energy, especially if you've just—it's also very monotonous. You have to look through—let's say you have to look through hours of footage just to find a few seconds to use. I always say I have a love/hate relationship with it."

Audrey enjoyed spending hours editing her content until she hit a "technical *snag*"—caught, halted, and, ultimately, coming up against the limits to creative labor's machine/body hybridity. Her inability to intuit the underlying logic of the software shaped her felt experience of the labor process, preventing her from having an aesthetic experience and meta-phorically entering into the machine. This relation between materiality and immersion points to a key component left out of research on affect and creativity in organizations and, more generally, "flow" experiences: the mutual mediation of material, often nonhuman objects and human sub-jects.[40] Audrey exerts "creative control" within her screen but only insofar as the software allows her to work toward that control. To do so, she must find software to be intelligible, a key point made by the science and tech-nology scholar Lucy Suchman when she argues that technology's "affect is an effect not simply of the device itself" but of the user's familiarity with the machine along with its materiality.[41] When the software "snags," Audrey felt deflated and stressed, a product of technological materialities and human subjectivity that provide creative labor's palpable meanings.[42]

Creators may desire technology-as-potential, but what of the immersive aesthetic experiences I discussed in earlier chapters? As Ed explained, "Yeah, when I edit it, I usually sit down for pretty much all day and night or evening and kind of do it. Once you get into it and you stop, then you have to step back and get into it again." While not as colorfully described as SoniCo's "disappearing" audio engineers, editing is something he must "get into," or, as Tammy the vlogger said, it is "an in-the-zone thing":

> It's kind of like mechanical in a way. Like you know what to do and you take this part out, you add the music, the title, copy/paste, the title with the same font, the same size, and the same place. And, you know, you really get

distracted by it, and that's all I do. I think otherwise, if I'm writing a blog post I get really distracted, I'm on Instagram. I'm texting my friends. I'm SnapChatting people, but whenever I'm editing, for some reason, if I'm not like completely focused in it, I can't do it.

Tammy's distraction implies attraction and focus because being distracted from one thing is to be attracted and focused by something else.[43] Tammy's distraction leads her to be "completely focused" on her editing tasks, blocking out other attractions, especially social media, the most ubiquitous of all attracting distractions. Tammy's description of a distracted focus also echoes Paolo Virno's discussion of workers' skill and disposition under cognitive capitalism. According to Virno, creative labor requires "the sensory learning of technically reproducible artifices," a form of learning empowered by distraction,[44] much like the "mechanical" arranging of text and sound that Tammy describes.

Leland—a creator and experimental video artist—described a similarly mechanistic loss of self during his editing process. As he said, "I definitely experience that all the time, and it's cool. I enjoy that feeling a lot. Just being like, I am like a machine or I am like a robot that is working through some sort of higher power or something, you know? I have no idea, but it's like still exciting regardless of all these different feelings I have about it. To make a thing, you know." Subjectively absent in his robotic repetition, Leland described something like an aesthetic experience where he felt like "a robot that is working through some sort of higher power," his body lost inside the screen. While enjoyable, these moments elicited conflicted and difficult-to-articulate affects ("all these different feelings"). Tammy and Jerry, another vlogger, shared Leland's can't-put-my-finger-on-it sentiment. He struggled to explain his experience and said, "I don't know if I'd classify them as enjoyable but they're not miserable. It definitely, maybe it is transcendental: just in the moment. Sometimes it's enjoyable. If I feel like—enjoyable wouldn't be the right word." Still, he felt "productive" in these moments and said, "I tend to get a sense of joy out of being productive." Further complicating his experience, he added that his productive "joy" involved "painful drudgery."

What to make of this complicated bundle of experiences? I could attempt to hammer down creators' accounts of the ineffable like nails that stick up and out, but that moves us away from how these accounts gesture toward the importance of work's affective or aesthetic dimensions. Social and political theorists posit these dimensions of social life as "thought and felt by the body's sensory and perceptive faculties," "pre-social but not a-social," "preverbal" or "infra-individual," "beneath . . . conscious knowing," or, more simply, difficult to articulate through language.[45] Jerry suggested as much. To be subjectively absent is not enjoyable but transcendent, not miserable yet painful, even productive—which is enjoyable.

Despite difficulties locking down their aesthetic experiences into language, creators were uniform in their post hoc interpretations. These were *productive* moments, aesthetic experiences that enrolled creative labor in managerial and platform projects of accumulation. This differs sharply from the few studies of earlier modes of capitalism that make mention of such experiences. For example, Donald Roy in the 1950s and Michael Burawoy in the 1970s both found factory workers who *zoned out*, lost in the rhythmic clicks of factory machines. Phyllis Baker's study of clerical workers in the 1990s found them to associate immersive absence with *escape* from the doldrums of data entry.[46] Rather than escaping from work, productive absence enrolls creative workers, providing the aesthetic experiences, or "flow," which they pursue in search of meaning.[47] As I will show later, The Future's office staff shared this interpretation of immersive absence as productivity. With that in mind, let's enter The Future, where full-time office staff shared creators' precarity despite their "standard employment."

AN INVITATION TO EXIT . . .

Moving upstream to The Future's offices, I find homologies between the interests of management and the platform, workplace churn, rapid technological change, and the material organization of the workplace. Even by media industry standards,[48] job tenure at The Future was short, following the same right-skewed, "superstar" distribution as creators' success, with a median length of employment at just under twelve months. Most who made it longer were men who held managerial or executive positions. The majority of the nonmanagerial staff I spoke with worked a mandatory fifty-hour week for just a bit more than the median annual income for a single person in the United States ($35,000); regular staff who survived longer than a year earned $45,000 to $50,000 per year. Their average pay shakes out to be between $14.60 and $20.80 per hour. The low end is less than the median U.S. hourly wage, while the high end still falls below the hourly wages for many public universities' teaching assistants—a notoriously low-paid position and one I held while conducting much of the research for this book. Keep in mind that while I was conducting fieldwork, Los Angeles's median monthly rent for a one-bedroom apartment hovered close to or above $1,900, roughly 65 percent of an average employee's gross monthly earnings.

Management and the Workplace Experience team (WE) considered The Future's rapid turnover to be "normal" for a digital entertainment firm in an ever-evolving "space," or industry. As a member of WE said, "It's normal, turnover's fast, usually, here. It's normal. Entertainment is a fast turnover, in general." "Form cannot come before function," explained the head of WE, echoing a similar statement from an executive at another firm, who said, "We cannot be precious about form." An executive concluded a staff meeting with a PowerPoint slide that read, "Buy into the process." He explained how "if you buy into the process, that will make you very valuable somewhere else," then paused—perhaps realizing the concerns this might raise—before he added, "if that's the route you choose. Right now, we've made it a point of getting rid of those that don't buy into the process."

The "process," though quite open, included meeting quotas, internal logging of activities in enterprise management software such as Salesforce, and near-constant, multimodal communication. Again, Lazzarato's theorization of work under cognitive capitalism appears instructive when he claims that management no longer concerns itself with work per se; rather, managers focus on "the organization and control of 'processes' essentially consisting of the application of methods, monitoring of indicators, verification of the uniformity of procedures, and the organization of meetings."[49] Management's "process" aids in the maintenance of the organization despite high churn. Illustrating a broad theme of expected exit, management ordered

TABLE 5.2
Job tenure at The Future by gender

	Median length of employment (months)	Number of respondents
Male	12	33
Female	10	45

employees to log completed tasks in Salesforce to maintain, as a manager said, "institutional knowledge" in the face of ever-changing employees.[50] Notably, this "process" became more prominent after the company's purchase by a global media conglomerate. Before that, The Future had been, in the words of one employee, "Like the Wild West. Like [that TV show about tech startups] *Halt and Catch Fire.*"

Churn stemmed not from the "natural" ebb and flow of the labor market but from managerial choices. These people were not simply free-footing members of the "creative class" caught up in the rapturous freedom of "boundaryless" careers.[51] Obviously, high churn seemed a logical way to keep labor costs low, a common choice in entertainment industries typified by what the media scholar John Caldwell calls attempts *"to get everyone to work for free,"*[52] and so churn at The Future mirrored the perpetual "squeeze" experienced by creators and other platform workers.[53] Phillip, a supervisor in his mid-twenties, suggested as much when he said, "We're expendable you know. They [management] don't have our interests in mind at all." Cooper added, "Yeah, no they don't. I mean, that's entertainment. In entertainment, unless you've reached a certain level, they don't care. You're expendable. Totally different from tech [companies]." I nodded, and Phillip added, "Right, I mean, they just do what's going to make them money." These comments contrasted sharply with SoniCo, where employees felt closer to management, given overlapping social relationships, and where management expected staff to remain employed there for well beyond a year. As a supervisor at SoniCo said, "The whole business feels a little bit more like a partnership than an owner/employee relationship." In contrast, The Future's management expected workers to be creative within a particular "process" which *might* make them more valuable upon exit, leaving Phillip to tell me how he wanted "to be a CEO someday. I want to own my own company in this space, and you know, I just want to figure out how to manage more effectively." Per the "process," Phillip's imagined future resided within the "space," not the firm.

. . . AND AN INVITATION TO EXPRESS

The invitation to exit came paired with an invitation to "express" from WE, the Workplace Experience team. Management by invitation is a rather common practice, on display at both The Future and SoniCo as well as several recent studies of call centers, in which management invited employees to "be yourself" as a means of obscuring more direct modes of control.[54] The Future's WE team invites all newly hired employees to create a playlist of their favorite songs, which would then be played over the office PA system. The head of WE described this invitation as a way for new workers to share "their personality, their taste" and to provide a "common ground," a "simple way of bringing people together," and an "equalizing device" by which he hoped to efface organizational hierarchy by allowing all the organization's members, even interns, to exert some degree of control over the sound of the office.

These playlists do, in fact, bind together otherwise transient employees—at least for a short time. As Garland, an "analytics" employee, said, "One great thing about the playlist is that you get a great sense of who a person is based on the music that they choose. So, for me I had a lot of '90s music, Disney music, NSYNC, Backstreet Boys, a lot of stuff I listen to now. Just a lot of my favorite songs. It was great because all throughout the day people came up to you and said, 'Oh hey I really love that song,' or 'Oh that was a really cool playlist.'"

Similarly, Laura and Donna discussed going out after work, while Lucy, a newly hired employee, sat at a nearby table.

LAURA: I don't know about going to a movie, but I could see myself having a drink after work. Are you down?
DONNA: Yeah, I could do that, for sure.

A psychedelic rock song came on over the PA system. This was Lucy's playlist.

LAURA: Oh, this song. I kind of like this song, guilty pleasure.
LUCY: Hey! It's a good song!
LAURA: Oh yeah, it is. It is. I totally did this song at karaoke last Wednesday.
DONNA: Oh, last Wednesday, huh?
LAURA: Yeah, well I was going to say over the weekend, but it was totally not the weekend.

Music brought comment and interaction among an ever-changing set of coworkers. Otherwise, they might enter and exit The Future, fleeting faces seen only briefly at bimonthly staff meetings, passing like data packets through a computer server.

The lyrics of songs chosen by employees sometimes provided oddly poignant commentary. Late in my fieldwork, the 2012 hit song "Oblivion" by the indie-pop singer Grimes[55] played almost daily over the PA. The singer's fragile voice whispered, "I never walk about, after dark. It's my point of view. 'Cause someone could break your neck. Coming up behind you, always coming and you'd never have a clue. I never look behind, all the time . . . always looking straight . . . See you on a dark night." This seemed like sound advice to The Future's staff, to always look ahead, toward the future, avoiding the danger of dismissal that perpetually lurks, hoping to catch you "on a dark night."

Music provided subtle advice and camaraderie, but the office's design—endlessly reconfigurable, lacking walls and fixed seating—made employees' transience palpable. Like the "office of the future" described in *Cubed*, Nikal Saval's history of workplace design, The Future's offices lacked desktop computers and other objects that anchor workers to a place that is "theirs."[56] Staff could ostensibly roam around the office freely with their laptops and smartphones or ditch the office altogether and work remotely from home. Deterritorialized and virtualized, The Future's office contained few, if any, cubicles. Instead, employees sat in bullpen-style desks, along walls at metal IKEA furniture tables, or in glass-walled "collaboration" spaces. Occasionally, they dipped out into common hallways for more private conversations. A comment from a new employee in his late forties was revealing:

> You know I came from a real corporate environment, you know? This is new. Sitting anywhere, working anywhere. I guess this is just how Millennial people work. You sit anywhere, just so long as you have your iPad or your MacBook or whatever. You can just sit wherever and do your work. It's, I guess they call this a startup? I got here and was like, "What's going on?" especially when I first got here and was out on intern row. I just thought, "man what is happening?" but I'm used to it [now]. I mean, that's how it is. Now they got me stuck on the side of a wall.

Some might think that this design facilitated fluidity and teamwork, but the open, unfinished, blank quality of the office seemed more likely to subtly reinforce management's invitation to leave.

According to employees, many rooms felt unfinished given the constant shifting of equipment, furniture, and people. Office décor was sparse, often haphazard, with white walls punctuated by a handful of puzzling artworks that evoked street art and heavy metal album covers (e.g., a dark figure holding a weapon, both made of dollar signs). The lack of color, suggestive of both culture industry professionalism and a lack of finality, also elicited displeasure.[57] As Desmond said, "It's a bit too white." As another male employee said, "We work in a really sterile environment. We try really hard to make our room the polar opposite of the rest of the offices. It's weird how blank everything is. It just feels very much like an [talent] agency in a lot of ways, which is a really boring, like hypercompetitive, Type-A [personality] environment. It just has a very dull, power-washed vibe." One employee even performed a bit of corporate espionage, sneaking into entertainment and technology firms around Los Angeles to take photos to convince management of the need to redecorate. "They're so cool and it'd be so easy. Why can't we be like that?" he asked rhetorically while showing me photos on his phone.

Was the apparent link between office design and churn just a coincidence, an unintended consequence of poor planning, or was it because of management's need for "flexibility?" Seeking an answer, I asked the decorator, Heather, a member of the Workplace Experience team. She echoed upper management's statements about "flexibility" and said, "Whatever can best fit us at that moment and that is nice to the eye but not too overtaking because our space is supposed to be eclectic where you could put things in it and it doesn't really change the whole vibe of it." Able to exert aesthetic agency over the space, she cited "the vibe" as her favorite part of work. So, what was that vibe? Well, The Future felt flexible and fluid, its people and furniture in constant flux. This approach had also been on display in WE's approach to technology; they favored subscription-based software hosted on the "cloud" (e.g., Salesforce, Slack, and Dropbox) rather than proprietary software hosted on traditional, on-site servers.

Management's expectation of exit, borne out in the aesthetics of the workplace, conflicted with employees' needs, and so the white walls were littered with subtle indications of employee discontent. Andrew Ross calls this subtle form of resistance "survivor art" in his ethnography of a web design firm with a similarly designed office in New York's Silicon Alley.[58] One such piece of survivor art, a handwritten sign, hung above a section of bullpen desks and read "SHELLYandLUCYspace." Simultaneously claiming territory amid deterritorialization and voicing dissatisfaction, a bulleted list below the sign offered instructions and advice for coworkers that might violate their attempted sovereignty. "Do not take our things, especially the chairs, they're very important" and "If you want the tape, fine, take the tape, but do not take our equipment. You may leave us things. We like candy. Not crappy candy, but good candy." Somewhat differently, Laura decorated her desk and its immediate vicinity with posters and action figures. Contesting work's aesthetic terrain, employees claimed space, something The Future permitted but did not officially condone. By decorating, Laura and her sign-making coworkers reclaimed territory in an otherwise deterritorialized office.

Departing employees left their mark upon the organization by posing for photographs with coworkers in the lobby's digital photobooth just after they were fired or had resigned. Left tacked to the lobby wall, the photos served as a sort of memento mori, reminders of just how fleeting "standard" employment could be at The Future. After a friend had been let go, Garland, a veteran employee (at nearly ten months), said, "So, Gordon's gone. Better add him to the wall of the fallen." "What's that?" said a manager. "Gordon, he's gone. So, I said we'd better add him to the wall of the fallen." While workers claimed space on the white walls, managers and executives maintained control over their offices, often with quite elaborate décor as well as dedicated landline phones and desktop computers that demonstrated their relative stability beside the tumultuous blankness inhabited by staff.

TECHNOLOGICAL BANALITIES AND ENCHANTMENTS

In this nomadic office, work required constant communication, via a veritable buffet of systems. While other scholars focus on how these systems leave workers feeling overburdened, "pressed for time," or temporally disrupted,[59] I want to continue to focus on how technological aesthetics shape workers' inclinations toward information and particular tasks. Some technologies at The Future felt "natural" and "normal"; others afforded immersive experiences. "Normal" systems tended to resemble social media and other technologies used in everyday life. These included communication systems such as Slack, a now widely used application that served as The

Future's main communication tool alongside enterprise software (Salesforce and Asana), email, Facebook's Messenger, AIM, Google Chat, texting, and phone calls. In contrast, blackboxed systems directly tied to The Future's core business evoked more intense feelings, either acute frustration or the sort of immersive experiences that aesthetically enroll workers in projects of capitalist accumulation.

The "Normalcy" of Constant Communication

Mundane, "normal" systems of constant communication demanded corporeal attention, emitting distinct sounds and sights that signaled new task assignments and other information. Eyes attended to the screen, with auditory support from earphones jacked into an Apple laptop like an umbilical cord. Ubiquitous, vibrating smartphones provided additional sensations, a short pulse against the body indicating a new email or a comparatively longer vibration indicating a text message—something I learned quite quickly when my phone silently buzzed in my pocket as I picked up lunches and ran other errands for executives.

Staff often described waking early in the morning, beginning work with a tap to their smartphones that retrieved a night's worth of accumulated emails, and their days often ended around 10:00 p.m. or whenever they decided to stop checking their phone.[60] In addition to email, they were encouraged to use Slack, a program that mimics the design and interface of popular social media platforms such as Twitter and Instagram by allowing users to tag messages (e.g., #productive, @TheFuture, #throwbackThursday, and #NewTalentTuesday) and easily share videos, animated GIFs, and other content. These systems felt quite "natural" and, for the most part, unworthy of comment. Garland said, "I guess I'm technically what they [call] a digital native. So, I mean, I always have my phone on me. I always have my email going. My email and Slack and Facebook and text. They all come to my phone anyway. There's no real break between [my phone and computer]. My phone is sitting next to me on the desk. It's not overwhelming because I grew up always using multiple forms of communication." Workers described "having a feel" for these systems or "quickly just picking it up."

Developing a "feel" without instruction requires quick acclimation to new technology, which includes associated sensations and interactional styles. Many of The Future's communication systems resembled or in fact were part of the sensed, everyday experience of many—though by no means all—young people in global cities (e.g., smartphones, computers, screens, social media, etc.). Just as reading a book or magazine while watching television might have seemed overwhelming to someone in the 1950s, The Future's dense array of communication technologies and associated sensations *felt* normal. Workers' blasé attitude toward dense communication technologies showed just how much, to borrow from Ben Highmore's analysis of everyday aesthetics in his book *Ordinary Lives*, their "senses have adjusted to intricate and heterogeneous" types of technologically mediated experience.[61]

Of course, work had been no less dense in sensation or communication at SoniCo. Smartphones buzzed and rang while computer screens flickered with information as SoniCo's staff answered phones while logged into Google's suite of cloud-based productivity software (Sheets, Docs, Calendar, Mail, etc.). They too found this density of sensation and information unremarkable, but even so, this level of everyday technological impingement upon the senses should not be taken for granted. Jason, a supervisor at SoniCo in his early thirties, illustrated this point when I asked how he felt about these systems.

JASON: It's been a learning process. Like the [Google] calendar took me a while to figure out.

MICHAEL: Did you use that in your everyday life or, no?

JASON: I've never used the Google calendar I don't think. A lot of the stuff I do now for SoniCo, like using Excel and stuff, I'd done before when I was working in restaurants doing payrolls and all that stuff. But, no it's like this was my first smartphone that SoniCo bought me, an iPhone. I had an Android before so that was kind of, I learned a lot about the really common tech communication because of this job.

MICHAEL: So, how did that feel coming in for you?

JASON: It seemed a little strange because I'd never had a job like that before where I was spending so much time on the phone and writing emails. Similar, I guess in a wider sense to jobs I had that were really service oriented when I was just talking to people that were coming up to my counter all day. Not the same bouncing between writing an email, talking on the phone, going outside and smoking a cigarette, writing an email on my phone or texting [while smoking]. I feel like I'm communicating through a screen pretty much all day at work.

By no means a common response, Jason's "learning process" suggests just how much effort these technological sensations require to become "natural" or "normal." Older than many of the workers whom I met at The Future and SoniCo, Jason provides an exception that supports a more general pattern of bodily attunement to communication technologies. The body attuned or entrained to this sort of "normal" is a *classed* body, possessing the sensibilities, dispositions, and tacit knowledge that, along with formal education, comprise a worker's labor power, or "human capital," and thus their position as a member of the "creative class." More succinctly, the banal sensuality of constant communication does not seem so banal to just any body.

Productive Escapes from Dull Scrapes

Workers tended to associate new processes and information with "creativity," which tended to be what they most enjoyed about their jobs. Here I want to press further on the importance of work's aesthetics by showing how technological materialities provide processual pleasures. Communication technologies felt "normal," but blackboxed search technologies elicited vibrant responses. Like a lot of people I met while conducting fieldwork, The Future's talent and strategy teams felt they had a close relationship with technology—sometimes immersive, sometimes frustrating. In this section I focus on the talent team who searched YouTube for potentially valuable creators and attempted to sign them to multiyear contracts—all duties that I regularly performed as a member of this team. Not all of YouTube's one billion users create content, but many do, and so The Future's key problem lay in figuring out where and how to focus employees' attention within the platform's ever-expanding ocean of digital content. Search tasks formed a core component of the firm's business, which hinged on consistent acquisition of new creators ("signing") to capture value from their content. The Future partially solved this problem through a quota system that oriented employees toward reaching metric benchmarks—a part of "the process." Quotas, along with the managerial invitation to "be creative," formed The Future's system of control, but how did workers become affectively invested in these quotas, and how did achieving these quotas relate to their creativity?

The talent team used proprietary and cloud-based systems for search and data analysis. This included finding ("prospecting") and recruiting creators ("outreach" and "signing") as well as formatting their content ("optimizing"). When I first arrived, workers searched for and contacted fifty to one hundred creators each week in order to meet a set quota. After a global media firm purchased The Future, management eliminated quotas and instead focused on monthly and quarterly metric benchmarks (increases in "Total Monthly Views" across the entire network). This change in strategy was not accompanied by a change in logic. The firm earned money from advertising derived from views, taking a percentage of creators' YouTube earnings as well as fees from brand deals, which were also tied to views. Thus, increasing the network's view count directly affected profits. The overarching goal remained one of capturing value from creators with a minimal expenditure of firm resources such as the office staff's labor power.

Most of my days were spent with the talent team, gathering and interpreting digital data about YouTube channels and their content so I could render a judgment—not of taste but of financial viability ("prospecting"). Based on this judgment, staff then developed "optimization" strategies by which creators might produce more views, and thus The Future might capture further value. Much like "normal" communication, this process required creative labor, presuming a high level of tacit knowledge and interpretive competencies to infer what is and what might be popular based on metrics.

We began prospecting by "scraping" data from YouTube. Generally, scraping refers to gathering or "pulling" user data and other information en masse from the databases of platforms and websites—a rather generic practice increasingly common to state and corporate surveillance, political espionage, and social research. Slack, The Future's primary internal communication software—housed the firm's web-scraping application. Ostensibly, this allowed seamless integration of internal communication and organizational search processes. Using Slack, talent team members (like me) typed a short line of code that initiated a data pull from YouTube. Several hours later, Slack would notify us that a CSV file containing the requested data was ready for processing. Among our team, we referred to these CSV files as "scrapes," as in "the crafting scrape" or the "Kids content scrape." Whoever ran the scrape would upload the file to Google Sheets, which allowed multiple team members to coordinate with one another as they collaboratively processed the scrape, despite working in different rooms and, occasionally, different continents.

Uploaded and shared, each scrape contained thousands of rows filled with YouTube channel names and URLs, view counts, and subscriber counts. Scrape preparation began by first sorting data by key metrics such as views or subscribers. Employees then made their way through these sorted lists, row by row, vetting potentially valuable creators with the hope of finding unsigned, already successful YouTube channels so as to "extract the maximum amount of value."[62] In Google Sheets, totem-like animal symbols appear on the upper-left-hand side of the screen. These avatars indicated which members of the team were actively mining scraped data. One team member might be a pink ostrich or a green antelope. Color-coded cursors indicated where each animal avatar worked on a sheet.

Scrapes were divided among regular employees and interns. Employees tended to focus on high-value channels with one hundred thousand or more subscribers; interns were tasked with smaller channels (ten thousand to twenty thousand subscribers). Even though the less popular channels tended to yield fewer viable "leads," unpaid intern labor provided a way for The Future to cover less visible portions of YouTube while focusing on potentially high-quality, high-yield channels. Workers color-coded each row in the scrape to render visible the channel's viability.[63] Green indicated a "qualified" channel, meaning that the channel was in English, had not been entered into the company database, and contained "some creative element." The last part leaves substantial room for workers' judgment and thus requires the creative labor of interpretation. The Future's attempt at outsourcing this process reinforces this point. For a brief period of time, the company contracted with workers in the Philippines to prospect, but that ended after a week because the overseas workers provided lists of channels that failed to meet what my supervisor called The Future's "simple" standards (i.e., original, English-language content free of copyright violations).

My team's typical screens was visually dense, including multiple open web browser tabs alongside all the aforementioned communication programs. I would open several YouTube channels in quick succession to process a scrape as fast as possible—something an intern called being a "tabmaster, where you have like a bunch of [Google] Chrome tabs open at once." When I did this, videos would play automatically, so I would often hear multiple languages and multiple genres simultaneously for a few seconds before muting all the tabs save for the one on which I wished to focus. Later, a design change in web browsers eliminated the need to take this additional step, but at the time I watched men complain about their bad dates, computer-generated voices read the Bible coldly without emotion, and young men instructing viewers how to clean vintage videogame cartridges. Women in South America, Europe, the United Kingdom, and the United States told me how to achieve a "smoky eye" look. Disembodied voices spoke awkwardly overtop of video game footage: "This is from my fifth playthrough. I didn't really understand the symbolism on my first time. This game has high replay value." Rocket-propelled grenades exploded the bodies of virtual animals, humans, and zombies. As the videogame violence wound down, Korean news overlapped with disembodied voices speaking in Farsi overtop images of Heath Ledger's Joker from the 2008 film *Dark Knight*.

My experience both seems mundanely familiar and evokes the scene in Stanley Kubrick's *A Clockwork Orange* where state officials hold open the eyelids of Alex, the antisocial protagonist, forcing him to watch reeducation films. Like everyday internet usage, processing a scrape included overlapping, often conflicting sounds along with screen environments manipulated by using a keyboard and a mouse or a laptop trackpad. Rather than dulling workers' sensibilities, the broader media environment heightens their ability to fluidly interact with and navigate sensorially dense technological environments.[64] Technology designers and management consultants publicly claim that these technologies replicate the everyday smoothness of communication, increasing productivity by engendering aesthetically pleasing "flow" experiences.[65] As a designer of one of these programs told me, "The goal of [our product] is to feel natural, to get out of the way," and allow workers to "feel immersed in their work." Likewise, The Future's workers spend much of their day on the web, where content producers and distribution platforms such as YouTube aim to produce what industry strategists call "limbic resonance" by using what The Future's optimization team called "flow architecture."[66] When I visited VidCon, a digital media industry conference focused on

YouTube in 2015, consultants and other industry gurus claimed (or perhaps just fantasized) that these web experiences enable smooth, continuous consumption of content by acting upon the brain through "limbic resonance." In addition to a dense, immersive sensory experience, prospecting provided unique access to far-flung regions of YouTube, and this excited employees. As a new hire said, "I'll have to get used to this internet illuminati shit." Another employee said, "Sometimes it's like holy shit there's a lot of crap on YouTube, and other times it's like wow, there's a lot of *great* crap on YouTube." I return to this "crap" in chapter 6 when I discuss how platforms reconfigure workers' judgment, but here I want to press further on the aesthetics of work at The Future.

Alongside scrapes, staff used cloud-based databases that aggregated social media data—most commonly a free-to-use, searchable database called Social Blade. Explaining his relationship with this system, a talent team member said, "I really like Social Blade a lot. It's a really interesting piece of software. It's very simple and it's very useful. It's not 100 percent accurate, but it gives you a ballpark. I don't need 100 percent accurate information. I need an idea." This "idea" came from Social Blade's various charts, which enabled him to infer the growth potential of a channel based on its past performance. Suggestive of the interdependence of technology and workers' skill, he added, "If I didn't have it, I wouldn't know how to do my job." As part of prospecting, Social Blade provides a rudder by which talent team members navigate YouTube's deep streams. Similar to creators, workers were neither "lifeless" appendages of a machine, as in Marx, nor wholly liberated, as in Blauner's iconic automated factory wherein workers were free to eat soup and walk around while on the job.[67]

The Future differed from SoniCo insofar as the platform and associated technologies oriented employees toward metrics, diminishing their need to rely on socially embedded conventions to guide production decisions. Even so, the information provided by systems like Social Blade often remained unclear to staff. How do these numbers arise, and what do they mean? From what calculative procedures did they emerge? Lacking access to the underlying logics that produce these figures, workers creatively guessed how the information came into existence. This guesswork made otherwise tedious tasks feel genuinely enjoyable. As Cooper explained,

I like looking at tools and trying to figure out how tools can help [me]. It's a puzzle. It's building things. It's trying to figure out how to use a hammer to build a house. Like, when you create a lever, there's something exciting about that. I like it. What I [don't] like is I have no control over the tools and the process. I still don't have control of the tools, but saying that I no longer want to run scrapes because we're not finding a way to use the system was something I just did.

Blackboxed technologies were fascinating, "exciting," yet never fully knowable given their position upstream. Cooper had no control over his tools, yet they enchanted him. Their hidden functions captivated him. What do they do? How do they work?

These cloud-based, blackboxed technologies captivated precisely because they evolve, change, and refuse to ever be fully knowable. They only partially fulfilled workers' *libido sciendi*, or desire to know and understand—similar to the relation between workers and technology in earlier chapters. Technology's design, its materiality exerted power over the staff insofar as figuring out how blackboxed technologies function required repeated, enjoyable interactions that enrolled Cooper and other staff into the larger organizational project of achieving metric benchmarks. In contrast, the feel of a scrape depended largely on its contents. Prospecting in a scrape could feel exciting, unremarkable, or, after hours and hours spent combing through a lot of useless information, intensely dissatisfying. As a talent team employee said, "To stare at a screen for hours is very painful," a comment echoed by an intern who said, "I'm tired of this list. My eyes hurt from looking at this screen" while he combed through a particularly "bad" scrape full of thousands of low-quality YouTube channels. Sometimes scrapes felt bad, yet workers enjoyed their attempts to understand how these tools functioned. Since these tools existed as networked, cloud-based platforms, they quite frequently changed, dynamizing work.[68]

When these changes stifled employees' ability to complete tasks, workers responded by engaging in productive refusals, often resulting in new ways of meeting organizational goals. Some, like Cooper, attempted to know, alter, and refine The Future's scraping system. This furthered the organization's larger project of rationalizing and quantifying content acquisition ("the process") in order to facilitate growth ("to scale"). More often, rather than scrape and scour data, the talent team improvised workarounds to reach growth goals. As Cooper suggested, workers improvised alternatives because organizationally prescribed processes blocked their ability to gather information, and so they got creative. As Desmond told me, every morning he "checks the most popular YouTube videos or what's trending to see if there's any viral [videos] or any videos sparking everyone's interest." He tacked back and forth between YouTube and Reddit while mining his Facebook feed for qualitative data. As he said, "I like to find other videos of other friends, what other really funny or interesting people are following."

Desmond aimed to enter "a wormhole of YouTube" with multiple open browser windows. After working with him for nine months, I intuitively knew what his terminology meant. In fact, the experience ought to be familiar to most internet users. Pursuing one piece of information leads to links to other bits of information. Without a clear sense of intentionality, you might end up quite far from where you started, with only a hazy clue as to why or how you ended up reading a lengthy Wikipedia entry on cookies or some obscure academic article. For me, the materiality of a wormhole consisted of combing through large lists of channels or clicking YouTube's "suggested video" links. As Desmond explained,

> Yeah, my coworker, when I was telling him how to do prospecting, I was telling him that I would just sometimes open up a window, I would say maybe that channel we've already reached out to or maybe they're not interested. I would then look at their channels and open a new window. Before you know it, I'd have twenty windows open and be super deep into some vertical [genre] where the channel might be popular and might be getting views, but you won't be able to find it.

First, Desmond is oriented toward organizational goals with only vague direction. He searched not for any particular *type* of content but for *any* content—so long as it met company guidelines for popularity, ownership, and language. Second, Desmond describes his subjective absence as productive. He went through a "super deep" wormhole, through numerous "open windows." This implies travel or being transported elsewhere, merging with the video streams, exiting the office, and occupying a sort of liminal space. Entering into the object and unlocking whatever meanings lie within, he brought back knowledge from the end of the wormhole.

As he went on to explain, "I'll spend maybe twenty minutes and find myself at a dead end and go 'Wow, I just wasted twenty minutes,' but [now] I know where not to go. So, that twenty minutes wasn't wasteful. It was impactful for me." Again, Desmond travels through the windows and finds the "dead ends" in the labyrinth of internet content. How does the hunter who travels across digital time-space feel when he finds his quarry? "There's nothing more satisfying than finding that untouched channel, just like, you know?" In unlocking the unknown secrets of YouTube or at least learning where those secrets cannot be found, Desmond's experience shared much with Cooper's enjoyable inferring of functions and SoniCo's "disappearing" office staff. Alongside his own judgments of quality, management's quotas and metric benchmarks guided Desmond's virtual journeys and so, even in these moments of immersive absence, creative labor appeared subordinate to organizational goals, free only to imagine paths toward increasing metrics. Growth goals set by management required workers to contact an increasing number of new channels each week, something made easier by wormholing. As Desmond said, "I find myself in that warp, that wormhole of just children[-focused] channels, I may reach out to fifty of them that week." These aesthetic experiences enroll workers like Desmond in management's project of metric accumulation and thus the accumulation of profit under cognitive capitalism.

Alongside wormholing, employees would "deep dive"—an increasingly widespread metaphor for gathering in-depth knowledge about a particular subject. They typically used the phrase when talking about in-depth data analysis. As the head of optimization and strategy said, "It's one thing to Google and grab a few things from the front page," but deep diving consists of "looking through the deeper analytics and extracting meaning that you might not see just at a top-level glance." Like wormholing, one goes "deep" into the screen in search of meaning, or as another employee said, "much further than those surface-level things." Practically, deep diving into a particular organizational problem involved using data and tacit knowledge to render a judgment and, ultimately, devise a strategy. A version of this process began by skimming the "surface" or looking at line charts within Google's YouTube analytics platform. YouTube touts "viewing time" as its search algorithm's most important metric, often displayed first among the other metrics in the platform's analytics interface. Employees use these charts to see the point at which audiences stop viewing a video. They then watch that point in the video to make a judgment or provide an "insight" about audience behavior.

Temporarily occupying an empty office, Diane, an optimization and strategy employee, explained how she felt during a deep dive: "Zen. I like the focus. It's easy for me to focus on numbers. Not everybody enjoys looking through numbers. I find it very interesting. To find, to dig meaning out of metrics. When I start digging, I just zone out from everything else. I'm very focused, very interested in it. That's why I'm moving my career in that direction because I enjoy it. I'm very focused. You could say zoned out." Being "zoned out," typically a language of disengaged distraction, becomes a process by which Diane unlocks the meaning of data. Like the "distracted" but "focused" creators, Diane described her immersive entry into a pleasurably productive state of intense work. Opening multiple tabs in a browser and clicking through link after link, diving deep, workers like Diane produced meaning or "insights" for use in organizational decision making.

Immersion, again, tended to be associated with productivity—something borne out in large-sample, quantitative studies of the relation between affect and creativity, where being caught up in the "flow" of work leads to feeling productively creative.[69] The interpretation of absence as "productive" differs from similarly immersive experiences among factory workers and white-collar clerks in earlier periods of capitalism; then, these immersive moments were recounted as *escapes* from work.[70] Under cognitive capitalism, yesteryear's escape from boredom becomes productive, pushing workers toward organizational goals (i.e., quotas, creatively developing new work processes). The Future's workers pursued these aesthetic experiences—part of the "game" they play in the labor process—and were free to do so as long as they followed management's "process," which required logging all activities involving search and outreach in Salesforce. As a department head explained,

> We need to have institutional knowledge established. That's why we've implemented things like Salesforce and BCC tracking. That's the big one, as much as the information that could be set as a logged call or keeping an email thread where I can go back and look at a channel for the last year and a half and see every piece of correspondence that's happened with it, that's the only way for that institutional knowledge to be passed on from one member of the team to another.

Free to improvise and achieve quotas however they choose, employees were asked to maintain logs to pass information on to other team members or, given the high rate of turnover, new employees. Both free and thoroughly captured, they retained creative control while management controlled creatively.

Metaphors such as "wormholing" and "deep diving" may seem overly specific to The Future, but they capture experiences common to screen-based work where technological systems provide desirable information and immersive experiences.[71] Rather than the factory's deadening assembly line or service work's prescribed scripts, interactions between workers and technologies, the human and nonhuman of creative labor, appear similar to other aspects of social life and, perhaps more strikingly, offer the possibility of immersion given their material affordances. Theorists of cognitive capitalism claim that work now produces and requires a deterritorialized, nonspecific desire to know, understand, and work within dense technological processes,[72] something readily apparent at The Future's positive pole, where immersion and absence partially satisfy an organizationally mandated desire to know and search ("prospecting") for nonspecific information ("content").

That this depends upon distinct technological materialities can be seen when employees remain subjectively present. While the following employee, James, said that he sometimes felt similar to Diane, Cooper, and Desmond, he said that more often, "It really does feel like I'm on the surface of things. I'm just like wading through, if you imagined it like a desk full of papers. It's like, 'oh, I need this thing,' and thankfully software lets me recall it much quicker than anything else. It really is with my trackpad, it's a lot of just swiping through stuff and like, 'Oh, I need this thing and [pause] cool.'"

James's explanation emphasizes the importance of the material, tactile, and ultimately aesthetic experiences that bind creative labor to precarious employment. James feels "on the surface" when swiping documents back and forth on the top of his desk. The other examples indicated travel, movement, and focus—essentially going to another place wherein meaning can be unlocked. James, instead, stays on the surface, his hand gesturing back and forth along a laptop's trackpad—quite literally skimming a surface in order to drag documents into an email without opening or metaphorically entering into the documents. He neither dove deep nor wormholed. James simply "skims," feeling dull and superficial, gliding across technological surfaces. Lacking the sort of sensual binding the other employees experienced, James refuses management's ideological gloss, declining their invitation to "be creative."

CONCLUSION

The Future's creators and staff work under what I call a quantified regime of creative labor. Quantified creative labor consists of waged work that requires interpretation and improvised action involving symbols and other abstractions, not unlike a social regime of creative labor. In contrast to the primacy of social conventions and status seeking under the social regimes found in more conventionally organized culture industries, such as music or film, metrics play an outsized role in structuring The Future's work processes. Though social scientists often find creative labor's productivity difficult to measure, the platform's metrics seem to work well enough to regulate creators and The Future's staff, and so, under this quantified regime, creative labor's potential economic value tends to be less dependent upon other modes of valuation (i.e., reputation and prestige, status, or other forms of "symbolic capital").[73] Thus, creative labor processes come to more closely resemble other modes of capitalist organization dominated by quantitative evaluations. At the same time that the platform reconfigures the economies of status or prestige found in other fields of cultural production, the omnipresence of metrics affords workers the possibility for asserting their worth in widely recognized terms. While social ties, status, or assertions of artistic value may be questioned, metrics, like other quantifications, hold a widely accepted facticity.[74]

Despite this fundamental difference between the social and quantitative regimes, there exist several similarities in terms of control, technology, and workers' subjectivities. First, the managerial invitation to "be creative" depends upon the interplay of humans and nonhumans, and so "creativity," as ideology, depends upon particular sociomaterial arrangements that, in this case, include the interface and the screen, their auditory signals and tactile surfaces, and, of course, the practices of workers and management.[75] Thus, capital's invitation to "be creative" requires more than disembodied *illusio*. To be accepted, capital's invitation requires excitement, engagement, or what I call aesthetic enrollment. Second, there is platform discipline, wherein the platform and downstream organizations encourage an entrepreneurial orientation focused on metrics. For creators, this began when the platform and The Future aim to discipline and educate creators so as to produce subordinate entrepreneurs that imagine their economic futures to be bound up in technology. Equally bound to technology, office employees entered a sensorially and technologically dense workplace that felt simultaneously "normal," exciting, and productive. These enchanting engagements with objects depend upon the interplay between technological materialities and the possibilities that they evoke in workers' imaginations.

Both types of workers accepted capital's invitation, and, crucially, their acceptance depended upon work's aesthetic dimension, an aspect of power largely ignored by many labor scholars and sociologists of work. The Future's technologies reproduce the texture, if not the goal, of everyday, screen-mediated life. Insofar as technology makes work *feel* similar to more desirable aspects of social life, this appears not wholly unlike what I observed at SoniCo. The Future differed insofar as the employing firm did not own or directly control the technology that captivated its employees. In both cases, workers imagined potentials that they perceived as embedded within technology and described this imaginative process as enjoyable. This enjoyable immersion depends upon the design of blackboxed, often cloud-based infrastructures.

Suggestive of The Future's negative pole, this chapter also showed how workers' collective self-identification once again tended toward the individual and entrepreneurial rather than as common, creative labor. In both the social and quantified creative workplaces, resistance occurred primarily in the form of simple, atomized refusal. Conflicts arose between workers and management, sure, but also *between segments of creative workers* because of divergent interests, divisions produced by the organization of the labor process. Even though both performed creative labor, these class segments did not understand their work as "in common," a stark contrast to assertions from critical political theorists such as Michael Hardt and Antonio Negri, who claim that class consciousness and collective mobilization might arise from the mutual interdependence of those who provide cognitive or creative labor.[76] The platform's inscrutability further complicates the development of class interests. Whom should workers organize against, and how? Google remains forever silent and opaque, The Future does not technically employ creators, and The Future's office staff was doubly in thrall to both Google's infrastructure and The Future's "process." Labor processes embedded within platforms such as those at The Future obscure whom workers would, should, or could mobilize against, aside from exiting the industry altogether. Viewed in light of part 2, a question remains: How do these workers manage their precarity when they choose, as they often do, to remain in the digital "space"?

THE FUTURE'S NEGATIVE POLE

Compound Precarity and the (Infra)structure of Alienated Judgment

Members of the Workplace Experience team passed out plastic flutes of champagne as Sister Nancy's dancehall reggae classic "Bam Bam" played over the office PA system during a farewell party for an employee. I stood next to Shelly, a new hire who was explaining to me how she had just moved to Los Angeles from the East Coast. She said she needed a change after she turned thirty, so she left a job at a traditional talent agency and moved to LA. She liked the city, its sunshine, and its relative abundance of space. She also enjoyed her new, "interesting" job, even if she could never quite "get a handle on" The Future, no doubt an issue for most in the ever-evolving "space" of digital content. Even as an experienced entertainment professional, she found the high turnover puzzling. "You know, on the East Coast, it's not uncommon to be an assistant for years and then hope for a promotion, you know. People stay in the same company, but here, here it seems that people come and go a lot more." Shelly's comment suggested a choice, but was that so? Management expected and even encouraged exit—something that was occurring even as we spoke. As Shelly and I talked, an employee walked out the door one last time. The farewell party's champagne and music had not been for him, but the occasion still marked his last day. "You don't know it yet, but you'll miss me," he said to us with a smile.

While Shelly and her coworkers tried to get a hold on digital media's amorphous and uncertain "space," creators grappled with another sort of precarity, one intimately tied to the platform and its algorithms. Ed, a construction worker who made YouTube prank videos in his spare time, said he disliked "the money aspect." "Trying to figure out how to fund things and explain it to my wife." It was not that Ed found money distasteful or somehow at odds with creativity; he just wished for more of it, at least enough to cover costs. Even so, he fared better than most, earning about $100 to $200 a month, $750 during his most active periods. Despite his meager earnings, he still tried to pay the friends who served as his camera operators and editors, usually $40 for a shoot plus food and beer. Ed's struggle resembled a lot of other independent contractors, such as the recording engineers discussed in part 2, but he and other creators faced many issues unique to platform-based work. Darren, a creator in the Southwest, voiced one of these distinct problems when he complained about the need to create content specifically formatted or "optimized" for YouTube's search algorithms to maximize views. YouTube often changes these algorithms without notice, and when this happens, his older content is no longer properly formatted, potentially decreasing his views and income.[1] Like other platform-based workers, Ed and Darren were in the dark about the algorithms and calculative procedures that govern their incomes. This made them anxious. Others were more frustrated, even angry.

Back at The Future, Katherine worked as an executive assistant, coordinating the few productions actually funded by the company—"integrated" content, what others might just call "advertising." Like many of the people in this book, she liked her job because she could "be creative," something she defined as the transmission and interpretation of information— exactly the sort of instrumental pragmatism desired by management. She drew upon her communicative knowhow, weaving a dense stream of signs and symbols in each email she sent every day. Despite this daily abundance of creative acts, Katherine struggled to find meaning in her work.

"Where's the meaning in our job? Where's the value in what we're creating? It's hard to say. I mean, at the end of the day, entertainment drives purchases, and that's in the best-case scenario," she said with a laugh. Even that justification seemed hollow. The Future's positive pole might engage the body, providing immediate, corporeal meaning, but upon reflection, work fell short. As she said, "I think about it in my own life, when we talk about eyeballs and likelihood-to-buy a product based on advertising. It's kind of hard to, you know, I don't really think so, I mean, I guess that's why I think about it a lot." As a teenager Katherine "fell in love" with the idea of working in media because of her "passion" for certain shows, *Gilmore Girls* in particular. Did the digital "space" elicit such deep affections from audiences? She did not think so. Instead, she imagined digital media's audiences as atomized, their engagement ephemeral at best. Maybe some younger fans felt strongly about vlogs and prank videos like she had about TV, but The Future's creators left her feeling distant. As she said, "I think that I'm a little removed from it because I don't feel the same attachment to it that Millennials do."[2]

As The Future churned, its staff and creators grappled with the opaque rules that govern the platform. They tended to associate their precarity with the ever-shifting terrain of an industry, or "space," built upon a constantly evolving, privately owned infrastructure. Even Shelly suggested as much in her befuddlement, her inability to "get a grip." Her work in traditional media had been precarious, sure, but not like this. Something seemed different, like feeling as though you may be on a bridge when you thought your feet were on solid ground, as if the floor might drop at any moment. Alongside precarity, there is alienation—Katherine's feelings of meaninglessness even in a workplace centered around media, arguably the most loaded with meaning of all consumer goods. Much like SoniCo, culture's abundance in the workplace does little to guarantee satisfaction or meaning.

These visions from The Future return us to creative labor's negative pole, now firmly embedded within a digital infrastructure. Recall that workers in part 2 diversified and stretched their skills while feeling distanced from the cultural products they produced. The Future's workers share these practices and sentiments, yet The Future differs in its structures of precarity and alienation. Workers' tactics for mitigating precarity depend upon platforms, which disrupt just as much as they empower workers. Creators and staff work-to-labor by acquiring skills but do so using the very same systems that seem most closely linked to their economic uncertainty, something illustrated in the preceding chapter's discussion of YouTube's training materials. Much of their work-to-labor occurred within a virtual, deterritorialized labor process, extending beyond any particular worksites and often including creators' private residences. Just as management expected and encouraged churn, workers' tactics for mitigating precarity were equally taken for granted, a common part of their working days.

The dominance of a single platform reconfigures the (infra)structure of alienation, directing workers' attention to quantitative measures of "eyeballs," to use Katherine's phrasing. Tensions surrounding judgment were significantly less social at The Future, at least in the most traditional use of the term. Rather than simply subordinating workers' judgments to the organization or clients, as in a social regime, platform-based work subordinates workers' judgment to infrastructure, specifically YouTube's algorithms and metrics. The platform determines these key means of valuing creative labor, and, as shown in chapter 5, The Future's office staff and creators orient, primarily, toward these quantifications. At the same time, The Future's organizational hierarchy, however minimal, tended to be dominated by white men, a stark contrast with the company's diverse creators and office staff. This lack of diversity at the top intersects with the platform to subordinate workers' judgment, revealing both the power of capitalist digital infrastructures and the persistence of gender and racial inequality despite platforms' supposed "democratization" of media.

MANAGING PRECARITY, COMPOUNDING UNCERTAINTY

"The [lack of] safety and security. It used to be [frightening]. I have healthcare. I don't have financial stability, but I do have faith in my abilities. I have financial *ability*," said Bobby, a comedic vlogger. Recall that in the previous chapter, he described his equipment as a bodily extension, providing new senses, new economic "ability." When we met in 2015, he was financially independent and enjoying a flexible schedule, even if that meant instability. His parents worried about him, offering money, something he repeatedly refused despite having previously depended on them to survive. Like others with economic and emotional support from friends and family, Bobby framed precarity as liberating and freeing, a bundle of opportunities to be realized.[3] He may be unstable, but he thought himself fully abled by his assemblage of equipment, skill, and social ties. Realizing the potential of these resources required a lot of work. He spent half of each day pursuing work beyond his YouTube channel. "If I need money, I will call someone [at a company where I do freelance writing] and say, 'I will work for you.' In that sense, I do have financial stability . . . I'll go in there twice a week to keep me alive."

As seen in the last chapter, most creators earn very little from their content, a common feature of "winner-take-all" labor markets in the culture industry. Most earned under $20,000 per year, an insufficient income to cover production costs and living expenses, whether they lived in LA or other parts of the United States, and so, again, there is a problem of reproduction. Unlike workers in conventional culture industries, creators' earnings tend to be tied directly to platforms' blackboxed inner workings. They worked for a piece rate, earning a number of cents per view, but creators remained in the dark as to how YouTube set their rates. More importantly, the payment structure and calculations underlying those payments could change at any time, without notice. Relatedly, The Future and other MCNs do not recognize their creators as employees.[4] Instead, YouTube and MCNs classify creators as independent contractors, and so, like most of the workers discussed in this book, creators are part of "the precariat," and YouTube structures creators' precarity just as Uber and Amazon structure the precarity of workers who use their platforms.[5]

How, then, does YouTube affect workers' efforts to offset precarity? Bobby's portfolio of on- and off-platform gigs may resemble the diversification tactics I found among music workers in part 2, but Bobby's situation is qualitatively different insofar as creators' attempts to mitigate their precarity were almost wholly embedded within platforms. They diversified across multiple platforms, used platforms to learn new skills, and constantly networked online and offline. In doing so, creators hoped to generate income beyond that provided by YouTube. Creators like Bobby interpreted this situation positively, toiling under the individualist banners of their personal brands as creative entrepreneurs rather than as members of the collectively oppressed precariat. While apologists for platform capitalism claim that stretching one's career across multiple platforms provides outsized opportunities in comparison to working in "legacy" culture industries such as music and film,[6] that line of argument ignores just how much creators' entrepreneurial diversification depends upon, produces value for, and remains subordinate to multiple platforms and their parent corporations. In a clear way, creators' "freedom" appears always already circumscribed by capitalist infrastructure in ways unseen in conventional culture industries.

Creators' diversification tactics included seeking out brand sponsorships ("integrations"),[7] joining affiliate programs with online marketplaces such as Amazon, and crowdfunding. Howard and Angela, vloggers in Los Angeles, earned quite a bit of money through brand integrations, but their incomes remained unsteady, fluctuating wildly from month to month.

HOWARD: I get paid once a month, so if you'd asked me a week ago, I would've said, "I don't get paid anything, man." Last month I made $500. This month I made $9,000.

MICHAEL: Is that just YouTube or brand deals?

HOWARD: Brand deals and [advertising revenue from] YouTube.

MICHAEL: And all of that, it varies quite a bit?

HOWARD: And I never know. I never know month in month out. It's not six figures. I'll say that. Learning now, it's ironic, after I left the big channel and [my] personal channel went down, that was my year of biggest earnings, and it's been on a trajectory up, and I hope it stays that way.

Chasing after these income streams required an abundance of time and a familiarity with the workings of the advertising industry—something The Future purportedly provided, but creators claimed otherwise, often recounting disgruntled tales of neglect. Just as SoniCo's lack of full-time opportunities "businessed" engineers, The Future's inaction coupled with YouTube's training materials encouraged an entrepreneurial attitude among creators, leading them to perform additional work-to-labor by finding, obtaining, or creating various income streams. In some cases, The Future claimed a percentage of gross revenues from both sponsorships and views regardless of who secured the deal, further enabling the firm to capture value produced by creators' efforts to mitigate precarity.

"Affiliate" programs run by online retail companies such as Amazon and crowdfunding platforms such as Patreon provided another avenue for diversification. Becoming an affiliate of an online marketplace mapped rather neatly onto certain YouTube genres such as product reviews, tutorials, and "unboxing" videos, in which creators open the packages of various consumer items, seeming to revel in the distinctiveness of commodities' materialities as they provide meticulous descriptions of the objects. Amazon allows creators to sign up as affiliated promoters, and, once affiliated, they receive special weblinks for products featured in their YouTube content. Creators place these links in the description of their videos and then tell their audience to click on those links (a "call to action") if they wish to purchase the items. Creators then receive a commission (3 to 8 percent) for each purchased product. This tactic can be quite lucrative, as evidenced by Hank, the Midwestern survivalist in his hardened basement studio. Only a third of his income came directly from YouTube. The bulk of the money he earned from his content came from Amazon affiliate commissions on hunting and camping gear, water-purification systems, and, most lucrative by far, solar panels. Earnings from Amazon's affiliate program and donations given by fans through crowdfunding platforms such as Patreon usually remained outside creators' contracts with The Future. While neither The Future nor YouTube directly captured value from these sources of income, both the network and the platform capture value from creators' reinvestment of their off-platform income into heightened production values, a strategy encouraged by both YouTube and The Future. Again, this provides global capital (the platform and The Future's parent company) with a means of capturing value from creators' equipment.

While providing additional earnings, this tactic provided little in the way of additional stability. YouTube frequently changed their policies regarding remuneration, just as Amazon can change its commission rates and Patreon can decide to take a larger percentage of donations without notice. Each platform possesses the power to change the rules of remuneration at any time, and so while each provides an additional income stream, none solve the core issue that heightens precarity for platform-based creative workers, which is the embedding of work within privately operated infrastructures built to meet the needs of and wholly controlled by capital. Instead, creators multiply their uncertainty across a complex portfolio of revenue streams embedded within digital infrastructures, each subject to the unknowable whims of capital.

Several creators with whom I spoke used YouTube as part of a broader business model wherein they produced content in order to drive consumers to other entrepreneurial ventures, not unlike the audio engineers who became microbusinesses in chapter 4. In doing so, they gained a margin of economic autonomy, if not stability. For example, two creators in the Midwest created videos that instruct viewers on how to play popular songs on an instrument. Save for the obligatory watching of advertisements, audiences may view these freely; however, each video also advises viewers to visit the creators' website if they desire more in-depth lessons. For $14.95 per month, viewers gained access to a vast catalog of off-platform music lessons on the creators' website. While the creators' YouTube channel generates sizeable advertising revenues from its millions of monthly viewers, the bulk of their earnings came from monthly paid subscriptions off-platform. This venture generated enough revenue to pay the two owners' yearly salaries of just over $70,000 and $40 an hour for their handful of part-time employees. While becoming an off-platform business provided some economic autonomy, the platform and The Future still capture a portion of revenues. Even if creators seem to be working for themselves, their creative labor, when embedded within platform infrastructures, generates value for global capital. Creators' attempts at skill building further illustrate this point.

BUILDING SKILLS, FEEDING GOOGLE

The Future's creators and office staff built skills as a way to offset their precarity, not unlike the studio workers in part 2, but the similarities end there. While SoniCo's workers built upon skills acquired through formal education and apprenticeships, few creators whom I met had formal training of any kind. Instead, they had "fooled around" with consumer video cameras as teenagers or begun their careers using built-in webcams on their personal computers. They figured things out as they went along, learning to write, shoot, edit, and promote high-quality videos by consuming YouTube's all-you-can-eat buffet of user-generated tutorials along with more formal advice from the platform and The Future.[8]

Even the few who had some formal training built up their skills through the platform. Bob, a professional editor and part-time creator, explained that he studied media production in college but "did not do exceptionally well," and so "that's where just going on YouTube and typing 'After Effects tutorial' [or] whatever the subject is I'm trying to tackle comes into play. Most often there is a tutorial for it." Another creator on the East Coast made videos in which he "fights" digitally inserted characters from popular videogames. This required sophisticated animation and computer graphics skills that he initially lacked but quickly acquired by watching tutorials on YouTube made by other creators. As he said, "I thought visual effects were really hard for me, but after I saw [YouTube star] Freddy W, he made a tutorial in After Effects. I started to learn this After Effects tutorial and started doing my action videos." Ed, the construction worker and prankster whom we met at the beginning of this chapter, had to learn a bit about microphones, cameras, and editing. When I asked how, he said, "YouTube is the new encyclopedia. So, anything you want to do or anything you ever thought about doing, you can learn how to do it on YouTube. But, yeah, I'd see something on another video and say 'Oh, that'd be kind of cool on mine,' and so I'd look it up on a how-to video and go from there." The platform enables self-directed learning by storing creators' knowledge, as tutorials, and redistributing that knowledge to aspiring creators. Compared to workers under the social regime at SoniCo, this process appears emancipatory but also less conventionally social. Recall that SoniCo's workplace provided opportunities for skill acquisition by way of interactions with other people. The platform's similar opportunities were embedded within content rather than people.

This situation shifts the practices of skill building away from social networking and toward consuming videos on the platform. Brooke Duffy describes the learning tactics of creators and other social media "influencers" as simply a "DIY approach to learning,"[9] a description that obscures the power imbalance in the relationship between creators and the platform. Skill building through content consumption generates value for the platform in direct and indirect ways. First, creators view advertisements while watching tutorials, which directly increases YouTube's total viewership and advertising revenues. Second, creators embed their skills within the platform when they produce tutorial videos, making their skills accessible to all able to view YouTube. Through these tutorials, capital captures users' skills and increases the number of skilled media producers on the platform. In this process, creators' skills become part of technology, housed on Google's servers, ready for use in the next product cycle and thus indirectly contributing to YouTube's revenues by increasing the overall quality of content.

Creators' situation also runs rough against contemporary discussions of cognitive capitalism's dependence upon the "general intellect," such as

Paolo Virno's claim that cognitive capitalism depends upon knowledge that cannot be separated from living labor. "Instead of being incarnated (or rather, *cast in iron*) into the system of machines . . . the general intellect manifests itself today, above all, as communication, abstraction, [and the] self-reflection of living subjects."[10] In YouTube production, infrastructure (technology) constitutes a repository of knowledge ("the new encyclopedia"), and so the relationship between dead and living labor (technology and workers) appears more similar to that described by Marx in the *Grundrisse*, a text referenced by Virno and other theorists of "immaterial" labor under cognitive capitalism. In that text, Marx briefly touched upon abstract knowledge embedded in machines (fixed capital) as a productive source of value. For Marx this no doubt referred to underlying principles embedded in automated machinery. Instead of automating processes, tutorial videos produced by creators and stored within technology educate and train future creators while also generating profit for the platform. The knowledge of living labor, congealed in tutorials, appears as dead labor separated from the living and incarnated in video files housed on YouTube's servers.

Creative labor may not be "cast in iron," but workers' knowledge may certainly be stored in glass and aluminum, the primary components of the hard drives that form YouTube's extensive network of servers. Creators access tutorials in the form of streaming video—in a sense liquefying ("streaming") and consuming dead labor. Not wholly unlike the 1999 film *The Matrix*, in which sentient machines liquefy the dead as a way to feed newborn babies, YouTube liquefies dead labor housed on its servers as video streams, feeding the dead to the living so that they may become polyvalently productive creative laborers. Insofar as Google/YouTube owns the means of distribution and storage of this information, the general intellect or knowledge embedded in the technology generates value for the platform on both ends of the production/consumption loop. Many of the creators produced content in addition to unrelated work in a variety of industries. In other words, they labored even in their "free time," and, as Virno argues, "What is learned, carried out and consumed in the time outside of labour is then utilised in the production of commodities, becomes a part of the use value of labour power and is computed as profitable resource."[11]

Acquiring these specialized media production skills via the platform requires both widespread computer skills and a desire to learn—Boutang's *libido sciendi*—which creators voiced as a desire to "constantly learn" or their need to always learn to be "better." That creators possessed production skills should be evident by now; nevertheless, their *desire* to learn requires some explanation. When faced with an absence of knowledge, all the people with whom I spoke explained how they searched YouTube for an answer or "Googled it." They described their first impulse as being one of knowledge seeking or self-directed learning aimed at solving a practical problem. As such, constant learning—what Jeff Sallaz calls "permanent pedagogy"—and dispositional ease vis-à-vis online search technology appear as necessary, if rather generic, productive skills.[12] To draw again from Virno, "all the more generic attitudes of the mind gain primary status as productive resources."[13] For Virno, these "generic attitudes" include most of what I defined as creative labor at the beginning of this book: human capacities for language, learning, memory, abstract thought, and self-reflexivity. Workers' deployment of these generic capabilities required close interaction with technology, and so, again, managerial and platform invitations to "be creative" depend upon particular technological materialities.

The social structure of creators' skill-building efforts differs from the social regime described in earlier chapters. Creators consult the platform or some other Google-owned technology much like early-career audio engineers consulted industry veterans. This structural difference enables YouTube to capture value from skill building as creators consult dead creative labor congealed in content housed on its servers. On one hand, this circuit of production/consumption evokes a grim, dystopian future wherein labor appears hemmed in on all sides. On the other hand, the platform ostensibly provides useful knowledge to all, independent of their position within a professional network, though still dependent upon their connection to the internet. Recall that skill building under the social regime often required dense social ties, potentially excluding those who lack social capital, who, in creative fields, tend to be women and those from less economically privileged backgrounds.

By transmitting skills to new creators for use in future cycles of content production, YouTube offers a diverse, global workforce what Angela

McRobbie calls "lines of flight," along which members of marginalized social groups might participate in creative careers,[14] controlling their representations and heightening their visibility. In providing these possibilities, YouTube also provides global capital (e.g., Google and MCNs such as The Future) with a means of capturing value produced by a globally distributed workforce and its personal property (cameras, lights, microphones, computers, etc.). Not specific to YouTube, this generic feature of all platforms (e.g., Uber, Lyft, TaskRabbit, Airbnb, MailChimps, etc.) enables both widespread increases in workforce participation and global capital's capture of value from a global workforce and its privately owned production technologies.

WORKING-TO-LABOR IN "STANDARD" EMPLOYMENT

While creators struggled to earn money across a variety of platforms, The Future's staff faced high churn, low wages, and minimal managerial guidance. At the same time, the very office they worked in provided visceral reminders of their disposability, as shown in the previous chapter. Despite their engaging sociotechnical interactions during the working day, employees' precarity provoked a certain nervous anxiety in their daily struggles to subsist on salaries near or below the U.S. median annual income. To do so in Los Angeles, they lived with roommates in small apartments, a not altogether uncommon situation for many adults worldwide, but certainly delaying one of the traditional markers of "adulthood" in the United States. Those who did live by themselves occupied small studio apartments or even smaller "bachelor" apartments that lacked kitchens.

In their efforts to maintain employment and make these rather spartan living situations possible, workers performed additional work-to-labor, engaging in two primary tactics. First, members of the office staff engaged in self-directed learning. Like creators, this included watching YouTube tutorials, which generated value for the platform. Staff also engaged in more conventional modes of learning on the job, such as reading industry news and sharing information with one another. Second, staff developed social networks to aid in obtaining and maintaining employment. Their networking echoes the altogether more social response to precarity found under the social regime in part 2, while their constant learning closely corresponds with the pragmatic creativity desired by management.

Just Figuring It Out

As one of my coworkers explained, working at The Future meant that "the answer [to any question] shouldn't be no, and if the answer is no, you should present another option. Don't ever say 'No,' just figure it out." Just figuring it out, "managing up," or "being creative" comprised a large part of Future's working day. This instrumental pragmatism shifts the burdens of training, or "human capital investment," traditionally borne by an employer onto employees, something illustrated clearly by my experience at The Future. After being in the field for six months, I began to train interns in webscraping techniques and in the use of Social Blade and spreadsheet software such as Excel and Google Sheets. As an intern said, "Cooper told me to ask you. He said you're real good with that [Google Sheets and Excel]." I never received formal training in any of these processes, only brief instruction from Cooper, and, technically, I was an intern being asked to train other interns.

Similarly, Harriet, an executive assistant, explained that she had not been trained so much as thrown into a complicated situation in which she used a combination of keen observation and publicly available information on the internet:

> I was trained by sitting on and covering some executive assistant desk [and phone lines] as an intern, and that gave me kind of training in terms of answering phones and maybe a little bit of scheduling. But other than that, it was kind of like learn as you go, just go as you get instructed with [the] project. . . . And actually, right now, I'm watching—well, I was watching—a tutorial. But then, also just asking around, trying to be as resourceful as possible. Going to people who may have the knowledge I'm seeking or that I need to finish what I'm doing and, yeah.

Harriet trained herself by watching YouTube tutorials at work. When this failed to yield results, she asked around the office, trying to "be as resourceful as possible" by drawing on the knowledge of coworkers. Garland described his entry into an analytics position in similar terms. He went to college for media production and marketing and said, "I didn't know anything about reading graphs or reading data or statistics." Still, "The learning curve actually wasn't too steep, and so technically I'm entry level in this position. There's some room for growth in that way. Just kind of hopped in and hit the ground running, learning things as I was doing it." Despite being overseen by an executive and a department director, Garland tended to rely on coworkers for training and direction. His coworkers had learned how to do the job by practically solving problems and acquiring skills as needed.

While Garland and Harriet accumulated skills specific to their jobs, Desmond described a more involved process, one that encompassed much of his life. He said his job required a sort of embodied data processing, what he called "learned intuition." As he said when he described his job searching for YouTube talent,

> [I] watched a lot of stuff, absorbed a lot of content. I watch a lot of film, TV, content. Every time I watch something I look at numbers. You just kind of keep putting in data. It's learned intuition, it's my own memory bank. I don't have some spreadsheet I use. It's just more so [that] I understand the current environment. I talk to a lot of people. I talk to a lot of people in the industry, outside of the industry. Usually casual conversations, just trying to get them, a sense of their thoughts on it, whether they're right or wrong. At VidCon [an industry convention], I talked to a lot of creators. At another industry event, I talked to a lot of our creators, asked them about their experience, asked about what they do. I think my learning experience is to amalgamate data. I cannot teach that process. My processing of the data is different from the next person. Someone will process that data differently than I can.

Recall that in the previous chapter Desmond "wormholed" his way through a number of screens, gathering and observing information. In doing so, he relied on his "memory bank," tacit knowledge gathered through watching, conversing, and calculating. Despite his abundant use of spreadsheets and other software, he highlighted his embodied, creative labor and the tacit knowledge needed to interpret information *his* way. He "processes" his "amalgamated data" while remaining dependent upon an assemblage of platforms, generic workplace information and communication technologies, and other tools. Still, the living, creative labor he provides remains his and his alone, a process he "cannot teach." As embodied, living labor, his processing capabilities cannot be separated from him, yet his process required a variety of inputs and support from a dense network of digital infrastructures and people.

Learning during their working days provided a way of feeling in control and lessening the anxiety of a workplace where one expects to be unexpectedly fired or laid off. Much of this work-to-labor could be performed during working hours, but those hours tended to extend beyond The Future's mandatory fifty-hour work week, given the constant connectivity afforded by communication technologies.[15] From workers' entrepreneurial point of view, each new day presented opportunities to enlarge, reinforce, and invest their cultural and human capital by learning skills that might, to use the phrasing of an executive during a staff meeting, "make you valuable elsewhere."

Advocacy Within Social Networks

Alongside constant learning, employees relied upon their social ties to offset the economic, emotional, and temporal strains of precarious employment. This may be seen quite clearly one unremarkable day during which I ended up in an elevator with Leo, Wally, and Laura on their way out for a smoke break. "Today's my last day," said Leo anxiously while wearing his backpack—an uncharacteristic sartorial choice for a smoke break. "What? Why?" asked Laura. Leo said, "The CEO just debriefed me. 'Leo, your position's been terminated.' I guess they fired my boss too. What am I going to do? What am I going to do? What am I going to do?" I remained quiet, unsure what to say, but his coworkers, having been through similar situations, began sharing advice on how to cope. "File for unemployment as soon as you get home," said Laura. "Yeah, but they offered me one more paycheck," said Leo. "Yeah, but [unemployment] takes a while," began Laura, before another coworker finished her sentence. "It takes a while to process, by the time it goes through—" Laura finished, "It'll be after your next paycheck. It lasts a year and it's like 80 percent of your pay. It's not great, but it's enough until you get another job. You'll get another job." Somberly, Leo said, "Guess I'll go back to selling drugs. When I interview for another job, they can ask what my background is in, and I can say, 'Uh, pharmaceuticals.'" "No, please, it's street entrepreneurship," I offered as a joke, trying to add a bit of levity to the situation. Leo cracked a smile, managing a short laugh.

Leo's reaction highlights a key economic reason for pursuing work at The Future despite relatively low wages. Office work may be precarious and uncertain, but occupying a position within the firm reduces the amount of work-to-labor required of freelancers, something to which crime seemed preferable for Leo. Precarious, standard employment temporarily relieves persistent search costs and uncertain investments in skills associated with freelance work.[16] In other words, precarious, full-time employment still offers some semblance of stability in comparison to the "freedom" of freelancing. As he said, "I don't want to freelance!" A coworker, trying to be helpful, said, "Well, at least in between things. You just need to make money until you find something steady." Leo's coworkers continued to tell him about potential job openings while expressing their shared dissatisfaction with The Future. Wally said, "Man, this comes after I heard Lucy complaining about how she only got thirty-eight [thousand] compared to my thirty-five. I'm like, 'Fuuuuuck you!'" Laura and I laughed. They all repeatedly told Leo that this was "bullshit." "There was no reason to throw you under the bus because of your boss," added Laura.

Leo asked Laura if she knew of anywhere that might be hiring. She had many friends working in media and film production and at Silicon Beach tech startups in West LA. Some of her friends were in the process of staffing a global media company's new LA office, and so Laura told Leo that she might be able to "hook that up," adding that he should not "underestimate LinkedIn for jobs. Sign up for their updates for whatever position you're looking for." Wally concurred and said that he had found his current job through that social networking website. Laura turned to me and said, "It's a revolving door around here," explaining that she had been fired in 2012 before being hired again in 2015. Leo fumed, repeatedly recounting his meeting with the CEO that morning as we made our way back to the offices. He greeted the receptionist gruffly as we entered the office lobby, and I returned to my communal worktable. An hour later, Leo headed toward the exit with a bankers box full of his personal items. His termination came along with the termination of his entire small team. When I left for the day, I shared an elevator with Katherine, who said, "Today, this place is a zoo. It's crazy here, today." From my perspective, this all seemed rather "standard."

A month later, Leo was still looking for work, and his friends at The Future continued to look out for him. During a conversation about who might serve as a producer for an upcoming bit of content, "Just use an intern. That's an, an intern can do that," said the executive. "No. No, not an intern," said Katherine, trailing off as she searched for a reason not to use an intern. "Sure. An intern," said the executive. Katherine, still searching for a line of reasoning, said, "No. Look, interns are here for what? Seven weeks? No. Look, if you want to find a job for Leo, why not give it to him?" The executive, seeming to remember that this might be an option, said, "Oh, right, what's he looking for exactly?" Katherine suggested that the executive hire Leo on as a line producer for the small project. The executive agreed and later emerged from his office to tell Katherine to include budget line items for Leo as a producer. He repeated this twice, seemingly for emphasis, as Katherine looked directly at him. The executive's suggestion that the company use free intern labor is consistent with the media scholar John Caldwell's claim that media management aims to avoid paying people.[17] Katherine's advocacy, much like other coworkers' offering of advice and potential assistance, attempts to mitigate or ameliorate their shared precarity.[18]

The working day at The Future contained networking opportunities and emotional support, given workers' physical co-presence, not unlike the social regime described in part 2. However, The Future's staff lacked stability. Management expected them to leave, and in light of this, The Future's staff worked anxiously to maintain employment. In response, they sought knowledge and information that might prove valuable anywhere in the "space." Like the workers described in part 2, The Future's employees exited the industry when the emotional and economic burdens of maintaining employment broke the tenuous bindings provided by aesthetic enrollment and managerial invitations to expression. Lena, the woman whose content-covered face greeted me when I entered The Future, returned to her hometown in the Southwest. As she was one of the few regular employees that had been with The Future for more than a year, I asked if she planned to stay in media. She said, "No, my hometown doesn't have any cool jobs." She hoped, instead, to work for an airline. A member of the Workplace Experience team left to work for her family's business in an unrelated industry. Others left to work as political campaign organizers during the 2016 election or for small startups in

Silicon Beach—a bit closer to digital media's "space" but mostly outside the orbit of YouTube.

MY "DUMB" CONTENT

YouTube adds to workers' precarity, capturing value all the while, but how does the platform shape the social relations that produce alienated judgment, the other major valence of creative labor's negative pole? While SoniCo's social regime subordinated workers' judgment to the firm and clients, the quantified regime subordinated judgment to metrics, algorithmic governance, audiences, and downstream firms. Recall that creators first encounter metrics through the platform's various education and training programs and via advice from The Future—what I called formatting. Here, YouTube resembles classic bureaucracies insofar as the platform attempts to build a rules-oriented workforce through education and training.[19] Platform discipline oriented creators toward metrics (views, likes, subscriber counts, watch time, etc.) and encouraged a variety of platform-specific practices, shaping content in accordance with YouTube's algorithms. Following the platform's algorithms and metrics ultimately subordinates decisions to global capital (Alphabet/Google) rather than combinations of market and community interests as presupposed by sociological theories of cultural production.[20] Thus, creators' production decisions, that is, their judgments, tend to be always already heteronymous, oriented and often conforming to the demands of others.

Becky, the wine/lifestyle vlogger mentioned in the last chapter, described this subordination of her judgment very clearly when talking about her most popular videos. She often received requests from fans for content that they want to see. Producing for the audience increases engagement metrics (comments, likes, etc.), benefiting her as well as The Future. So how did she respond to these requests? "I'm just like, 'Ew, I don't want to do that,' but then I'll just do it." Explaining why fans' suggestions elicit such a response, she said,

> I just want to have quality content that's entertaining and informative. And I'm not trying to get a viral YouTube video, although my manager would like me to have one. You can't go in thinking, "I'm going to make a viral video."

A lot of my most watched videos are ones that are just kind of dumb. Like, my drunk dating advice or my haul videos, where I go to a store and get a bunch of shit and drink it and give my opinions on camera. Those aren't even informative.

Becky's aversion to fans' suggestions may bear a passing resemblance to the jazz musicians famously described by the sociologist Howard Becker. Those musicians dismissed audiences' opinions about their performances, focusing instead on their peers' opinions,[21] but the materiality of Becky's interactions with fans significantly differs. The platform's interface mediates her interactions with fans. She does not orient to physically co-present fans as a musician might in a nightclub but instead focuses her attention on a screen, where she encounters a sociomaterial assemblage of human and nonhuman elements that shapes her production choices.

Rather than a charming example of community formation or "connection," Becky's statement suggests a rather fractious relationship between the content demanded by the audience, the content valorized by the platform, and her judgment of quality content ("entertaining and informative"). She tends to produce content that she finds distasteful ("Ew") when she orients primarily toward engagement metrics (likes, number of comments, watch time, etc.), fan suggestions (comments), and indicators of audience size (views, subscribers). Here, alienation stems not from strictly social relationships but from a sociomaterial assemblage of capitalist infrastructure, creators, and consumers. At the end of the day, Becky, accepting YouTube's invitation to expression, might not have a "boss," but she still called her most popular videos "dumb."

YouTube, like other social media platforms, encourages a rigorous production schedule, which tends to reduce creators' attachment to any one of their products—another facet of alienated judgment.[22] Creators were less attached to their products, even if they cared very much about their personal "brand" and were aesthetically enrolled in their production processes. While this might seem part and parcel to those that create for others, remember that creators create, ostensibly, for themselves, working in support of their self-devised personal brands. Theirs was a willful disentanglement of creators from their creatures (workers from their products), stemming from an inability to maintain both quality and production's rapid pace. As Angela, a lifestyle vlogger, said,

A lot of times I just don't have enough time, so as soon as I come up with the idea I'm just like, "OK, I'm going to go do it," which has been really hard for me. I like things to be perfect, but I can't do that with YouTube, especially with my timelines of every Tuesday and Thursday. I'm posting a video today because I didn't have time to post it yesterday. It's supposed to be out yesterday, but sometimes it just happens that way.

Similarly, Bobby expressed concern over his use of time. Short videos that could be done in a day enabled him to maintain a regular, daily release schedule and keep his engagement metrics high, but he preferred working on longer, more intricate videos that require more time.

When you're a one-man show, you have to do the editing as well. I have to justify to myself that you're doing the right thing by being inside right now. You're doing the right thing by sitting down for five hours, and you're doing the right thing by taking a week to make a video. When I'm doing the news, that's a video a day. Here, [working on longer projects] I'm sacrificing four videos for the sake of one. When I look back, I'm always happy I did it, but in the moment there's that panic of "are people going to forget about me." You know?

Somewhat differently, Leland (the video artist) strived to balance speed and quality. He wished for "perfect" content, but his early attempts at "perfection" required an unsustainable amount of effort:

My relationship with creating is very different now. I know what I can do to hide things. I know how to hide, like shortcuts. I used to just be, like, It's important that I work forever on this thing and make this beautiful thing, and who cares if nobody notices all those little things. Now I've gotten a lot better at being, I'm not going to do that because that's killing me. You know? So, I need to not work for twenty hours. In the process, it's made me like things less. Maybe? And maybe like kind of hardened me in certain ways to the realities of being a creator that needs to be successful and productive. I can't edit a video for three months and be like, that one-minute video is [whispered] perfect.

Workers of any kind become faster and more efficient as they gain production experience. That part of Leland's account seems rather insignificant on its own, but Leland, despite his heightened efficiency, wished for more time to attend to craft, to perfection, rather than the "realities of being a creator that needs to be . . . productive." Even though he makes his own schedule, YouTube's "advice" nudges them toward rapid production, demanding speed. In some contexts, this speed gives rise to stylistic choices that dovetail with creators' lifestyles, producing new meanings and associations between style and modes of living. For example, in *Ballad of the Bullet* Forrest Stuart describes how "drill" musicians crank out songs and their accompanying music videos as quickly as possible, hoping to saturate YouTube and other social media platforms with their presence. Stuart describes their approach as "rough" in comparison to the polish of traditional rappers or rock musicians, something they perceive as a direct representation of the rough lives they live as poor Black men on Chicago's South Side. While Stuart interprets this as a "quality" arising in opposition to the quantitative orientation favored by social media platforms, drill musicians' approach bears more than a passing similarity to creators like Leland or Becky who learn not to care about any particular piece of content because of how quickly they must work to stay ahead on the platform. Like Stuart's musicians, their content need only be "good enough," suggestive of how an orientation toward quantity produces a particular quality, one that drill musicians and their fans interpret as authentically "rough" or "street" and other creators such as vloggers and their audiences might interpret as part of social media's "authentic" amateurism.

Dennis, a European animator, shares this sense of diminished time and attachment to his work. When Dennis spoke to me via Skype from his rural home and production studio, he claimed not to think too much about what seemed like quite intricate and complex videos. Puzzled, I asked him to elaborate:

MICHAEL: You don't think that much?

DENNIS: I don't feel [that I care] so much. I just want to get it done so I can start with the next project.

MICHAEL: So, in some way, you don't feel attached to any single video?

DENNIS: That I've done? No, I don't think so. [Laughing] Maybe in the future. Maybe if I do something that goes to the, how do you say, cinema? Yeah, the cinema. It will probably never happen, but you never know. [Laughing] That would be quite cool.

Like Becky and Leland, Dennis simply wants to move on to the next project. In what he sees as a hierarchy of cultural forms, his is not a product for the ages. It is not "something that goes to the . . . cinema." Content is content is content, undifferentiated so long as it generates views. Dennis's distinction draws attention to material differences in how audiences consume media, debatable as his hierarchical classification may be. Cinema, like music, literature, and art, tends to be consumed far beyond its initial release, with many films, songs, and artworks finding audiences later. "No one cares until you're dead" is a cliché in a number of cultural fields for a reason. Content, in contrast, tends to be fleeting, in the moment, interchangeable, disposable, or, to use an industry term, "snackable."

SLOPPING THE TROUGH

If content is a snack, then The Future's employees help satisfy audiences' urge to munch, a sentiment summed up when Laura squeakily exclaimed, "The Trough!" one day as she, Wally, and I stood outside the office talking. "The Trough. That's what we call it. The Trough, such a great metaphor!" Wally continued to riff on the phrase, "Sometimes I'm overwhelmed by the Trough. I mean, it just builds up. There's no drain, so it just sediments I guess." Another time, he called The Future's content "a constant stream of trash" and said, "I can't imagine anyone knows everything that we represent. I mean there's no way to be familiar with all the thousands of people that we deal with here." Laura agreed. "Well the same goes for all the other MCNs, right? Thousands, tens of thousands of channels. You can't realistically deal with them all," I said. "And they don't!" exclaimed both Wally and Laura, almost in unison. So long as creators properly formatted their videos while avoiding copyright infringement, YouTube and The Future remained content with any content. The Future focused more on "optimization," or formatting processes, and as part of the team in charge of formatting creators, Wally and his coworkers attempted "to figure out why things get big" and how to avoid the "the tennis ball drop graph." By this, he meant an initial spike followed by several, exponentially smaller spikes until viewership reaches zero—much like a tennis ball's bounce. He explained that regardless of formatting, some videos never attained the desired degree of popularity. The Future's staff could not explain why because, according to Wally, "we don't pay attention to *what* the content *is*" and because the platform's algorithms lie upstream from The Future. As Wally said, "Yeah, so we don't, we can't see anything, but, you know, if it's not recognizable to the algorithm the turd just drops to the bottom of the Trough." Remember that Desmond, the wormholing analytics employee, still referred to content as "crap" even if it was "great crap." If Wally felt overwhelmed by the "turds" to which he tended, Desmond and others dove deep into oceans of "crap" with great enthusiasm.

Scatological metaphors aside, workers enjoyed the process of finding and aiding in the production of content, even if they found it distasteful, ugly, and, ultimately, cheap. They did so by following the platform's logic of valuation and categorization as mediated by management's monthly metric goals. As The Future's CEO said in a staff meeting, "Scale, in the budget, is the biggest line item. We need to scale." In social media and the increasing number of other industrial "spaces" where people speak the tech sector's distinctive patois, to "scale" is to grow, often as large as possible. For The Future, this meant increasing "inventory," another industry gloss, this time for eyeballs or, more abstractly, quantitative estimates of monthly views. This generalized emphasis on "scale" further shifts the focus of the culture industries toward strictly quantitative assessments and away from regimes of value revolving around "quality." Goals set by management orient workers toward quantities of views, subscribers, and other engagement metrics rather than any particular piece of content. Workers may "be creative" in reaching these goals as they seek to understand the platform's inscrutable algorithms—disappearing as they attempt to unlock the underlying logic by which videos might rapidly accumulate views. Doing so required that workers withhold or subordinate their judgment to a distinctly quantitative logic borne of the platform's metrics.

While working with the talent team, I found myself in relentless pursuit of content that, upon reflection, left me puzzled or, in the case of prank videos, offended. Aesthetically enrolled, I felt engaged yet alienated. The period during which my team made an effort to meet management's quarterly growth goal of one billion views provides a clear illustration of this experience. During this time, we began to focus on smaller YouTube channels (fewer than ten thousand subscribers) with "fast-growth" potential. Management sanctioned our purchase of Bent Pixels' "Locator," a cloud-based industrial search program developed specifically for companies like

The Future. We were excited about this because it meant we could avoid using the glitchy, unreliable webscraping tool that had been developed in-house and often gave us bad results, preventing our efforts to wormhole our way to "great crap." For a few weeks, my supervisor Cooper and I tested Bent Pixels' search tool and discussed our finds. Early on, I mentioned some videogame channels that seemed to be gaining momentum. These channels depicted recorded gameplay of *Agar*, a game where players take the role of bacteria in a Petri dish, and *Five Nights at Freddy's*, a horror game that had been wildly popular at the time.

"Kids these days. Who knows what they're into," he said before returning to our new tool and its latest search results. Cooper, as usual, focused on the numbers and rules for signing new talent, not the content. "It's showing channels that are starting to pop, and this one shows steady growth. So maybe, maybe we run the popping [search] every week and the other one every once in a while. These are all great. Original content, good views per video." We went through each report, brainstorming ways to alter our search strategy to find channels with either fast or steady growth. "The way I see it, we need a threshold for views or subscribers, and then we need a growth metric. These are great [search results]." Cooper looked up each channel listed in our search results on Social Blade to check for recent histories of growth, eyeballing trendlines of channel data displayed on the website. "Look at that! The slope is really high. Great!"

We spent a few minutes theorizing the relationship between metrics and audience behavior before Cooper decided to set a minimum sub-scriber threshold and then focus on growth rates. Offering his own micro-sociological theory of audience behavior, he said, "Well, subscribers, that requires more effort on the audience. You have to initiate a call to action and get them to subscribe, so that's a fanbase. Views could just be a viral video or something, so we definitely want to use them together." He drew a two-by-two table on his whiteboard. "Way I see it is we have four ways of setting this up. Either a subscription threshold or a views threshold and then growth rates in subscribers or in views in the short or long term," he said before asking me for input. I told him that subscribers might be good for the short term since subscriber growth suggested repeated viewing.[23]

Cooper later asked me to use the search tool to focus on children-oriented, or "Kids," channels. This marked a major change from previous weeks, when we had not focused on any particular content category, a

decision that followed from industry assumptions about children's viewing habits. Executives and industry "experts" claimed that children tended
to be relatively passive, repeat viewers who, according to Cooper, might
help us meet our quarterly growth goal. Again, Cooper focused on the
numbers. "We need to get those growing channels early, as low as a thousand subs, doing well with views." I asked if he thought a thousand minimum subscribers with five hundred thousand or more views seemed rea-
sonable as thresholds because a low subscriber count with a relatively high
view count suggested a rapidly growing, "new" channel. Cooper liked the
idea, so I got on with the search, which generated a list of several thousand
channels. I adjusted some filters and still ended up with more than two
thousand channels.

I knew neither of us wanted to comb through two thousand channels
manually, so I filtered the results by keywords that I hoped might ferret out
children's content. This narrowed the list to eleven channels that met our
metric thresholds, half of which fell into what I called "Finger Family" videos. These videos consisted of poorly produced computer animations set to
a nursery rhyme or children's song, usually sung in English by a non-native
English speaker. Songs included "Monkeys on the Bed," "Wheels on the
Bus," and, my personal favorite, "Finger Family." The lyrics go something
like this: "Father finger, father finger, where are you? Here I am. Here I am.
How do you do?" with "Mother," "Brother," "Sister," and "Baby" replacing
"Father" with each repetition. I sometimes thought the singers' accents
sounded South Asian, but I could never really tell for sure. The animations
contained a computer-generated Caucasian hand whose fingertips represented the father, mother, brother, sister, and baby, starting with the thumb
and moving toward the pinky. Heads of superheroes, cartoon characters, or
inanimate objects sat atop each fingertip. The hand could be a family of
Incredible Hulks, Spidermen, Batmen, characters from Disney's *Frozen*, or
airplanes, all of which were popular at the time. These had most likely been
chosen for their popularity as indicated by Google Trends or some other
source of information on popular web searches. Though this ran rough
against IP policing, they were original enough to warrant that Cooper and
I reach out to whoever ran the channel.

I contacted Cooper on Slack and asked if he had seen the Finger Family
channels. "Finger Family stuff is great. Just hard to get in contact with, but
we'll keep being persistent," he typed, adding a second later, "the views are

there." Just that morning the CEO reminded us of our need to scale, something Cooper reiterated to me just before the following exchange on Slack:

COOPER: That channel is doing 37M views a month . . .
MICHAEL: Yeah, with 12k subscribers.
COOPER: We want to double down on these.

Two years later, in 2017, videos like the relatively benign, hypnogogic Finger Family and its more extreme, unsettling relatives gained international attention when news outlets began reporting on children's YouTube in panicked tones. The *Atlantic* said, "The platform's entertainment for children is weirder—and more globalized—than adults could have expected"; the *Onion*'s AVClub column called children's YouTube content an "automated hellscape"; and National Public Radio asked, "Is YouTube's Algorithm Endangering Kids?"[24] Cooper and I, if asked, might have said, "Yes," but that question never came. Instead, we put our creative labor toward The Future's "process" and its profitable, if dubious, ends.

While Cooper and I went about our days with a certain amount of absorbed indifference, others actively vocalized their displeasure. Laura, who mostly worked as an editor at The Future, had much to say when I asked what she enjoyed about her job. Displaying a rather romantic, ex nihilo view of creativity, she said, "Assembling something from nothing and trying to make it look like a TV show is fun. I do just like, as an editor you do have creative control over the final product and what it looks like." For her, even "polishing turds" could be "fun," just as long as she had "creative control" with no one telling her what to do. As she said, "I feel like [The Future] is a company where people are expected to be self-directed in terms of finding projects and pursuing them. I like that. I know some people, that it freaks them out, but I like that." She clearly enjoyed her job, experiencing pleasurable immersion in her tasks. As she said, "I just get into this headspace where I like, lose sense of time. I'm editing and it just becomes about color and motion." She enjoyed that feeling but, perhaps recognizing that she might sound a bit odd, laughed as she explained further: "I like things that put me into that headspace where I lose sense of what I'm doing and get into the feel of it and sit back and say, 'Oh look! I made a thing!' [Laughing] 'Ha, look at that.'"

Laura found work immediately pleasing and actively enjoyed her tasks, but when I asked what she disliked, she focused on content:

> Well, the opposite [of what I enjoy] is a lot of our channels are absolute garbage. A lot of the talent is garbage. The pranks are garbage, misogynist, racist garbage. Actual garbage. I had to cut a sizzle [promotional montage videos] for some prank channels, and I actually, it was the worst thing. Even another channel, I hate them. I generally hate a lot of the talent and don't want them to be successful. So there's that. I have to cut sizzles for stuff that's garbage that I think shouldn't exist. So there's that. [Laughing]

Laura felt as though she possessed "creative control" in her productive moments of subjective absence, but in doing so she became the means to someone else's ends, hating the end product of a highly enjoyable process. Similarly, Leo, whom we met earlier on his last day, enjoyed providing optimization tips to creators, but he still said,

> Most of the stuff we do is garbage. It's garbage! That really popular vlogger? I didn't know who the fuck he was before I came here. Most of this stuff, I don't know who that is. It's some guy talking about his fucking life. What do I care? I hate that. And pranks? Man, that's crap too. Yeah, some of those are funny, but it's all mean-spirited. It's just going into public and fucking with people or provoking men. Or they're like, "It's a social experiment." OK, you pissed someone off by being weird, and then you say, "Oh, it really makes you think." What the fuck were they trying to make you think about? I mean, seriously.

Leo and Laura both refer to prank channels wherein creators engage in the more or less abandoned sociological method known as "breaching," most notably used by Harold Garfinkel and his students. In these videos, creators go into public and break social norms, but unlike Harold Garfinkel, they do so in pursuit of views, not sociological theory.

These "experiments" can be absurd, and they can be glaringly problematic, often with sexist or racist content. For an example of the former, one wildly popular video depicts a spandex-clad, mustachioed man who insistently plays the iconic horn riff from George Michael's 1984 hit song

"Careless Whisper" on a saxophone to confused, amused, and angry onlookers in malls and grocery stores before being escorted away by security guards. I encountered someone shooting a similar but less inventive version of this type of video when a man snuck up behind me in a park and poked me with a carrot while his friend recorded my rather intense reaction and laughed. More troubling were the many videos produced by creators promoted heavily by companies like The Future, the "stars" who often graced YouTube billboards around town and actually received professional services from MCNs and other industry intermediaries. One channel featured hundreds of videos of a man propositioning women for sex. In another, a man wiggled his behind while bent over digging around in his car's trunk wearing spandex exercise pants. When other men passed by, he stood up and asked, "Were you looking at my ass?" On another popular prank channel, a man played gunshot sounds from loudspeakers while driving through Black neighborhoods that the creators called "The Ghetto." The sounds caused people to duck for cover, which the pranksters caught on camera.

Office workers developed coping practices that resembled the alterations to and refusals of music listening described in part 2. As Cooper said, "I really feel bad for the people that are really into YouTube and really love the stuff because after a while they don't love it so much anymore." Desmond, wormholing his way through the working day, made distinct efforts to avoid YouTube outside of work: "When I'm at home I try to not be on YouTube. I try to focus more on traditional media. I kind of feel that what we're doing here is going to combine with that soon. Almost, kind of predicting that by looking at what's popular, what's popular on Netflix. I'm not someone who consumes cable. I don't even have cable. You know?"

Despite limiting his YouTube watching to the time spent in the office, Desmond still worked around the clock. Even in his leisure hours he attempted to predict the future of media, using the embodied data-processing practices that he described earlier. Echoing SoniCo's employees who sat in silence or read books at home after a long day of being bombarded by sound, he said, "I've been staring at a screen all day. I throw it off to the side, and I pick up a book. I read a book. I'll draw. I'll paint. Anything to take my eyes off the screen." The Future's screens bombard the eyes with a dynamic flow of images much like the "noxious" sound flooded music workers' ears. In response, The Future's staff dove "deep," losing themselves during the working day and finding solace at home in off-screen consumption just as SoniCo's workers found reprieve, disappearing during their working day and sitting in silence at home. They enjoyed their work processes, yet the content they helped produce confronted them as excrement, something far less "alien" than Marxists might presume. Upon reflection, they found little joy in the products to which they contributed their labor. Though they could "be creative" and exercise judgment, they judged in accordance to standards that were not theirs.

JUDGMENT'S INFRASTRUCTURAL AND HIERARCHICAL ALIENATION

While the platform's emphasis on metrics shaped the orientations of The Future's creators and staff, the organization's internal power structure mediated these metrics, dually shaping the structural conditions of workers' alienation. While the platform determined much of creators' choices in their content, The Future's predominantly white male leadership seemed to determine who received the most attention from the company. This affected creators' careers, no doubt, but also the relationship between The Future's staff and the content they helped promote. For instance, Lucy enjoyed working at The Future but forcefully expressed distaste for the "sexists and racists" represented by the firm. She wished the firm would take a stand against this sort of content but conceded that controversial content tended to perform best. "That kind of baiting makes us a lot of money. To denounce it makes us lose money, which is a really bad financial decision." Lucy seemed a bit fatalistic, peppering our conversation with the phrase "it is what it is," but she hoped digital media might still usher in change. She rationalized The Future as a sort of Robin Hood. As she said, "I take comfort that as a result of the incredibly racist and sexist stuff, the money we make off it is going toward people of color, gay people, and Jewish people [in the office]."

Was it simply, as Lucy suggested, that sexism and racism sell? Certainly, but YouTube also shapes the field of options available to audiences. Rather than providing a transparent, objective indicator of consumer preferences, YouTube actively attempts to shape content production, encouraging creators to orient toward metrics and to format their content to better match the platform's algorithms. In doing so, YouTube subordinates judgment to quantification, favoring the popular above all else, which leads to both YouTube and Google promoting extreme, often sexually suggestive and racist content, which is what both Lucy and a growing number of researchers, journalists, and creators suggest.[25] In fact, that is precisely why Black creators filed a class-action lawsuit against Google, YouTube's parent company, in the summer of 2020. They claimed that the platform's algorithms actively discriminated against people of color, a well-documented bias also seen in Google's search algorithms.[26]

In addition to potential algorithmic bias, The Future's power structure tended to favor a particularly white male taste, which further alienated workers' judgment along lines of both gender and race. Despite the diversity of The Future's lower-level employees, noted by Lucy, executive positions tended to be held by white, heterosexual men. Some came from the tech sector and others from "Hollywood"—industries known for their misogynistic work cultures and, in recent years, widespread revelations of sexual assault, most notably Ronan Farrow's reporting on Harvey Weinstein and the ongoing revelations in film, television, music, and digital media spurred by the #MeToo movement.[27] In this context, it should not come as a surprise that the content most heavily promoted by The Future includes racist and sexist videos, typically from pranksters or gamers.

Staff meetings clearly illustrated The Future's male-dominated power structure. In the meetings I attended, nineteen people sat the center conference table, with an additional thirty to forty people sitting on benches around the main table or on the floor. Usually only three people at the main table were women, sometimes just one. The remainder of female employees sat in the periphery, quite literally on the sidelines with no seat at the table. In one meeting, a junior executive sat next to the CEO, describing a recent video made by a prank channel in which an older woman becomes the punchline. The video featured a young, bikini-clad woman asking a man to oil her up on the beach. She brings the man back to her towel and lies down beside an older woman, asking the man, "Could you do my grandma too?" He obliges, and the older woman makes suggestive comments: "Oh, I haven't had hands on me like this in years." The executive explained that in one iteration, the older woman kissed a man on the lips to further the "prank." "We should give her a channel," said the executive. "No, we should incorporate her into more content on existing channels and then maybe spin her off," said the CEO. Someone suggested that

the woman needed a name, and another man at the conference table suggested "Naughty Nana." Another of the men laughed and repeated the
name. Though many people in the room laughed, only men offered up
potential names, riffing on the "humor" of an attractive, openly sexual
older woman.

This sort of talk occurred frequently at The Future and, as is well known
among scholars of humor inside organizations, jokes facilitate camaraderie while also establishing group boundaries.[28] Participating in affirmative
performances of masculinity provided ways for men to socialize and
potentially develop their careers. Similar to SoniCo in part 2, crude,
often sexual humor was a notable part of performed masculinity at The
Future, suggestive of a micromechanism that produces systemic gender
inequality in the culture industries alongside other noted sources of gender inequity in the creative sectors, such as pervasive negative stereo-
types of women in the workplace, the entrenchment of men in positions
of authority, and the boundedness of gendered professional networks.[29]
Katherine suggested the last two of these when she said, "Sometimes it's
easier to connect with other women and have them look out for you."

"She's hot!" exclaimed a VP the day after the "Naughty Nana" meeting.
He said this while I "worked his desk"[30] as he discussed a recent talent
prospect with some of the staff. "I spoke with her and then with someone
else [on the phone]. She sounded great, very smart, intelligent. I was thinking of a way to ask how she looked, and then I saw her. She's so hot!" You-
Tube, like most contemporary media, is an image-based business where all
bodies tend to be scrutinized regardless of gender, sex, or age. Even so,
women tend to be more scrutinized than others, and so, while unsurprising, I remained struck by the VP's comments. Even in 2015, women were
"Naughty Nanas" or "So hot!" Even differences in self-presentation seemed
to reflect persistent masculine dominance. Female employees wore high
heels, heavy makeup, and business attire, while men tended toward
hooded sweatshirts, jeans, and sneakers, in a style reminiscent of Facebook's Mark Zuckerberg. Men held the privilege of informality whereas
women tended to be both more formal and to present as heteronormatively feminine.

Toward the end of my fieldwork, an executive told me to come to his
office with my laptop. He asked, "Are you good at writing? Can you
write? I mean, be honest." I told him that I had published in academic

journals and had written some music reviews in the past, so, yes, I could write. He asked me to write pitch sheets for some shows featuring The Future's most popular creators, some of whom produced highly questionable (though not necessarily sexist or racist) content. First up, he envisioned an "episodic movie" to be shot in vérité style, similar to *Cloverfield* or 1999's *Blair Witch Project*, but featuring a YouTube prank star. "It's like, he's out with young kids and they accidentally capture something, some sort of bad thing, you know, like, organized crime or the government. Like that movie with Gene Hackman and Will Smith, but with the prank guys." I asked if he meant *Enemy of the State*. "Exactly, but it's found footage, you know, because they're young, so it's all shot on phones," he said, waving his large iPhone 6 Plus in the air. "The other one is like a mockumentary, but about Millennials and done by a sketch comedy star. You know, like there's the guy that's like PewDiePie, but banging bitches and drinking booze, maybe light drug use. Also, maybe a vegan, you know, Millennial types."

John, a twenty-something with a perfect tan and permanent stubble, entered the office. "Did you say my name? I heard you talk about banging bitches. If you're banging bitches, that's me. I'm there, man." The executive paused and then carried on as if nothing had been said. "And then the other, you know the trailer for that fake movie? Like that, but a full movie. Pitch it as a movie. Think you can do that?" I told him that I would try. He brought Denise, a project manager, into his office. "Nice outfit, boss," said Denise. "Are you being sarcastic?" Denying any sarcasm, she added that his choice of colors was a "classic combination." "Well, you can't tell around here sometimes. Denise, Michael should work with your people. They know what to do with this, but they're both writing right now." "Lord knows we could use good writers here," said Denise. "Well, this might be your guy." I could not tell if he was serious, but they never asked me to write again. I guess I had not been their "guy."

In sum, inequalities linked to gender, race, and place persist despite illusory promises of "participatory" media and platformed entrepreneurialism. Though all may feel alienated by what the platform's metrics reward and privilege, I found that women, people of color, and members of the LGBTQ community faced an additional subordination of their judgment. They faced leadership's hegemonic interpretations of those metrics in both staff meetings and everyday interactions. Though here I focused on office staff, I also found this in some interviews with creators. For example, one of the most popular vloggers I met explained how they felt that their career was in a holding pattern because they are a queer person of color, a feeling echoed by a white vlogger whose content focused on his experiences transitioning. Both felt that they were often passed over when it came to lucrative brand sponsorships and, despite their high earnings, had to advocate for themselves rather than receiving managerial services from The Future. Their viewership numbers gave them some leverage but provided no guarantees when they demanded attention from higher-ups at The Future. Similarly, content created by and for people in rural areas, though quite popular, tended also to be absent in The Future's roster as well as at industry events such as VidCon.

Despite platforms' oft-praised democratization of media, the tech sector and the industrial "spaces" around social media platforms remain dominated by white men, something seen clearly at The Future. Coupled with the quantitative regime's general orientation toward metrics, inequality linked to sexism, racism, and heteronormativity persists given white male leadership and algorithmic biases. This, in turn, both genders and racializes alienated judgment. In response, women, people of color, and other marginalized groups sought opportunities to promote content that more closely aligned with their judgment as best they could. Laura and Lucy pushed to work on "Young Adult" content, a genre often focused on young women, the difficulties of youth, and, increasingly, LGBTQ issues. In stark contrast to The Future's racist pranksters, a Black woman who worked at The Future encouraged her Latina coworkers to find ways to promote content focused on ethnic communities within and outside of the United States. She explained that African films were quite popular among diverse groups of Black Americans. As she said, "You go to New York. You get your hair done. They have them on and people get excited. They get wrapped up in the story. Why not the same for telenovelas and Spanish films? You need to do that for Spanish." She suggested that they might best accomplish this by producing "small, cheap films." Angela McRobbie theorizes moments such as these as "lines of flight," that is, pathways toward advancing the interests of marginalized groups from within the walls of the culture industries. YouTube and The Future may offer lines of flight, but only through great efforts were women able to traverse them. The authority of white, often heterosexual men remained firmly in place despite digital media's supposed openness, and so The Future's staff routinely slopped the "trough" with the most rotten, "snackable" content.

LEAVING THE FUTURE

Describing a precarious workforce as aesthetically enrolled may seem only to reinforce critical social science's darkest dystopian daydreams, but the fragmented experience I am describing here should provide us with hope, something missing from dire predictions about the full subsumption of labor and the supposed elimination of workers' capacity for critique.[31] In contrast, I argue that judgment, however alienated, provides room for critique even if it ends only with workers' casual complaints or isolated, often passive refusals rather than with organized resistance. The Future's creators and office workers loved their jobs but rarely pretended to be doing much more than transforming excrement into gold.

In research on labor in culture industries, Hesmondhalgh and Baker argue against the concept of alienation in favor of a standard for the normative assessment of labor conditions—a rubric for "good and bad work" similar to Kalleberg's "good" and "bad" jobs. For Hesmondhalgh and Baker, "good work" includes contributing one's labor toward "human flourishing." These rubrics may be analytically useful for sociologists, but their connection to work processes remains unclear. More importantly, determining how and when workers contribute their labor toward that end requires a value judgment rife with ambiguity. The "garbage," "trash," or "turds" in the Trough certainly contribute to the economic success of certain creators and the enjoyment of some, often male, employees. For others, the snackable slop seems distasteful, if not wholly detrimental, to humanity. This demands a conceptual category beyond "good" or "bad," something for which I hope alienated judgment serves.

Differences between SoniCo and The Future provide entry into a discussion of how platforms, as privately owned infrastructures, shape work. Infrastructure provided a crucial explanation of variations between the labor processes described in parts 2 and 3. The Future's negative pole resembles SoniCo's: workers perform additional work in order to reproduce themselves despite their precarity, and judgment tends to be subordinated. The similarities end there. Whereas SoniCo's social regime subordinated judgment by means of social relationships, the quantified regime found at The Future does so through infrastructural relationships. This structural difference changes the relationship between workers' precarity and global capital.

First, platforms contribute directly to workers' precarity because fluctuations in how the infrastructure calculates and determines metrics affect how people get paid. Radical uncertainty may be a general feature of all creative industries, but the uncertainty of selling cultural products embodied in tangible objects (ticket sales, books, physical music media, etc.) differs from earning a living from views. The definition of a view (or any other relevant metric on a platform) and the means of payment for views may be altered at any time by the platform's owners. In the context of YouTube, this leads to an uncertainty in measurement, which leads, ultimately, to uncertainty in income, given the shifting definition of pieces in this piece-rate payment system. That creators spread their productivity across multiple platforms simply compounds rather than reduces this uncertainty. This holds for those involved in YouTube content production as well as for organizations and workers in digital publishing who use Google-owned advertising infrastructures and, more broadly, for all work processes embedded within platform infrastructures.[32]

Second, the platform captures value from efforts to evade precarity. As creators and The Future's staff work-to-labor, they watch YouTube videos to gain new skills, and so even when entrepreneurial workers labor for themselves, they produce value for the platform by supplying their eyeballs. This holds true for both creators and their counterparts in The Future's offices, where the networked technologies that allow them to pragmatically solve organizational problems or "be creative" also embed them within YouTube's circuit of value production. Third, the platform alters the structure of alienation. The Future's creators and office staff use their judgment in evaluating content's likelihood to increase relevant metrics. Metric-based decision making with regard to the production and valuation of content serves the pecuniary interests of creators and capital (YouTube and The Future) but not necessarily the aesthetic interests of workers (office staff and creators). As such, workers are alienated from their taste by way of infrastructure, a social structure of alienation that differs markedly from the subordination of judgment to clients' agendas under the social regime.

These differences arise clearly from each case's political economy of infrastructure. Music production exists within diffusely owned infrastructures and institutions and thus continues to resemble most other creative industries. Music, in its industrially produced form, flows from small production teams in studios like SoniCo to a variety of distribution outlets. While these outlets certainly include YouTube and other platforms, music may still just as easily accrue economic and cultural value elsewhere in stores, magazines, websites, and other outlets for sales and critical evaluation. YouTube content, in contrast, appears coterminous with an infrastructure owned and operated by a single, global corporation: Google. The quantitative valuation of creative labor on display at The Future and with its creators stems directly from their inextricability from YouTube and its metrics. Whereas those in conventional media production may seek valuation through a plethora of infrastructural and institutional outlets, YouTube content, by definition, exists only on YouTube. The Future thus occupies a structurally dependent position vis-à-vis Google's global infrastructure of production and distribution, not unlike other forms of digital media production wherein Google-owned infrastructures and other platforms exert power at the level of working day. Embedded within these infrastructures, work at The Future and other platform-based employment follows the logic and interests of global capital.

PART IV

Conclusion

Chapter Seven

TOWARD A THEORY OF CREATIVE LABOR AND A POLITICS OF JUDGMENT

This book began by asking how organizations appropriate and control creative labor and how creative workers come to enjoy precarious employment. Through the comparison of conventional and platform-based media production, I also addressed how the digital infrastructures commonly called "platforms" shape these processes. While working on this book, I often came in contact with people who viewed the project with more than a bit of suspicion. To the question of control, they said that these workers were "not controlled at all" (a "common-sense" idea of which this book hopefully dissuades its readers). To the question of pleasurable precarity, they offered a two-word explanation: "It's culture." Culture—in the limited sense of "the arts" or "media"—may well be the "ideal commodity," the one providing the shimmering sheen that "sells all the others," but time after time, I found that culture failed to sell workers on precarious or low-paying work. Instead, I found workers deploying their creative labor to produce culture from which they felt alienated. So, what made their precarity make sense? At the risk of vulgarizing myself, it seemed to boil down to work being "cool" and "creative," but what did those words mean? Were those meanings emergent from workers' practices or imposed from the top by management? The answer, of course, is both: the managerial invitation and its acceptance by workers.

Read this way, this book provides an empirically grounded analysis and critique of creative or "cognitive" capitalist labor processes, one that attends to key components needed for a theory of creative labor such as control, (re) production, alienation, and (the absence of) collective resistance. Thus, this book stands in contrast to untethered critiques of cognitive or creative labor as well as those empirically grounded investigations that lack critique. The key point, of course, is that power in cognitive capitalist economies operates at two levels usually ignored by labor scholars: the aesthetic and infrastructural dimensions of work. Thus, "cognitive" capitalist organizations dominate workers, at least in part, by enchanting them, by engaging them sensually, by setting parameters upon their actions, and, like other examples of properly neoliberal power structures, by offering them positive freedom, what I called the *managerial invitation*. Capital invites, enchants, and sets the boundaries within which one may do as one wishes—so long as profits accrue.

Recall that I began by describing the profound ambivalence that marks creative labor processes, the multiple, simultaneously occurring valences that I call creative labor's positive and negative poles. Tracing these polarities, I sought to avoid speaking of "contradictions" or anything that might be so neatly parsed. As should be evident throughout, the positive and negative poles only appear neatly separable in my chapter headings; they are never so tidy in my ethnographic rendering. Each pole contained its opposite, and thus capital's creative control over labor never obtains "consent" to "contradictions"—a resolution of opposites—but instead achieves temporary stabilizations of opposing polarities, which, however entangled, never resolve to consent or erupt into resistance. Instead, they merely hang together, loosely bound by work's aesthetic dimension. This book, of course, extends beyond the level of the working day and beyond the individual sites of my ethnographic research to the level of infrastructure. If each case represents an instance of creative labor, each case also represents creative labor under conditions of diffuse (music) and monopoly (YouTube) infrastructure, highlighting the importance of the political economy of infrastructure upon the working day.

In this brief conclusion, I first present a conceptual map of creative labor, a theory that draws out the common contours of this book's two cases. I then return to one of this book's key themes—the importance of work's aesthetic dimension—to argue that scholars and organizers need to seriously consider a labor politics of judgment rather than a politics of affects and aesthetics. Having sketched these contours of creative labor, I then offer some concluding thoughts regarding the "digital divide" and labor policy in the United States and suggest directions for potential future research on platform-based employment.

TOWARD A THEORY OF CREATIVE LABOR

As I said in the introduction, creative labor consists of commonplace but unevenly distributed skills and habits needed to interpret and mobilize signs, symbols, and material artifacts (often technologies). It also involves improvisation using these same signs, symbols, and objects. In other words, creative labor consists of the most distinctly human capacities for productive activities—what Richard Sennett calls "character" and what Franco "Bifo" Berardi more provocatively calls the "soul."[1] Positing a theory of creative labor first required this definition along with a theorization of the specific valences or polarities and modes of control or power exerted at the level of the working day. The *control* in controlling creative labor is one of focusing knowledge accumulation and directing its deployment, spurring interpretive and improvisational capacities into action toward some organizational or managerial goal. Management tends to accomplish this task by inviting self-expression ("be creative") and by modulating the sensorial, felt experience of work. This includes some of the more pleasurable, aesthetic experiences vis-à-vis technology as well as the anxiety produced by inviting "free" expression in the absence of clear rules save for the directive to generate profit.

Far from the free, unfettered creativity so often imagined by the more romantic among us, creative labor under cognitive capitalism tends also to be alienated creativity. Capital may invite and depend upon workers' judgments, but those choices remain subordinate to the demands of dominant actors (management, clients, or the platform). In addition, resistance tends to be atomized and fleeting. Workers may withdraw or exit, they may crack jokes in backrooms or while on cigarette breaks, but broader mobilizations were mostly absent or, in the case of recent attempts to mobilize YouTube's creators, failing.[2]

Conventional explanations of these situations center on ideology. These include Bourdieuian explanations that focus on the *illusio* or belief that justifies the "game" within fields of cultural production as well as arguments about "creativity" as capitalist ideology or *dispositif*. In the latter, capital responded to refusals of labor in the twentieth century by inviting workers to participate in managerial decision making, which in turn led to today's invitations to "be creative." These invitations frame even the most routine jobs as expressive, perhaps even artistic, pursuits, and thus ideology alone supposedly controls creative labor. In the popular Bourdieuian explanation, workers (or "artists") consent to low wages and exploitative conditions because of an omnipresent *l'art pour l'art* ideology wherein art and commerce do not mix. Operating under this *illusio*, creatives supposedly value status or symbolic capital more than they do money. Symbolic capital may be converted into economic capital, and thus forgoing immediate economic returns supposedly seems a fair tradeoff for long-term gains.

Though convincing, these arguments primarily depend upon ideology as a key explanatory factor, which leaves a question unanswered: how do workers become attached to these beliefs in their daily routines? What binds workers to these beliefs, to their "faith," or, in the terminology of contemporary critical theorists, what process of subjectivation produces workers willing to freely provide their creative labor? Focusing on the aesthetic, affective dimensions of the labor process, I argue, provides scholars with a felt, material, and ultimately interactional basis for these ideologies to feel "true"—a requisite explanation for belief and passion dating back at least as far as Durkheim.[3] If "creativity" controls labor, then this discourse's power or control over the labor process seems to be exerted through and dependent upon *things*.

Creative labor tends to be managed loosely, with managerial authority depending on neither prescription nor prohibition but instead invitation. Workers' acceptance of the managerial invitation requires modulation of work's affective and aesthetic dimensions. Management and the platform may invite creativity, but the material experience of the working day enables workers to accept this invitation. The work's materiality and associated embodied experiences bind or attach creative labor to the labor process. While chapter 2 illustrated capital's invitations to "be creative," chapters 3 and 5 illustrated how workers became affectively invested in their working days and thus offered examples of the process of binding workers to work under the social and quantified regimes of creative labor—what I termed *aesthetic enrollment*. In both, management exerted power over the labor process by shaping how work feels. Chapters 4 and 6 examined creative labor's negative valences of precarity and alienation. In both cases, workers attempted to mitigate their precarious conditions by developing multiple streams of income; this illustrates how the managerial invitation produces entrepreneurial workers. Expressive and routine workers engage in constant networking and self-directed learning both inside and outside of the workplace in order to maintain employability. Constant networking and learning were necessary but unpaid tasks performed to maintain and reproduce creative labor.

These features of creative labor processes span both cases, but only creative labor embedded within digital infrastructures appears always productive. While not always "working" in the sense of laboring in a workplace and performing tasks assigned by management, workers at The Future tended to produce value for the owners of infrastructure even in unpaid efforts to reproduce their creative labor power. Consuming online content for the sake of self-education and skill building produces value for the platform by way of advertising revenue, and so even the work of reproducing creative labor generates value that capital captures. This constant learning leaves workers with increased skills that they retain while generating value for both the platform and the employing firm.

In both cases, workers' capacity for free autonomous judgment tended to be subordinate to others. SoniCo's social regime subordinated workers' judgment to the demands of clients—a social relationship in the most traditional sense—while The Future's quantified regime subordinated workers' judgment to the demands of the platform's metrics as mediated by management. In the latter, expressive and routine workers rendered judgments upon content in terms of quantitatively qualified qualities. These qualities were defined as desirable or valuable based on metrics defined and controlled by the platform. So, again, the key difference tends to lie in The Future's dependence upon global infrastructures of production and distribution (in this specific case, the YouTube platform). This infrastructure enables the mass production of mass entertainment while also allowing the platform and downstream firms to capture value from a global, creative workforce. Infrastructure also constrains organizations and labor through metrics and algorithmic search functions.

Taken together, these key points from this book's empirical chapters provide a contour map of creative labor processes under cognitive capitalism.[4]

The ideology of creativity depends upon a distinct, material structure of feeling, something lost in Bourdieuian analyses as well as by theorists who claim that cognitive capitalism "seeks to prioritise . . . creativity, distributed through the entirety of the population" while attempting to get "the multitude to work for free whenever it has possibility."[5] Though insightful, theorists of cognitive capitalism tend to leave out how this occurs. In doing so, they paint a rather seamless portrait of capitalist domination, often leaving out the processes by which capital *invites* and *compels* creativity, a problem addressed by this book.

COGNITIVE CAPITALISM AND A POLITICS OF JUDGMENT

Even "normal" or "routine" work increasingly resembles work in creative sectors. More people in routine jobs are being invited to "be creative," to use their innately human capacity for judgment, and fall in love with even the most routine of jobs. At the same time, employers are adopting nonstandard work arrangements, forcing more and more people to become precarious, entrepreneurial workers.[6] Alongside these managerial invitations to be creative, entrepreneurial workers, business consultants now advocate the adoption of technologies that promote immersive, integrative "flow" experiences. Why? To increase productivity, of course. One can quite clearly see capital advocating aesthetic enrollment—alongside heightened workplace surveillance and quantification—as an increasingly widespread mode of controlling labor.

Given these circumstances, this book provides an ethnographic examination of the micromechanisms that enable cognitive capitalism. To be read in that mode requires a brief definition of cognitive capitalism, the clearest of which appears in Vercellone's "Hypothesis of Cognitive Capitalism."[7] For Vercellone, three characteristics define cognitive capitalism: the labor process, the source of value, and mode of controlling labor. First, workers appear increasingly autonomous within cognitive capitalist labor processes, especially in comparison to the twentieth century's Fordism and Taylorism. Second, value depends upon cognitive or creative labor, which appears in abundance thanks to the expansion of education opportunities in developed countries over the course of the twentieth century. Put differently, *labor puts the "cognitive" in "cognitive capitalism."* Third, capitalist control over labor depends upon the production of subjectivity, with desire goading workers' "free" provision of their creative labor. This shift flows from capital's recuperation of what Boltanski and Chiapello call the "artistic critique" of capitalism. The artistic critique—most closely associated with the 1960s' "New Left" and political art groups such as the Situationists—focuses on capitalism's supposed expulsion of meaning, beauty, passion, and "authentic" living. Boltanski and Chiapello argue that capital incorporated this critique into the labor process when managers began inviting "participation," not unlike what I call the managerial invitation.

Through these managerial invitations, capital "humanized" the labor process and, as shown in this book, cognitive capitalism dominates at the level of affect and aesthetic experience—an assertion for which this book provides much needed empirical support—not by alienating our emotions, as in studies of emotional labor, but by modulating our senses via technology, producing innumerable daily moments of low-level, atomized effervescence. This leads contemporary critics such as Christian Fuchs to claim that "play and labour are today indistinguishable,"[8] an interpretation that seems to shut down the possibility of opposition. This is why others argue for exit[9] or "selective engagement" as labor's main options under cognitive capitalism.[10] Should we leap so gleefully into such a critique, one so eager to shut down the possibility of resistance to what Fuchs terms "hyper-exploitation"? Though insightful, these critiques seem perched a bit too safely within the comforts of the "Grand Hotel Abyss."[11] Instead, my goal has been to understand fractures and possibilities internal to the working day through a detailed ethnographic rendering of creative labor processes. In doing so, I found that the experiences and understandings had by living, breathing labor, that is, by my informants, run quite rough against the seamlessness suggested by theories of cognitive capitalism as well as by a related strand of social and political theory that emphasizes affect as a site of potential resistance.

While work demands workers' full subjectivity, their feelings and judgments, the body and its mind, labor's full subsumption produces its opposite: alienation. Precarity and alienation persist alongside dynamic, sensually engaging labor processes. More pointedly (and in contrast to arguments from economists and sociologists), these tensions find no resolution, neither a balanced mental spreadsheet of psychic and economic wages nor an eruption of collective resistance. The embodied dynamism of work engages and drives workers to provide their creative labor, but this merely masks economic anxiety. Any "psychic wage" earned at the positive pole tends to obscure rather than balance out the negative.

In traditional Marxist critique, the negative (exploitation, alienation, etc.) provides a basis upon which class consciousness might be built. What possibilities lie in creative labor's negative pole? Precarity produced entrepreneurialism and atomization, a sort of neoliberal creativity. Even workers' provision of mutual aid revolved around either highly individualistic circumstances (e.g., one's social network) or improving their entrepreneurial capabilities (e.g., skill sharing among engineers and creators). Collective mobilization of creative workers as *workers* failed to emerge in response to exploitative economic circumstances, but what of alienation? What possibilities lie there? Creative labor processes alienate judgment. This runs counter to two quite common claims with regard to workers and the affective or aesthetic dimension of social life. Theorists of cognitive capitalism such as Berardi and Fuchs along with more empirically grounded scholarship claim that creative workers tend to be overabsorbed by their sociotechnical milieu to an extent that precludes the development of critical subjectivities, thus precluding resistance.[12] To be alienated from one's labor is to be at least somewhat critical. Aesthetically engaged, creative workers reflect upon their product with disdain, judging their product to be undesirable. These particular, irresolvable valences or tensions mark creative labor as distinct from emotional and manual labor as well as the labor of what Christine Williams and Catherine Connell call "looking good and sounding right."[13]

Workers are both aesthetically enrolled and alienated. This finding highlights a problem with critical theory's turn to affect over the past several decades. Affect theorists—most notably Brian Massumi in his calls for a "politics of affect"—posit the affective or aesthetic dimension of social life as a key, potential wellspring of sociopolitical resistance and, by extension, political mobilization, for example in the forceful critiques of cognitive capitalism influenced by autonomist Marxism.[14] In these approaches, affect, aesthetics, or sensation—the precognitive, prerational, and asocial (but not presocial) dimension of social life —remain autonomous from ideology, from being located or classified within the boundaries of accepted discourse. One's ability to affect and be affected supposedly remains autonomous vis-à-vis discourse or ideology and thus potentially resistant to power.[15] Even in somewhat more grounded research on algorithmic cultures, the aesthetic experience of technologies—what Taina Bucher calls "algorithmic affects"—provides opportunities to resist or oppose capital predicated upon the embodied decision making of the flesh.[16] In contrast, the organizations examined in this book dominated workers precisely at this affective or aesthetic level of experience. My point, then, is not to discredit these theorizations of affect or aesthetics but to highlight how capital's power, exerted through invitations to "be creative," depends upon this affective or aesthetic dimension.

Creative labor's negative pole produces the conditions of possibility for a collective *politics of judgment* rather than a politics of affect.[17] Divisions run rampant within and between the many sectors dubbed "creative," but as shown in this book, creative workers share much in terms of alienation. They may possess autonomy, they may be aesthetically enrolled, and, in some cases, they may even be well compensated, but they all lack control over their judgment—what used to be considered the most "human" of cognitive faculties. Now, any such politics of judgment must be tempered by the simultaneous consideration of both capitalism's affective or aesthetic dimension *and* the long-known sociological insight that judgment tends to be shaped by social position.[18] Workers' critique tends to be based in their value-rational judgments and economic interests. Thus, organized opposition to capital, were it present, might mobilize under the banner of judgment as well as economic inequality, as it has in Europe.[19] Rallying in support of judgment, decision-making authority, and not simply the right to express, speak, or "be creative"—rights already freely given by cognitive capitalism's "conversational" firms[20]—provides a common cause around which class fractions might unite. To reiterate, I am arguing both with and against theorists of cognitive capitalism and affect theory insofar as I find social life's aesthetic or affective dimension to be of crucial importance when discussing power. As William Mazzarella writes, "any social project that is not imposed through force alone must be affective in order to be effective."[21] Aesthetic experiences provided an affective binding, eliciting workers' consent to precarious employment, but that bandage falls loose when workers reflect upon the products of their labor.

Though cognitive capitalism may invite creative participation, the labor process excludes workers' judgment, often foreclosing the possibility of truly meaningful work. Platforms exacerbate this process, embedding work within privately held infrastructure and, often, subordinating the judgment of workers in a variety of social contexts to the interests of global capital. More broadly, platforms appear disarticulated from what Jose van Dijck and her colleagues call "democratically agreed upon public values."[22] That alienated judgment might provide a common cause for creative labor may be seen at SoniCo and The Future as well at major tech firms such as Google and Facebook, where workers increasingly demand to be able to choose projects in line with their "ethics."[23] At the same time, there exist enormous disparities in earnings and numerous occupational cleavages within the "creative class" despite the workers in the field all generally providing a similar type of labor to their employers. What I am arguing is that a potential for collective mobilization lies in workers' shared experiences of that which cognitive capitalism denies, that for which so many continue to fight. Struggles for creative control remain, ultimately, struggles to reclaim judgment. Future research might do well to trace both failed and nascent efforts at collectively mobilizing creative labor, asking how and around what common causes organization occurs.

While this book focused explicitly on the class antagonism between labor and capital, there remains important work to be done on the persistent inequalities stemming from race, gender, and place. My findings suggest key differences in how people use platforms based on location as well as social position. Women and people of color continue to face diminished opportunities because of the dominance of white men both at the level of infrastructure and in organizational hierarchies. Content creators outside major cities tended to view YouTube as an alternative means of employment, using the platform to escape or mitigate the diminished employment opportunities of the rural Rust Belt and the United States' deindustrialized and depopulated cities. In contrast, those in Los Angeles tended to view the platform as a gateway to Hollywood. These findings dovetail with Forrest Stuart's research on the use of YouTube among Chicago's "drill" musicians. Despite access to digital infrastructure, Stuart highlights how young Black men still lack many digital opportunities, often chasing views in ways that put their lives in peril. Taken together, these findings run counter to popular narratives of technological emancipation and the supposedly diminished importance of place in the digital economy.[24] While I focused on commonalities across a diverse group of informants, future research might ask how these intersecting forms of inequality shape both creative labor and workers' interests vis-à-vis platforms while being especially attentive to the interrelatedness of infrastructural biases, place, race, and class.

POLITICAL ECONOMIES OF INFRASTRUCTURE
AND THE FUTURE OF WORK

Having provided a conceptual map of creative labor, I now turn to differences between conventional and fully platformed work to extend from SoniCo and The Future to the distinct political economies of infrastructure in which each were embedded. The darkest predictions for the future of work hinge on the expansion of what Nick Srnicek calls "platform capitalism," that is, the increased capture of valuable data and other information enabled by digital infrastructures owned by global capital.[25] Platforms such as YouTube enable this capture—something illustrated quite clearly in part 3 of this book with YouTube's near-monopoly ownership of infrastructure for distribution and remuneration. As more and more types of work become embedded within platforms, more and more workers may become precarious in ways similar to those who produce content for YouTube.

The emerging, quasi-monopolistic infrastructural context of cultural production has two implications for a theory of creative labor. First, the degree of concentration of infrastructure in each case directly affected processes of cultural production and thus creative labor. Music production tends to be embedded within distribution infrastructure diffusely owned by a (small) plurality of firms, not unlike film or book publishing. This political economy of infrastructure, with its competing information regimes and sources of valuation, lead to workers' and organizations' continued concern with *social* valuations (professional status, genre conventions, reputation, etc.). Thus, music continues to resemble prior research in numerous sociological studies of cultural production. Though platforms increasingly dominate conventional cultural production in terms of revenue, there still exist a variety of distribution networks that enable workers in conventional or "legacy" media to bring their wares to market. If a media conglomerate or some other distributor refuses to release a song, producers and musicians may sell it online through a platform such as Bandcamp or offer a streaming version through Spotify,

SoundCloud, or YouTube; they may also choose to bypass platforms alto-gether, selling physical products in brick-and-mortar stores, via mail order, at live performances, or any other space where people congregate to consume. Likewise, there still exist institutions that provide critical, qualitative evaluations of creative products—what Bourdieu called "con-secration."[26] Together, these provide multiple pathways to revenue and distinct, competing valuations. Music, like film or publishing, contains multiple infrastructures for distribution and valuation, and thus creative labor's products may still succeed symbolically, if not economically. A Grammy or a positive review from *Pitchfork* or *Rolling Stone* may, in the long run, result in status-building acclaim despite less than stellar perfor-mance in the market.

In contrast, YouTube production is, by definition, embedded within a single distribution and remuneration infrastructure owned and operated by a global corporation. Google/Alphabet's YouTube controls both the primary system of remuneration as well as metrics that affect supplemen-tal incomes (e.g., sponsorships) and the platform's regulations, which, at present, allow for promoting crowdfunding and other off-platform income sources. Aside from the platform's metrics, few if any alternative valuations exist as of this writing. Though platforms' quantification of creative labor provides some power to workers in negotiating contracts, platforms reduce culture to "content," and quantification reduces the value of "content" to market success or popularity—an issue discussed by the filmmaker and activist Astra Taylor in *The People's Platform*.[27] Taylor notes how platforms tend to promote the popular at the expense of the culturally or politically "important," which may be unpleasant or difficult and thus unpopular. For example, political documentaries or innovative and thus difficult-to-digest content may fail where a makeup tutorial or a dat-ing vlog may succeed. So, for example, Taylor's feature-length films *Žižek!* and *Examined Life*, both of which examine complex ideas through inter-views with philosophers and social theorists (e.g., Judith Butler, Cornel West, and Martha Nussbaum) might not fare so well in a quantified regime of cultural production where "quality" tends to be qualified by quantities. She calls for a reimagining of platforms alongside building institutions that might balance platforms' rationalization of cultural pro-duction with judgments of "quality." Taylor implicitly calls for a politics of judgment, and I am obviously sympathetic to her argument. Still, she never specifies how we might arbitrate "quality," an important question given how often experts in the arts have used their definitions of "quality" to exclude the cultures of women, people of color, the working classes, and other marginalized groups. Perhaps more central to this book, Taylor never theorizes the distinct regime of labor introduced by platforms, instead focusing on how platforms disrupt conventional media producers' revenue sources. Instead of lamenting this lost past, sociologists of labor and culture need to ask how these new infrastructures affect the valuation of labor and products in both emerging and existing occupations and modes of media production. Examining how people value what they do may provide further insight into how judgment provides a potential rallying point for collectively mobilizing creative labor.

Platforms rationalize production in terms of their metrics, which always remain under control of the platform's owner, shaping workers and their products in the image of these measures. As shown in part 3, capital actively sought to produce a metrics orientation among creative workers just as yesteryear's capitalist sought to engender a rules orientation among workers in bureaucratized labor processes. Metrics tend to be the sole source of valuation—while remaining blackboxed and under the complete control of capital. Platforms' blackboxing of metrics and payments effectively shuts down quibbles over pay rates while directly linking production choices to the whims of capital. Production tends to be oriented toward what the platform measures, a situation not wholly new to scholars of science and technology. Concerns over reputation tend to be reduced to a reputation for garnering incredible amounts of views. Team formation and repeat encounters on projects tend also to be dictated solely by histories of market success. All actions lead to more views leading to more users leading to more data captured by the platform.

This certainly illustrates how platforms extract and capture value from users' data—what Srnicek describes as platforms' key business model—but what I wish to highlight here is how much the platform shapes the production of that information. Doing so illustrates why we need to consider users as labor. Discussions of platforms tend to treat data and content as resources ("just like oil") or natural byproducts ("datasweat"), but capital actively controls and shapes the processes that produce that resource (users' measured activities). Platforms mold the "natural" resources that they "extract," producing rather than merely reflecting the social structures in which users work.[28] Users' data, including media content, may never be "raw," but platforms go one step beyond data processing by actively shaping workers' subjectivities. As illustrated in chapter 5, YouTube and downstream firms guide content creators so as to produce content that elicits particular behaviors from viewers. Fostering a metrics orientation alters the desires and actions of those downstream from the platform.

How this occurs varies from platform to platform, and so users' data or content cannot be thought of as a "natural" resource or a thing independent of the infrastructures capturing it. YouTube content (and data produced by users on all platforms) represents actions oriented at all times toward what Google requests or invites. Platforms do not extract so much as they guide the production of, and thus they fundamentally alter the very "resource" they depend upon—as if Exxon could educate oil and then, somehow, extract refined gasoline straight from the earth. What I am saying is that the platform attempts to control users' creative labor, and so rather than "free participation," creative labor, embedded within platforms, emerges in the image of these capitalist infrastructures. Moving forward, labor scholars need to ask how and through what processes do platforms and other work infrastructures "fabricate" labor, shaping workers understandings of their labor power and thus the possibilities for collective mobilization.[29]

This leads to my third point. Platforms' blackboxed governance compounds workers' precarity. YouTube's algorithms, remuneration structure, and calculation of metrics remain obscured from downstream creators. The platform allows much, but its governance tends to be absolute, final, and difficult to appeal to, like a silent god. As such, working for YouTube resembles work on other platforms that pay their "users" (e.g., Uber, Lyft, Amazon Delivery, and Postmates).[30] Collectively, platforms comprise one of work's emerging futures. YouTube and these other platforms rarely give direct orders; instead they nudge, incentivize actions, or suggest more profitable "best practices" by which one may articulate an "authentic" branded self. All the while the platform maintains a structural advantage over workers by maintaining their status as "users," by promoting "entrepreneurship," and by lobbying against the classification of "users" as employees.

Findings presented in this book reinforce broader calls to consider digital inequality as more than simply an issue of access and the issues raised by how technology makes workers overly accessible. These jobs require creative labor—a set of very human skills that often depend upon technologies. All of the work processes in this book required technological competence, fluency, and ease. It should be clear that most creative work occurs within smartphones, texting, email, instant messaging, social media, Apple and Microsoft computers, and Google's search and suite of cloud-based office applications, along with industry-specific, specialized technologies. Beyond their creativity and technical fluency, workers' skills include all the unspoken, tacit knowledge of each system's distinct communication etiquette (when and how to email, length and frequency of communication, etc.). A key implication for policy, then, is that regardless of access and technical proficiency, there remains a widening gap in social fluency within these systems, one experienced by the body and as a lack of knowledge. The expansion of access to and usage of the internet and smartphones does little to guarantee the tacit, embodied knowledge required to be fluent in the dominant modes of using these technologies at work. Some may never *feel* comfortable in heavily mediated work environments, and many more *may* feel comfortable but lack enough knowledge of the dominant modes of digitally mediated communication in work contexts.

In the densely mediated contexts described in this book, the workers I observed always seemed to be working. Even when they were not working, they were producing value for some firm, though not always their direct employer. I set myself the task of explaining why they participated in this process, but for policy, it might be better to ask what time constraints ought to be placed upon constant communication—a rather generic feature of contemporary work[31]—and platforms' round-the-clock capture of value. The expectation of being available around the clock for relatively low-paying jobs effectively drives down hourly pay rates below the legal minimum wage. Working in excess of forty hours a week is common for salaried workers in the United States, but platforms such as those described in this book push this common practice to its limit. Platforms continually blur the line between work and other activities such as education and leisure insofar as we produce value for social media platforms both when we produce and when we consume content. This blurring points to the need for serious policy discussions in the United States about constant workplace communication and the ongoing erosion of the boundary between work and nonwork.

DIMINISHING THE POWER OF PLATFORMS

What does this mean for the future of work? Regulating the content on social media and providing consumer protections for users of service platforms seem all the rage since 2016, but in serious discussions about regulating big tech and their platforms, labor rarely comes up. Sure, some critical scholars may claim social media users as "exploited" laborers in the "playground and factory" of the internet, but alongside such claims, one finds a growing body of celebratory writings from liberal scholars clutching the tech sector's bosom. Critical scholars may seem tone-deaf, too focused on capital's "full subsumption" of labor at the expense of potential for opposition, but at least they sing a tune of their own. In contrast, corporate apologists sing in harmony with their masters' voices, championing platforms' ability to bring consumers and producers together in new communities. Sure, they add just a touch of dissonance, so as not to seem too on the nose, but they dare not take seriously users' labor. Instead, they claim that platforms derive their profits from "content moderation" and by enabling community—a bit like saying that any company derives profit primarily from its managerial functions.

Silicon Valley remains happy to discuss issues of misinformation and "privacy" concerns, but we need to seriously consider social media platforms' power in terms of *labor* rather than toe the corporate line. Otherwise, we do little to truly understand the changes or "disruptions" wrought by Silicon Valley and provide little challenge to dominant discourses of platforms' "democratization" of media and enabling of entrepreneurship. Some argue that we must call upon the state to develop publicly owned platforms or band together to develop platform co-ops.[32] While I side with them, developing alternative infrastructures to rival those in current use seems a long-term goal. The long game may be necessary, but we also need the short-term goals of updated labor regulations that support workers over the demands of cognitive capitalism. In 2019, California passed legislation aimed at forcing transportation platforms such as Uber to recognize their "users" as employees. The legislation attempted to do so by forcing companies to treat as an employee any worker who performs tasks that supports a company's core business. This step in the right direction could be followed up by regulating "user" agreements as one might regulate labor contracts and by developing new regulations for platforms' blackboxed pay rates. Platforms' blackboxing of labor relations creates a situation in which workers may and in fact are subject to wage changes and dismissal without prior notice, justification, or process of appeal.

Here, some might claim that "users" do not qualify as employees, a defense of capital that falls flat when considering creators' centrality to YouTube's core business (i.e., using user-generated content to sell advertising slots) and YouTube's attempts to discipline and control creators' labor. Consider the degree to which YouTube's revenue would vanish without creators' investments of time, labor, and production technologies. The same may be said for every platform, from Uber to Airbnb to TaskRabbit and Postmates, and so while YouTube may be unique as a social media platform, it shares a similar opacity in terms of its inner workings and payment practices. On YouTube, there appears to be no baseline rate at which the platform pays content creators, and, contrary to regulations in the United States, the platform's advertising-based piece rate does not correspond in any way to the number of hours spent producing content or producing the inventory of audiences sold by the platform for profit. Additionally, the platform officially forbids discussion of wages earned by its "users." Though this does not legally shut down discussions of individual piece rates, the platform's stipulation forms part of the "user agreement" and thus, at present, may be enforced regardless of legality in terms of labor law.

As it stands, the official line is that creators do not work for the platform. They are simply users. As users, they may be denied the ability to earn income from the platform if found to be in violation of the terms of service laid out in the user agreement. Just as Amazon delivery drivers may be "deactivated," YouTubers may be "demonetized," with only a minimal and often difficult chance of appeal. Some researchers advocate this practice as a means of regulating platform workers and their content, as in recent discussions regarding regulation of extremist political content on YouTube.[33] Some platforms publicly bristle at that idea, claiming that it sets a dangerous precedent for "free speech" and thus perpetuating the more acceptable framing of platforms as transparent conduits of communication. Instead, we need to press further on how such a practice might set a dangerous precedent for labor, one in which capital may alter the wage relationship without any explicit specified procedure or established process of appeal. Without the aid of an intermediary organization, platform workers can rarely appeal decisions made at the level of infra-structure, at the level of the platform's owners—for example, Google/Alphabet, for YouTube. A union or guild might have served as such an intermediary in the past, but YouTube's creators depend upon for-profit corporations as representatives, and these for-profit mediators profit from the platform's lack of responsiveness, siphoning portions of creators' reve-nues, a bit like priests who required medieval Christians to pay indul-gences when asking forgiveness from their god.

All this points to the need for more research on how intermediary organizations serving workers' interests might offset platforms' power over work. Platforms' power far outstrips disparities commonly found in more traditional forms of employment in terms of speed, scale, and scope. Here, scholars and activists remain divided on how workers might orga-nize, debating the effectiveness of forming new unions or guilds and new modes of organizing such as platform co-ops and publicly owned plat-forms.[34] Both approaches presuppose a need for platforms. To this, we might ask how and under what conditions do these approaches succeed, or, even better, ask why platforms inhabit all the imagined futures being put forth by academics and technologists alike. Is this so for workers, and, if so, what futures do platforms such as YouTube enable workers to imagine?

Cooperatives and public platforms strike me as long-term solutions, and while workers certainly need a long game, they also need short-term gains. Guilds and unions fail to gain momentum in the face of widespread pushes for entrepreneurialism and rampant antiunionism in the tech sec-tor.[35] Researchers might trace these failed efforts at collective mobilization in order to better understand why creative labor and platform workers remain among the most unorganizable. Practically, workers might make more immediate demands upon platforms, applying pressure upon the state to classify "users" as workers and then, from there, ensuring that these workers receive appropriate labor protections. The degradation of labor protections in the United States certainly complicates this matter, but the platformed organization of work demands a three-pronged approach, one that includes short-term and long-term goals such as expanding labor regulations and protections to include "users" and cover round-the-clock work schedules, collective mobilization efforts, and the development of alternative organizational forms.

Capital's modes of controlling creative labor, through invitation and aesthetic enrollment, may prove instructive in efforts to mobilize creative labor around a politics of judgment. Whether this be a guild, union, or cooperative organization, any attempt at collective mobilization of creative labor needs to enchant or aesthetically enroll workers, providing material pathways by which labor might imagine viable, potential futures. Efforts to mobilize against global technological capital then requires not simply new infrastructures controlled and operated by workers but new infrastructures that aesthetically enroll workers in a project of emancipation, one that provides them with the creative control that capital denies.

ATTENDING TO DIFFERENCE IN SIMILARITY AND THE GENDER OF MY ACCESS

Ethnographies of the creative, cultural, information, or knowledge industries usually conclude with appendices in which the author discusses their difficulties with access or the shared precarity of researcher and researched.[1] The latter, of course, highlights how social scientists study "sideways" or examine those with whom we share a roughly equivalent social position when we study workers in the knowledge, information, or culture industries. This differs from the more common practice of studying "down," in which researchers often intend to give voice to the voiceless, or more recent efforts to study "up" as a way of exposing the powerful. By studying sideways, I hoped to show the routine, "humdrum" labor so often ignored by those who purport to study "art worlds" or "fields of cultural production" and, more importantly, how even the "heaven" of working in the "dream factory" offers little respite from the increasing uncertainty of the global economy. In doing so, I too had difficulty obtaining access and, speaking to the issue of precarity, critical qualitative sociologists such as myself verge on being unemployable, a point well noted by Gina Neff in the appendix to *Venture Labor*. Rather than simply reiterate what others have said, I want to use this appendix to contemplate how elements of my personal biography as well as my gender affected research in two fieldsites dominated by men. In doing so, I describe, linger, and prod but never fully come to a conclusion about these issues.

Still, a methodological appendix somehow seems incomplete without at least a brief retelling of my entry into the field. I approached over one hundred organizations before beginning fieldwork at SoniCo. Even then, I was only able to secure access there because a colleague introduced me to one of the owners. When I decided to expand the project to include a digital media firm, I contacted nearly one hundred media companies before gaining and losing access at a digital publishing company and then finally entering The Future as an unpaid intern, a strategy I borrowed from Laura Grindstaff after reading her now classic ethnography of daytime talkshows.[2]

Most companies never responded to my phone calls and emails. Of those who did, most declined to participate. One seemed to think I was asking for a job and said that they "had no open positions at the moment." A few even laughed at me, scoffing at the idea that a sociologist might observe the goings-on of their business. While I was on a call with several executives from a digital media company, their chief officer of operations exclaimed, "Wait, you don't just want us to give you data to analyze? We're happy to do that! But, wait, you want to see how we work and what goes on here?! No, no. We can't do that." The conversation immediately brought to mind the scene in *Dr. Strangelove* in which General "Buck" Turgidson, played by George C. Scott, refuses to let Russian diplomats see "the big board" in the war room. In hindsight, the conversation seemed closer to home in economic sociology. Marx had, after all, described capitalist workplaces as the "hidden abode" into which none shall enter unless invited for official business. So, yes, like others, I found it hard to gain access, and, yes, leaping from one temporary academic contract to another for several years while writing this book meant that I shared a precarious economic position with those whom I studied.

JUST ANOTHER MAN IN THE STUDIO?

Rather than belabor these points, I want to reflect on how both my history as a participant in music production and my gender informed and influenced the research process. Before becoming a sociologist, I spent fifteen years involved in "underground," or DIY (do-it-yourself), music scenes. During that time, I performed in punk and noise rock bands and in a number of one-off performances in various group improvisation projects. I released records, toured the United States, served as a co-director of a cooperatively run venue, provided recording services to other musicians, and worked in the warehouse of a music distribution company.

While rather unremarkable, my past involvement in music provided me with a skill set that facilitated my "deep hang" with the guys at SoniCo. This certainly helped a lot, as did being heteronormatively male, because I could blend, so to speak, in at least two ways. Rather than take this as (wholly) an asset, I often wondered if my familiarity, my ability to blend, prevented me from understanding that which remained specific to organizational life at SoniCo. This is an old question for ethnographers but one worth asking as more sociologists focus on groups similar to themselves and as more and more people (sociologists included) become media producers, given the proliferation of audio recording and imaging technologies and the shift to remote teaching during the COVID-19 pandemic. I offer no definitive statement here, simply a reflection on my experiences.

When I entered the field, I could easily perform various tasks that required a bit of specialized knowledge. This reduced the degree to which I "got in the way"—a common reason for denying access that I encountered when speaking to managers and employees at other companies. During my first day of fieldwork at SoniCo, an owner briefly introduced me to the staff, and then I got straight to work setting up microphones and guitar amps for the live concert described in chapter 1. Later, I needed little instruction to assist the staff when tidying up rehearsal rooms or doing basic setups for a recording session. I had spent years loading and unloading my own equipment when I gigged in nonstandard, sometimes illegal venues or when I engineered recordings for friends' bands, often recording in rehearsal rooms similar to those at SoniCo. In those spaces, I learned common techniques for tearing down and caring for equipment (e.g., following the curves of the wire when wrapping cables to prevent damage) and basic troubleshooting for equipment malfunctions (e.g., checking fuses and faulty cables, matching impedances on amplifiers and speakers, etc.).

On one hand, my background made fieldwork feel comfortable, even easy, as if returning to a world I had never fully left, but, like I said, my familiarity seemed just as likely to obscure SoniCo's specificity. Even if it felt "normal" to me, their world was *not* mine. First off, I had never been a studio employee; second, but more importantly, I had never worked in Los Angeles, a global city and one of the biggest hubs for cultural production, or "entertainment." Of all the global hubs of cultural production, LA remains most synonymous with "Hollywood," a shorthand for corporate greed and artificiality, the heart of the "culture industry" that made Hork-heimer and Adorno bristle in Brentwood, where people chase after thrill and spectacle so hard, so fiercely, that Baudrillard thought they might ask, "What are you doing *after* the orgy?"[3] I had performed in smoky Pitts-burgh bars and sweaty Chicago warehouses, selling records in the thou-sands, not hundreds of thousands or millions. I occasionally worked alongside darlings of newsprint zines and obscure blogs, not the Grammy winners and rising stars whom I encountered at SoniCo. So differences in education aside, the guys at SoniCo were also different sorts of male music workers. "Oh, you were one of *those* musicians, like the Part-Time Punks people," said Jack, referring to an LA concert promotion company that, indeed, had put on events for groups with whom I had previously shared bills. They could locate me socially, and they located me as someone only on the edge of their occupational subculture. You might say I was some-thing of a cultural "halfie" in this occupational world, though my usage differs somewhat from the typical use of that term.[4]

In response, I found myself engaging in two methodological procedures. First, I took care to describe the mundane aspects of fieldwork in such a way so as to account for skills that I might otherwise overlook as "just what you do." My notes aided in interrogating my experiences, estranging the everyday as I thought through my tasks, asking myself what I had needed to know in order to get through that day of fieldwork. I also used these notes to formulate the questions I asked later when I sat down with the guys for more formal interviews. Second, I followed the extended-case method, which, for those unfamiliar, begins with the researcher's extension outward to those whom they study.[5] I tried to bridge the gap between myself and the engineers by anchoring our conversations in our shared yet divergent expe-riences. My goal in doing so had been to avoid projecting my experiences onto those whom I studied—a common pitfall among those who research music communities.[6] I had worked as a musician and had even been paid to record a few singles and demos for friends' bands, so I attempted to mini-mize my potential to read my experiences onto my informants by actively inserting my experiences into our conversations. When we spoke, I might compare a recording session observed during fieldwork to one I had run in the past. This led to corroborations, clarifications, or elaborations from engineers and staff (e.g., "Yeah, you get it!" or "No, not exactly. It's more like . . . ," "Yeah, but also . . . ," etc.).

Even so, could I ever get it right? Maybe, but maybe not. Employees read earlier drafts of the article that led up to this book. Robert and Hersch said the drafts "read very well," and, later, I heard that one employee had used my findings to demand a raise. He succeeded. When I returned for follow-up research in 2016, one of the owners alluded to there being some employees and at least one owner who had been put off by my writeup but that they had left before I returned. Had I gotten something wrong? I could not ask them, but those who remained seemed happy to have me back.

ANXIOUS IN THE CONTENT REFINERY

Between my two stints at the studio, I attempted to extend my findings from SoniCo to The Future, hoping that a comparison might provide further insights into creative labor and into the "problem" of my subjectivity. My work history and research experience again eased my entry as an intern at The Future. During the initial interview, I explained my wish to conduct ethnographic research within the firm and quickly received an offer to start as an intern thanks, in part, to my experience at a music distributor and my brief stint at a blog publishing network (an earlier fieldsite to which I lost access).[7] Being "out" as an ethnographer allowed me to stay within the firm for ten months rather than an intern's typical seven-week appointment. I refused offers of full-time work (just as I had at SoniCo) for two reasons. First, full-time work interfered with research insofar as my role as an intern afforded flexibility. I could roam about more freely and ask a lot of questions—points noted by Alexandre Frenette in his study of music industry workers and, somewhat differently, David Halle in *America's Working Man*.[8] Second, I thought it ethically problematic to take jobs actively sought after by many people who were more committed to careers in these industries.

If SoniCo presented a problem of perceived social proximity despite distance, then The Future presented the inverse problem. I felt anxious, even repulsed, by The Future's business model, in part because of my history of involvement with communities opposed to "corporate" cultural production.[9] I suppose my feelings echoed those of Peter, an engineer quoted in chapter 2 who expressed distaste with what he called the "biz." The Future felt very much like the "biz," especially during my first month, when I faced the burdens of being an intern for the first time. This included running errands for staff like driving hard drives full of YouTube content around town or picking up $40 club sandwiches and $20 vitamin-B-infused wheatgrass smoothies for C-level executives. I felt contempt, something reflected in my early fieldnotes, in which "I hate this place" and "I hate coming here" appeared often.

Even if I managed to find a bit of humor in braving LA traffic to fetch an executive's favorite "Chinese Chicken Salad," The Future's entire business model ran rough against the sensibilities I had developed during my time in underground music scenes. As an old rock song says, "Those were different times," a not altogether bygone era during which many people attempted to eschew global media by developing alternative, often local or regional modes of organizing cultural production, often with the implicit goal of breaking down the walls between consumers and producers. YouTube and other social media platforms may promise just that to users, but as I found out, that promise, the invitation to "be creative," is always already circumscribed by global capital's demands.

Was I just being a snob? Was I just letting my past pretensions get in the way? Perhaps, but I also grew to enjoy many of my coworkers, especially the people whom I call Cooper, Laura, Wally, and Garland, and so I think the ethnographic story told in chapters 5 and 6 provides a sympathetic view into their world while also illustrating how I came to be complicit in the company's project. The Future may have made me feel uneasy, as if I was operating behind enemy lines, but I also found joy in chasing after numbers, in supporting that which I actively disliked. I did so in spite of my personal history and sociological training.[10] This experience produced what I consider to be a more fully rendered portrait of life at The Future as compared to SoniCo. If I felt uneasy, why? If I felt pleasure, how? Whereas I understood something about life in music production and could see something of myself or my friends in Robert, Marcus, or Wanda, I had a hard time getting a handle on The Future, not unlike Shelly, who says as much in chapter 5. Again, my attempt to develop an understanding began by following the extended case method, by moving from myself to The Future's staff. Doing so opened me up to the unexpected, to the gaps in the discourse of "creativity" and thus to the chance that The Future's staff might be just as conflicted as I was about their situation.

GENDER AND ACCESS

The culture industries remain dominated by men, gendering access, more obviously at SoniCo, with its mostly male staff, but no less so at The Future, despite its diversity and supposed openness. When I began fieldwork at The Future, their hiring manager asked me which of the company's internal teams I might want to join. He explained that the talent acquisition team, or "Network," worked with a variety of the company's other teams. I requested to join them because, as a central node within the organization's networked structure, I might be better positioned to interact with a variety of people in the company. He offered me that choice because of my role as a researcher in addition to me being an intern, but also seemingly because of the company's gendered hierarchy and the gendering of work teams described in chapter 6. All employees in the Network team were men. They worked in the "Men's Room," and about half of their interns were men, as compared to the all-female "Beauty" team, who managed creators in the beauty/lifestyle "vertical," or genre. One of Beauty's interns implied that gender affected her placement. She complained that she had told the hiring manager that she wanted to work with either the gaming team or the music video team but was instead assigned to Beauty. I often heard my team referred to as the "smart *guys*" but rarely heard active praise of Beauty aside from general acknowledgment of the staff as a whole, further reflecting The Future's gendered power structure. Even if I still had to go fetch lunches for executives or occasionally clean dusty storage rooms, my access as a researcher benefited from my gender identity.

Creative workers can be difficult to track down, and, as any resident of Los Angeles will tell you, it can be hard to schedule a meeting with close friends, let alone a sociologist. While I had privileged access within the office, scheduling interviews with female workers whom I did not see every day (i.e., audio engineers and creators) proved more difficult. After exhausting SoniCo's small stable of engineers, I used snowball sampling to obtain additional interviews. While effective, I found it nearly impossible to schedule interviews with female engineers. Statistically, women represent a small portion of all engineers in the industry, making them hard to find anyway, but even when mutual acquaintances referred me to female engineers, they usually declined to return calls or emails. Luckily, an acquaintance whom I call Wanda moved to LA while I was doing research. She gladly took me up on the offer to chat about her work over lunch.

In contrast, I had little trouble finding men to sit down and talk with me. Was this caused by the quantitatively low numbers of women in these industries, or was I just a bad ethnographer? My experience with YouTube creators suggests a possible answer. I sent countless messages to creators through email and direct messages on YouTube and other social media platforms. I explained who I was and my purpose for wanting to talk about their work. Some responded promptly; a few even seemed enthusiastic. Most never got back to me or, worse, stopped returning my emails or phone calls on the days just before our scheduled interview. One creator in the Midwest attempted to shake me down for a few hundred dollars (they assured me that their fee was "standard for this sort of thing," but even so, I declined).

I strained to find a pattern in creators' elusiveness. As the social world becomes more embedded within digital technologies, we might easily leap to the conclusion that email and other digital modes of communication simply make it easier for people to ignore social scientists. Some claimed to be too "busy," a fair excuse given what I said before about life in LA. While this may be the case, a single sentence from a female vlogger whom I interviewed suggested gender as an equally likely explanation. As she said, "I get a lot of strange emails from *men*," a sentiment echoed by a number of my other female interviewees. In this regard, my web presence helped. Like a lot of my informants, she had Googled me, and I suspect my topping the list of Google results for "Michael Siciliano Sociology" certainly helped.

ATTENDING TO DIFFERENCES BETWEEN SIMILAR CASES

My experiences of course highlight the importance of social position and personal biography in gaining ethnographic access, but also the need for continued engagement with and attention to difference in contexts wherein the ethnographer appears to be studying "sideways." Subtle variations within a class or subculture, occupational or otherwise, must be attended to in order to overcome what might otherwise appear to a naïve researcher, colleagues, and readers as iterations of similar groups. Attending to gaps between my experience and those at SoniCo and The Future required that I extend myself to their experiences, to allow their work to interrogate my own just as much as I attempted to interrogate them. This may seem quite standard, methodologically speaking, but I think it's a point in the process of being forgotten.

Second, and following from this first point, organizational structure further mediated my already gendered access, varying between two relatively flat, male-dominated organizations within male-dominated industries. The Future seemed actively to prohibit women from entering certain parts of the organization despite the company's apparent diversity. SoniCo had few female employees, but the women who did work there occupied roles in all parts of the organization, even if they ended up leaving more quickly than their male counterparts, in part because of the overwhelmingly masculine work culture. In the end, different microsocial processes resulted in the reproduction of male dominance within the culture industries. Sure, the guys at SoniCo were heteronormatively masculine in their mostly male workplace, but at The Future, despite the company's diversity in terms of gender, race, and sexuality, men had been more overtly misogynistic, quite literally relegating women to the back of the room in some instances. Just as my informants and I were differently similar, these two sites differed, even in their similarity.

NOTES

1. CREATIVE CONTROL?

1. See, e.g., Bell (1976); Castells (2010); Florida (2002); Hardt (2005); Reich (1991).
2. Florida (2002); Reich (1991).
3. Kealy (1979).
4. Here I am referring to a loosely assimilable set of political, social, and media theorists (e.g., Boutang 2011; Fuchs 2011; Marazzi 2011) who tend to take the "social factory" thesis (i.e., we are always working, even when not at work) put forth by Italian autonomist Marxism (see Tronti 2019 [1966]; see also Hardt and Negri 2001, 2005) as a key orienting problematic. The capture of value generated by networks of workers and nonworkers (e.g., social media users) and their cognitive-linguistic skills (what I am calling creative labor) tend to be the generative locus of value under "cognitive capitalism."
5. Berardi (2009).
6. Mills (1951).
7. Hochschild (2003 [1982]).
8. Braverman (1974).
9. E.g., Aneesh (2009); Huws (2014).
10. Paul Willis (1990) calls this "symbolic creativity." I use this definition because it remains adequately generic so as to encompass all the work examined during the ethnographic research that informs this book and, as mentioned in this chapter, as a way of gesturing toward the rather fraught history of the term "creativity."
11. Adorno (1991, 47).
12. Willis (1978); see also Hall and Jefferson (1975); Hebdige (1978).
13. Lloyd (2006).

14. Boltanski and Chiapello (2005).
15. Burawoy (1982).
16. Menger (1999).
17. Mears (2011, 69, emphasis added).
18. Gell (1992).
19. E.g., Horkheimer and Adorno (1947); Kracauer (1963).
20. Williams (1978).
21. E.g., Massumi (2002); Clough and Halley (2007); Sedgwick and Frank (2003); Ahmed (2006); Stewart (2007); Gregg and Seigworth (2010a, 2010b); see Leys (2011); Mazzarella (2010) for critique.
22. Strati (2003, 54).
23. Massumi (2015).
24. Durkheim (1995); see Mazzarella (2017a); Barnwell (2017) for discussions of Durkheim vis-à-vis affect theory.
25. See Mazzarella (2017a); Newell (2018); Rutherford (2016).
26. Gagliardi (1996).
27. Cetina and Bruegger (2002).
28. Burawoy (1998).
29. Hirsch (1972).
30. Gillespie (2010); Terranova (2017).
31. Chambers et al. (2018).
32. There are, of course, terrific studies of cultural production and creative work based on rigorous participant observation (e.g., Frenette 2013; Mears 2011; Ross 2004), but more often this line of research draws primarily from interviews, leaving the labor process behind (e.g., Gerber 2017; Gregg 2011; Hesmondhalgh and Baker 2011).
33. I made field recordings of the sound at both fieldsites and conducted a weekly survey while at The Future. The field recordings guided informed my interview questions regarding workplace aesthetics. Edited versions of these recordings may be heard at the Sound Ethnography Project website (soundethnography.com). I based the survey instrument on the workplace affect survey reported in Theresa Amabile's study of affect and creativity (2005) as well as on several open-ended questions about what workers found enjoyable or unenjoyable about the days on which they responded to the survey. By no means representative in a statistical sense, I used the data primarily to guide my observation, develop interview questions, and develop a rough estimate of average job tenure. In their open-ended responses, employees frequently identified their day-to-day tasks as what they most enjoyed about their work. This influenced my decision to focus on the minutiae of those tasks when I discuss work's positive pole.
34. Powell (1990); see also Adler (2001).
35. Caldwell (2008); Curtin and Sanson (2016); Gill and Pratt (2008); Ross (2009).
36. See Burawoy (1985).
37. Miège (1989), but note that Raymond Williams made a similar observation in *Sociology of Culture* (1981), wherein he developed a typology of cultural production not wholly unlike that put forth by Miège.
38. See Srnicek (2016) for discussion of platforms' reliance upon "network effects."

2. CONFLICTING CREATIVITIES

1. Examples of the positivist study of creativity may be found in psychology (e.g., Amabile et al. 2005; Csikszentmihalyi 1990) and economic sociology's business school variant (e.g., Godart, Seong, and Phillips 2020). These approaches endeavor to measure creativity, most often in hopes of providing managers with levers by which they might increase workers' creativity. The recent "sociological" version of this research trajectory strikes me as especially problematic insofar as the authors argue for a "sociology of creativity" focused on the "central" question of market outcomes for products, claiming that "creativity" emerges only in the social relationship between buyer and seller. In their effort to treat creativity as a social process, they emphasize a single set of nested market relationships between consumers, distributors, and cultural intermediaries while ignoring the social processes involved in production. Ultimately, this managerial line of research reproduces a fetishist view of cultural products, one devoid of labor.
2. Deuze (2019, 132).
3. For secular fundamentalism, see, e.g., Boellstorff (2010); Comaroff and Comaroff (2000); Gielen (2013). For the advertising industry, see Frank (1998). And for Silicon Valley, see Barbrook and Cameron (1995).
4. Boltanski and Chiapello (2005).
5. I.e., Kozlowski, Kurant, and Sowa (2014); Raunig, Ray, and Wuggenig (2011).
6. McRobbie (2016).
7. Adler (2001); Damarin (2013); Tolbert (2001); Hesmondhalgh and Baker (2011).
8. Fouch (2006); Mayer (2011); Pang (2012); Willis (1990).
9. See Irani (2015b, 2015a,(2019); Mayer (2011); Pang (2012).
10. Dijck (2013); Gillespie (2010); Srnicek (2016); Zysman and Kenney (2014).
11. See, e.g., Schumpeter (2008 [1942]); Adorno (2004 [1968]); Bourdieu (1993).
12. Williams (1983).
13. Joas and Sennett (2002).
14. Joas (1997).
15. Marx (1978a, 77).
16. Marx (1978b, 160).
17. E.g., Hall and Jefferson (1975); Hebdige (1978); Willis (1990).
18. Dewey (2005, 63–64.)
19. Dewey (2005, 64).
20. Dewey (2005, 78–79).
21. Kant (1951).
22. Vaneigem (2001 [1968]).
23. Boltanski and Chiapello (2005, 203).
24. See Lazzarato (2011) for critique.
25. For all that is made about the artistic critique's emphasis on *styles* of life by Boltanski and Chiapello, it should be noted that Vaneigem makes a forceful argument that the critique presented by art must defend itself against its "weakest, most aesthetic side" (Vaneigem 2001, 201).
26. Vaneigem (2001, 91).
27. Vaneigem (2001, 202, 55, 159–62).

28. Guy Debord's (1981) creation of "situations" or Vaneigem's (2001, 202) microsocieties of passionate, unmediated living are just two examples.
29. Vaneigem (2001, 55).
30. Schumpeter (2008, 142, 132).
31. William Whyte made a similar argument in *Organization Man* (1956), in which he voiced concerns over growing corporate and state bureaucracies as stifling entrepreneurship.
32. Adorno (2004, 32–33).
33. Amin and Thrift (2013); Nowotny (2011).
34. Florida (2002, 38, 39, 16).
35. Amabile et al. (2005, 38).
36. Amabile et al. (2005, 38).
37. Gielen (2013, 95).
38. Joas, Sennett, and Gimmler (2006, 12).
39. Gielen (2012, 95).
40. Gielen (2013, 94); see also Sewell (1998).
41. Gielen (2013, 94).
42. McRobbie (2016).
43. See Arthur and Rousseau (2001).
44. Mears (2011); Menger (1999).
45. Bourdieu (1993); see also Caves (2000).
46. Venturi, Izenour, and Brown (1977).
47. Friedman (1977).
48. Virno (2004).
49. See, e.g., Fuchs (2010, 2011).
50. As explained to me by other, more accommodating informants, the refusal to be recorded stems from a more general avoidance of transparency and documentation in media and entertainment. For example, older executives and managers tended to favor phone calls over email because email leaves a trace of the conversation, one to which they might be held accountable.
51. Here I mean to indicate those professions such as law and medicine discussed at length by Abbott (1988). I do not indicate the particular profession so as to ensure my informant a degree of anonymity.
52. Edwards (1979).
53. See Gillespie (2010); Siciliano (2016).
54. Hern (2016).
55. Hanlon (2006).
56. Rosenblat (2018).
57. "Struggles against chaos," a perennial theme in the creation myths in many religions.
58. Cf. Irani (2015), which fully draws out this point about the interdependence of "creatives" and low-wage, low-status "micro-taskers."
59. Gielen (2013).
60. This distinction appeared more often among those with some degree of artistic training, a finding that suggests that education actually resists rather than reinforces the creativity *dispositif* (cf. McRobbie 2016).
61. Gielen (2013).

62. Virno (2004).
63. I.e., Gielen (2013); Kozlowski, Kurant, and Sowa (2014); Raunig, Ray, and Wuggenig (2011).
64. Kozlowski, Kurant, and Sowa (2014).
65. Gouldner (1982, 246).

3. SONICO'S POSITIVE POLE:
AESTHETIC SUBJECTIVITIES AND CONTROL

1. In *Commodity Aesthetics* (1987), Wolfgang Haug recounts Hannah Arendt's famous report on Adolf Eichmann's trial in Jerusalem to suggest how ideology depends upon a distinctive material culture. As Haug said, "[Eichmann] reports that he was only able to drive away the thoughts of the mass murder—which he himself had organized but could not bear—when he caught sight of the Lemberg railway station. Its image comforted him. Destabilized by the direct experience of bloodshed, he lets himself be reconciled by the aesthetics of the Austrian official baroque. It is as if this architecture were a bandage on the wound which the murder afflicted upon the official murderer" (131).
2. Horning (2013); U.S. Bureau of Labor Statistics (2013b).
3. See Caldwell (2008); Mayer (2011).
4. U.S. Bureau of Labor Statistics (2013a).
5. According to Arne Kalleberg (2011), "good" jobs include control over working hours and exit from work, room for career growth within the organization, and worker input into processes and tasks, along with retirement and health benefits.
6. See, e.g., Fleming and Sturdy (2011); Turco (2016).
7. Gagliardi (1996).
8. Horning (2013, 15).
9. Kealy (1979).
10. Lingo and O'Mahony, (2010).
11. The importance of technology as synecdoche for engineers' skill and quality can be observed in the way that studios tend to advertise. For over forty years, studios have tended to list their arsenals of equipment and previous clients rather than the expertise of their engineering staff. See Kealy (1974, 102).
12. DeNora (2000).
13. See Becker (1982); Finnegan (1989).
14. Rossman, Esparza, and Bonacich (2010).
15. With few exceptions, I consistently found myself more excited by proximity to particular musicians than any employee.
16. An informant referenced the late 1990s science-fiction film *The Matrix*. Partially inspired by Jean Baudrillard's *Simulacra and Simulation* (1981), this film depicts a dystopian future wherein machines enslave humanity by trapping human minds inside the film's titular artificial reality.
17. Though somewhat antiquated, Blauner's (1967) discussion of automation and the belabored arguments that followed clearly illustrate these alternating interpretations of technology.
18. Théberge (2016, 80–83).

19. Cetina and Bruegger (2000).
20. In Edward Kealy's (1974) ethnography of recording engineers in 1970s Chicago, an engineer is asked why he chose to pursue a career in engineering. The engineer said, "Just a feeling. It's hard to describe. It all turned me on. Course all I saw was the glamour, I didn't see the pitfalls then, I knew what it was what I wanted to do. The music board, the recording console looked very impressive. It all turned me on" (85).
21. E.g., Caldwell (2008); see also Anteby (2008).
22. Oldenziel (1999).
23. Goffman (1959).
24. Simondon (2012, 3).
25. Nationally, revenue from recording studios has been increasing steadily for the past twenty years, and, by U.S. Census estimates, more studios exist now than ever before. While no form of steady employment exists, plenty of revenue-generating sessions happen every day in Los Angeles, New York, and other cities across the United States.
26. Here, I refer, implicitly, to Callon and Law (1982), who theorize enrollment as any process by which one set of actors attempts to translate or transform the interests, "desires, motives, and wishes" of another set of actors" (622). Successful enroll-ment processes result in temporary stabilizations of control or order within some domain of social life. Combining this with a key insight from the sociology of art, *aesthetic* enrollment provides a fragile form of control by "aligning particular, spe-cific actors with generic and non-specific modalities of action," as in DeNora (2003, 126).
27. E.g., Burawoy (1982); Roy (1953).
28. Sallaz (2015).
29. Adorno (2004, 14).
30. Burawoy (1982, 87).
31. Chun (2005); Hesmondhalgh and Baker (2011, 132); Quinn (2005).
32. Csikszentmihalyi (1990, 53).
33. Latour (2007); Molotch (2004).
34. Adorno (2004 [1970]); Dewey (2005 [1934]); Gell (1998).
35. Gell (1992, 1998).
36. Gell (1992, 43).
37. Gell (1998).
38. Gell (1998, 52).
39. Gell (1998, 71). Emphasis added.
40. DeNora (2000, 20).
41. The recalcitrant scrivener to which I refer appears in Herman Melville's "Bartleby the Scrivener: A Tale of Wall Street" (1856). In the story, Bartleby says "I'd prefer not to" whenever his employer asks him to perform a task. His boss refuses to fire him, and, for most of the story, Bartleby refuses to leave.
42. See, e.g., Cohen and de Peuter (2018).
43. Turco (2016); Cable, Gino, and Staats (2013); Endrissat, Islam, and Noppeney (2015); Fleming and Sturdy (2011).
44. Cf. Teresa Amabile's study of affect and creativity (2005) and, more critically, Andrew Ross's (2004) description of the tech sector's elaborate parties, which he argues bind workers to the organization.

45. Willis (1978, 178).
46. E.g., Hesmondhalgh and Baker (2011).
47. Duffy and Wissinger (2017).
48. duGay (2005).
49. This differs markedly from the sort of work experiences first emphasized by Roy (1953, 1959) and later theorized by Burawoy as components of control in *Manufacturing Consent* (1982). In both of these classic studies, workplace games played by workers produce what, drawing on John Dewey's aesthetic theory, Roy called "*an experience*"—a memorable experiential moment amid undifferentiated tedium. In Burawoy, these experiences—bolstered by economically interested competition among coworkers and the machinations of management—serve as a form of social control at work. For Dewey, "*an experience*" or memorable moment differs from aesthetic experiences. Dewey (2005 [1932]) defines an experience as aesthetic when "no such distinction of self and object exists in it, since [experience] is aesthetic in the degree to which organism and environment cooperate to institute an experience in which the two are so fully integrated that each disappears" (259). This definition appears instructive in explaining my informants' accounts and draws a sharp line between the experiential components of work delineated in earlier research and the experiences described in this book.
50. Chun (2005); Hesmondhalgh and Baker (2011, 132).
51. Boutang (2011).
52. I.e., Hardt and Negri (2005).

4. SONICO'S NEGATIVE POLE: MITIGATING PRECARITY AND ALIENATED JUDGMENT

1. Here I am referring to the sort of balancing act argument made by Menger (1999), wherein "psychic wages" somehow balance out economic precarity for those in creative careers. This sort of argument may also be seen in research such as Mears's *Pricing Beauty*, wherein symbolic capital somehow fulfils the same role in workers' mental ledgers.
2. Alienation tends to be seen as problematic for at least two reasons. First, classifying some labor as alienated presumes other, nonalienated labor. Whether the latter exists remains a matter of debate. Second, and more importantly, alienation from a "self" presumes a certain stable, singular self. Costas and Fleming (2009) argue that alienation in current work contexts ought to be thought of as alienation from personal narratives of the self, which change and evolve. Following from this, I define alienation as an objective subordination of creative labor and workers' perceived distance between their preferences and the ends to which they put their creative labor.
3. Lukács (1971); Horkheimer and Adorno (2007 [1947]); Boutang (2011); Vercellone (2007); see also Gill and Pratt (2008). With the "social factory" hypothesis, I am referring to Mario Tronti's *Operai e Capitale*, from 1966, in which he argued that "the specific traits of the factory are lost amid the generic traits of society," when "all of social production is turned into industrial production" (2019, 27). "When capital has conquered all of the territories external to capitalist production,"

capital must "possess [labor power] ever more totally," and so subjectivity becomes the focal concern of capitalist control, a process Tronti called capital's "inner-colonization" (31–32).

4. Kalleberg (2009). Unions represent only 6.7 percent of all workers in the U.S. private sector (Bureau of Labor Statistics 2016). From 2000 to 2015, union representation in culture industries saw a 7 percent decline, from 16 percent to 9 percent (Bureau of Labor Statistics (2015).

5. Ross (2009).

6. Hesmondhalgh and Baker (2011).

7. Menger (1999); Barley and Kunda (2011); Hesmondhalgh and Baker (2010).

8. de Peuter (2011, 419); see also Sennett (2000).

9. See, e.g., Hardt and Negri (2005); Huws (2014); Standing (2016).

10. Situationist International (1981, 85), emphasis added.

11. Boutang (2011, 133).

12. Wright (1998).

13. Boutang (2011).

14. Fuchs (2010, 2011, 2013).

15. duGay (2005).

16. Neff (2012); Umney and Kretsos (2015).

17. Levitt and Venkatesh (2000).

18. André Benjamin, the occasional movie star and vocalist for the hip-hop group Outkast.

19. Berg and Penley (2016).

20. See Deuze (2007, 194); Storey, Salaman, and Platman (2005).

21. Storey et al. (2005).

22. Gershon (2017).

23. Foucault (2010); Boutang (2011); Virno (2004).

24. Foucault (2010, 224–25).

25. See Caldwell (2008); Mayer (2011).

26. Emily Lazar was the first woman to win a Grammy for production for her work on Beck's *Colors*.

27. Mix engineers, as opposed to recording or session engineers, handle postproduction "mixing" of a song's constitutive tracks (i.e., bass, guitar, drums, synthesizers, etc.).

28. Berlant (2011).

29. Standing (2016).

30. Barley and Kunda (2011); Sallaz (2015); Standing (2016).

31. Granovetter (1973); Rossman, Esparza, and Bonacich (2010).

32. Reflecting its location within a global city, the studio frequently worked with musician clients from the United Kingdom, Europe, Asia, and Australia, though clients from California were most common.

33. Sallaz's (2015) study of post-Fordist call centers suggests that consent may be entirely absent from contemporary labor processes, with management aiming to only elicit effort. Workers temporarily expend an incredible amount of effort before finally giving up and leaving. While my findings exhibit some similarity, I find a partial, fragile form of consent in the attachment that workers develop to work's materiality and their coworkers.

34. Berlant (2011, 27).
35. See, e.g., Melissa Gregg (2011) and Andrew Ross (2004), along with Luc Boltanski and Evé Chiapello on workplace participation (2005).
36. I.e., emotional and creative labor; see Hardt and Negri (2005).
37. E.g., Hesmondhalgh and Baker (2011). Hardt and Negri's (2005) painfully slim discussion of the topic in *Multitude* illustrates this fairly well: "Alienation was always a poor concept for understanding the exploitation of factory workers, but here in a realm [the regime of immaterial labor] that many still do not want to consider labor—affective labor, as well as knowledge production and symbolic production—alienation does provide a useful conceptual key for understanding exploitation" (111).
38. Despite Mills's (1951, 150) keen observation regarding the subjugation of "intellectual" or creative labor to the demands of industry, his discussion of "self-alienation" in *White Collar* focuses primarily on the alienation of personality among sales and service staff—something more clearly stated in Hochschild's *Managed Heart*.
39. This may be found in both management research—e.g., Adler and Obstfeld (2007); Amabile et al. (2005)—and in theorizations of "cognitive capitalism": Boutang (2011); Lazzarato (2014).
40. My claim is only that workers' judgment serves organizational or clients' needs, not those of the worker. However, in a less grand way, this appears similar to remarks made by Horkheimer and Adorno in the *Dialectic of Enlightenment* (2007 [1947]). For them, technology and mass media deformed or nullified human capacities for critical thinking, a hypothesis for which I find no support. As they said, "On the way from mythology to logistics, thought has lost the element of reflection on itself, and machinery mutilates people today. . . . In the form of machines, however *alienated reason* is moving toward a society which reconciles thought" to form an unreal unity (29, emphasis added). Similarly grand and problematic, Horkheimer (1947) claimed that "Reason as an organ for perceiving the true nature of reality and determining the guiding principles of our lives has come to be regarded as obsolete" (18).
41. See Bourdieu (1993).
42. Blauner (1967). See, e.g., Hull, Friedman, and Rogers (1982); Leiter (1985); Vallas and Yarrow (1987).
43. Blauner (1967, 27).
44. Blauner (1967, 27).
45. See, e.g., Paul Willis's *Common Culture* (1990), "audience studies" research such as Jenkins's *Textual Poachers* (1992), and the innumerable books and articles that build upon this line of research.
46. Bourdieu (2000); Kant (1951).
47. DeNora (2000).
48. Berlant (2011, 35).
49. Adorno (2004, 15); emphasis added.
50. For example, Lukács (1971) claimed that workers' (journalists) creative abilities "are reduced to an abstract mechanism functioning autonomously and divorced both from the personality of their 'owner'" (100). Like the early Frankfurt School, Lukács presents reified or alienated thought as a permanent mental deformation caused by capitalism.

51. Weber (1978, 25).
52. Knights (1990).
53. Melissa Gregg makes a similar point in *Counterproductive* (2018), where she argues that self-reflection (e.g., meditation or "mindfulness" practices) provides a similar way of escaping or resisting labor processes that demand round-the-clock attention.
54. Massumi (2002, 2015).
55. Kant (1986, 165).

5. THE FUTURE'S POSITIVE POLE: PLATFORM DISCIPLINE, TRANSIENCE, AND IMMERSION

1. Other firms in the field refer to this as "white glove" service (Craig and Cunningham 2019).
2. The Future's focus on metrics may seem similar to a variety of industries wherein companies track products digitally via barcodes, data entry, and other forms of monitoring. These along with "algocratic" regimes (see Aneesh 2009) and the more general practice of accounting are, in fact, means of quantifying, tracking, and, ultimately, controlling labor. The differences between those practices and what I observed at The Future hinge upon the use of platform-based technologies. First, as a cloud-based infrastructure, platforms possess the ability to alter or remove these quantifications without warning and explanation. Imagine how different life might be if the manufacturers of barcode scanners retained the ability to instantaneously invalidate all forms of barcodes without warning. The power of the platform's metrics differ in speed, scale, and scope (Gillespie 2010, 2014; Srnicek 2016; see also Siciliano 2016a). Second, and following from the first difference, the structural relationship differs insofar as the platform—as infrastructure—embeds the interests of the platform's owners within the practices of all individuals and organizations that make use of the technology. Third, and more specific to cultural production, the platform's metrics tend to reduce the value of cultural products to popularity. This, in turn, alters the conditions of possibility for a field of cultural production's autonomy vis-à-vis market logics (cf. Bourdieu 1993).
3. Turkle (1997).
4. Turkle (1997, 62).
5. Burgess et al. (2009); Jenkins (2006).
6. Scholz (2013).
7. Wallenstein (2012).
8. If you are unfamiliar with this firm, have no fear. As an executive from Bertelsmann explained at an industry conference, "If none of you have had heard of us, you've gone to college with us." Their subsidiaries include Penguin Books and its Penguin Classics imprint.
9. Ball (2014); Cooper (2014).
10. YouTube (2017).
11. Dallas Smythe (1977) and critical communication scholars call these saleable representations of audiences the "audience commodity" (see also Napoli 2003).

12. Though this agreement officially prohibits discussion of wages, creators frequently discuss CPM and MCN contracts on numerous online discussion boards such as Reddit's "YTPartnered" forum.

13. I first noticed this change in May 2017 when creators first started to tell me about how they had been affected by changes in YouTube's content moderation policies. Before this, informants mostly talked about removal because of alleged copyright violations, but after 2016, informants began discussing removals due to violation of community guidelines. This occurred just as the platform's algorithmic moderation systems began flagging and removing right-wing extremist and white supremacist videos. My informants described how their videos were removed without warning, explanation, or pathway to appeal. YouTube simply stated that the video violated community guidelines, but never which guideline.

14. YouTube refused to share summary statistics when I contacted them. An automated email response from the platform said, "We're sorry that we cannot interface with you directly, but please check our press website." Many of my informants described similarly one-sided interactions with Google.

15. Caves (2000).

16. See Zysman and Kenney (2014).

17. Data for YouTube as a whole remains unavailable. Publicly available data on the Top 5,000 YouTube channels from Socialblade.com (2017) illustrate a similar "superstar" distribution; however, the 5,000 largest channels represent a different range, wherein the bottom 10 percent corresponds to the median channel size among creators with whom I spoke. The channel sizes of my informants ranged from 35 to just over 1,000,000, with a median of 54,616.

18. Weiss (2020).

19. Jones (2020); Rosenblat (2018).

20. In short, YouTube creators may be considered what Michael Hardt and Antonio Negri (2005) call a "multitude," or a potentially political collectivity that retains difference. As a concept this differs from "the masses," a "crowd," or a "mob," wherein individual difference tends to thought of as absent (e.g., "mob mentality" or the mass/individual dichotomy).

21. Grint and Woolgar (1997); Chun (2011).

22. Cetina (2009); Cetina and Bruegger (2002).

23. Mazzarella (2017); see also Durkheim (1995).

24. Foucault (2012); Haraway (1991); Chun (2011).

25. Exerting power through structures of information follows a more general managerial trend of focusing workers' attention, often by way of technology, in lieu of direct or bureaucratic control (Rennstam 2012; Sewell 2005). The training programs coexist with guides to YouTube success published by third parties, which began to appear early on in YouTube's existence. These earlier guides often served the purpose of educating users on the professional practices of video making (Müller 2009), and so the guidebooks included technical advice on lighting, editing, and the use of cameras. At the time, the platform made few if any attempts at educating and disciplining the production of content. Instead, YouTube presented itself by and large as "a cultural space of community building and shared experiences" (Müller 2009, 126). Even if users tended to adopt entrepreneurial strategies

for success (Burgess and Green 2009; Vonderau 2009), these strategies were not actively promoted by the platform until later.

26. Burgess and Green (2009, 97).

27. Karpik's judgment device (2010) may be thought of as a subtype of what Muniesa, Millo, and Callon (2007) refer to as "market devices," or objects that reduce or mediate uncertainty in order to enable market transactions to occur. In Karpik, judgment devices tend to be more closely associated with relatively singular commodities with radically uncertain use and exchange values, such as books, music, and films.

28. Burgess et al. (2009, 89), emphasis added.

29. See Siciliano (2016).

30. Callon (1998).

31. Cf. Craig and Cunningham (2019).

32. Bourdieu (1993).

33. See, e.g., Gray and Suri (2019); Jones (2020).

34. Baym (2015); Duffy (2017); Craig and Cunningham (2019).

35. Marx (1978b, 279).

36. Gell (1998, 74).

37. Lazzarato (2014, 51).

38. Hesmondhalgh and Baker (2011); Bourdieu (1993); McRobbie (2016); Mears (2011).

39. At first, I thought Nadine's lack of enthusiasm might stem from the more general, historically specific masculinization of technology (Oldenziel 1999): "Boys and their toys." I found this explanation less satisfactory in part because of the passion for technology described by several of The Future's female employees introduced later in this chapter and by Wanda, the female engineer from chapter 3. Considered together, these data suggest that occupational training, not simply gender, explains differences in orientation toward technology. Nadine even said as much while highlighting her preference for videogames, another traditionally masculine activity, over production equipment: "A lot of YouTubers that are my friends came from a film or camera, audio background so they get really excited about that. I'm just like 'Nah, I'd rather play video games.'"

40. Cf. Amabile et al. (2005); Csikszentmihalyi (1990).

41. Suchman (2007, 246).

42. Suchman (2007) further emphasizes this point in her discussion of Susanne Bødker's analysis of interfaces: "[Bødker] observes that when unfamiliar, or at times of trouble, the interface itself becomes the work's object. At other times persons work, as she puts it, 'through the interface,' enacted as a transparent means of engagement with other objects of interest (for example, a text or an interchange with relevant others)" (279).

43. Ben Highmore (2010), in his discussion of everyday aesthetics, argues that to be distracted is to be attracted and focused elsewhere.

44. Virno (2004, 93).

45. Strati (2003, 54); Massumi (2002); Lazzarato (2014, 31, 124); Gregg and Seigworth (2010, 1); Warren (2008).

46. Roy (1953); Burawoy (1982); Baker (1991).

47. Studies of capitalist labor processes typically center on "games" developed by workers in order to make their jobs meaningful—most famously the "making out"

game played by machinists in Burawoy's *Manufacturing Consent* (1982). Pursuing immersive, aesthetic experiences forms part of the game for creative labor, not unlike Benjamin Snyder's (2016) claim that pursuing moments of "flow" or "unification" form the "work-games for financial workers" (166).

48. Job tenure in the United States averages 4.6 years across all occupations. As of 2016, the average length of employment was 2.4 years in the sound and film industries and four years within information industries as a whole (U.S. Bureau of Labor Statistics 2016).

49. Lazzarato (2014, 119).

50. This dovetails rather well with findings that suggest that enterprise software like Salesforce and other ICTs capture workers' knowledge, which makes them less irreplaceable (Griffith, Sawyer, and Neale 2003; Klobas and Jackson 2007).

51. Arthur and Rousseau (2001).

52. Caldwell (2008, 324).

53. Pasquale (2015, 85).

54. Cable, Gino, and Staats (2013); Fleming and Sturdy (2011).

55. Grimes (2011).

56. Saval (2015, 274–75).

57. Zafirau (2007).

58. Ross (2004).

59. Gregg (2011); Snyder (2016); Wajcman (2016).

60. In contrast to U.S. workers, European workers collectively bargained for a stop to constant communication and recently proposed labor legislation calls for workers' "right to disconnect" (*Economist* 2014; *USA Today* 2014; *Washington Post* 2016).

61. Highmore (2010, 128). My reference here, obviously, is to Simmel (1995), who made a similar argument regarding modernity in his discussions of sensory perception and cities while also making an early claim regarding the sociological importance of the sense in general (see Swedberg 2011).

62. It is also common in the industry to celebrate the relative cheapness of digital video content—especially American-produced, English-language content. Most brands that choose to advertise with The Future and similar firms prefer English-speaking audiences. As a venture capital investor told the audience at the 2015 VidCon industry conference, U.S. content "travels well."

63. Over seventy years ago, Horkheimer and Adorno (2007) observed a similar process of dividing up consumers: "On the charts of research organizations, indistinguishable from those of political propaganda, consumers are divided up as statistical material into red, green and blue areas according to income group" (131).

64. Most writings on work and labor ignore the relation between media and work. For example, Michael Burawoy, in his classic ethnographic study reported in *Manufacturing Consent* (1982), argues explicitly against the importance of the broader media environment as a mode of social control over work. In reference to Frankfurt School–style neo-Marxism, Burawoy argues that the alteration of cognition and the modern sensorium associated with media or the "culture industry" has not "managed to shape our very character in accordance with its rationality." He goes on to state that "just as in the turn to the state, so in the turn to psychology the transformation of the labor process gets left behind" (201). In contrast, The Future's dense sensory environment resembles that of everyday life in the world's

overdeveloped nations. This situation echoes a classic, if slightly overstated, passage from Horkheimer and Adorno's *Dialectic of Enlightenment* (2007) wherein the "culture industry" fulfills "the single purpose of imposing on the sense of human beings, from the time they leave the factory in the evening to the time they clock on in the morning, the imprint of the work routine which they must sustain throughout the day" (104).

65. Johnson, Voce, and Garberg (2017).

66. Cash (2011); Gahan (2014).

67. E.g., Marx (1978a, 1978b); see also Sennett (2000, 2007). Blauner (1967).

68. Siciliano (2016).

69. Amabile et al. (2005).

70. E.g. Burawoy (1982); Roy (1953); Baker (1991).

71. For example, Cetina and Bruegger (2000, 2002) describe the experiences of stockbrokers in much the same way: pleasurable immersion in a world "appresented" or made interactively present by way of a screen. These experiences bind or "attach" workers to tasks.

72. Boutang (2011); Lazzarato (2014).

73. What I am suggesting here is that these disciplinary vectors reconfigure the oft-made distinction between "art for art's sake" (autonomous art) and commercially oriented production (heteronymous art) that exists in a variety of fields, including journalism, fashion, popular music, and, most obviously, fine art (see, e.g., Benson and Neveu 2005; Bourdieu 1993; Mears 2011; Negus 1999; O'Connor 2008). Aside from metrics, the field of YouTube production lacks other modes of valuation aside from quantitative success, and so, again, the ideology of "art for art's sake" does little to explain why creators desire to be precarious, subordinate entrepreneurs. The various disciplinary vectors described in this chapter simultaneously orient creators toward quantified measurements of audiences' desires and invite creators to take on an entrepreneurial disposition. Creators, insofar as the platform is concerned, appear always already heteronymous or, as I have been saying, subordinated, quantified, and bound by global, technological infrastructures. YouTube's quantified invitation to "be creative" may be linked to "an ideology that, above all, privileges self-expression *and* self-efficacy in the perpetual reimagining and rebranding of the subject," (Rey 2012, 410); however, this ideology depends upon and exists within an infrastructural context that encourages creators to produce content in algorithmically recognizable forms tailored to audiences' quantified desires and advertisers' economic concerns.

74. Porter (1996).

75. Cf. Duffy and Wissinger (2017) and McRobbie (2016), wherein this ideology seems to function indpependently of any particular material experience.

76. Cf. Hardt (2005); Hardt and Negri (2001, 2005); Virno (2004).

6. THE FUTURE'S NEGATIVE POLE: COMPOUND PRECARITY AND THE (INFRA)STRUCTURE OF ALIENATED JUDGMENT

1. YouTube has made limited moves toward wage transparency in recent years by releasing guides to "monetization." These guides resemble the various training

materials described in chapter 5 and, as of the summer of 2020, do not explain how the platform determines payrates.

2. "Millennial" generally refers to young people born sometime during the early 1980s and the mid-1990s. During my fieldwork at The Future, Katherine was twenty-four, and I was thirty-three. Though nearly ten years separated us, we were both what many consider to be Millennials. Curiously, neither of us felt an affinity for the term. Many of the staff at The Future were Millennials, but they used the term to denote someone that was younger, self-absorbed, internet-obsessed, and unwilling to work. No one is a Millennial, and yet everyone loathes them, even Millennials.

3. Umney and Kretsos (2015).

4. In the fall of 2019, California passed legislation that may force some platforms to recognize their contractors as employees. The bill takes aim chiefly at ridesharing and delivery services such as Uber, Lyft, and Amazon. How this law affects YouTube's creators remains to be seen, but this does highlight how resistance to platform-based employment requires, first, government regulation.

5. Standing (2016).

6. Craig and Cunningham (2019).

7. According to those with whom I worked at The Future, "brand integrations" differ from traditional product placements or sponsorships insofar as the content revolves around the product rather than being merely inserted into unrelated content. An "integration" differs from a normal advertisement or product placement insofar as the product to be promoted appears fully "integrated" in the content produced. Creators do not simply hold up a bottle of Coca-Cola or announce the availability of an iPhone so much as they build original content that revolves around a branded good or service. These integrations may be as simple as an entire video that explains how to use some particular computer accessory to short CGI films that utilize characters from existing intellectual properties to tell new, original stories.

8. This complicates Angela McRobbie's (2016) recent assertion that higher education in the arts serves as a key instrument or vector of discipline. Instead, the platform, The Future, and, more broadly, media consumption (i.e., other creators' YouTube content) generate value as they discipline creative labor.

9. Duffy (2017).

10. Virno (2004, 65).

11. Virno (2001).

12. Sallaz (2015). To some, my conclusion may seem to be an overgeneralization, one that ignores the complex interplay of class, race, and gender. However, I make this claim based on a diverse group of informants and drawing from several recent ethnographies of platform-based cultural production, which, taken together, illustrate just how widespread these skills may be. Alongside my informants, young black men who make "drill" music (Stuart 2020); people of color and white people who perform online sex work, or "camming" (Jones 2020); and women who earn money as "influencers" (Duffy 2017) all acquired these generic technological skills in the course of their everyday lives and continued to develop their skills as they went along, often in the ways I describe here.

13. Virno (2001).

14. McRobbie (2016); see also Deleuze and Guattari (1987).
15. See Gregg (2011); Wajcman (2016); Wajcman and Rose (2011).
16. Barley and Kunda (2011).
17. Caldwell (2008).
18. Officially, I occupied an intern position. Many employees and a few managers consistently brought my name up during meetings as a potential internal hire. They also frequently encouraged me to submit my resume. I never did this for methodological and ethical reasons. First, my intern position enabled me to move with relative freedom throughout the offices. Second, it seemed hardly appropriate to take a position away from the small army of other interns and job applicants waiting for a job at The Future. Still, my coworkers generally seemed hopeful that I would take up work in the "space" and continued to volunteer my name whenever openings arose. On my last day, one manager said, "You better apply for a job here when you're done with that PhD!"
19. Cf. Gouldner (1964).
20. Cf. Becker (1982); Bourdieu (1993).
21. Becker (1963).
22. See Duffy (2017).
23. At the time, the platform notified a channel's subscribers when new content had been posted to a channel, increasing the likelihood of viewing. YouTube later stopped notifying subscribers and by 2018, during my second visit VidCon, creators were justifiably annoyed, voicing their concerns in many of the conference's creator-led panels.
24. Madrigal (2018); Gerardi (2017); Wamsley (2017).
25. Fisher and Taub (2019); Lewis (2018); Tufekci (2018).
26. Albergotti (2020); Nover and Winicov (2020); See also Noble (2018).
27. Farrow (2017).
28. Fine and Soucey (2005); Lerum (2004); Linstead (1985); Plester (2009).
29. Eikhof and Warhurst (2013); Hennekam and Bennett (2017); Hesmondhalgh and Baker (2015).
30. To "work a desk" is industry terminology for answering someone's phone calls while managing their digital calendar. For example, an assistant to an executive might be said to "work at the desk" of that executive.
31. E.g., Ross (2004).
32. See Siciliano (2016).

7. TOWARD A THEORY OF CREATIVE LABOR AND A POLITICS OF JUDGMENT

1. Berardi (2009); Sennett (2000).
2. Alexander (2019); Weiss (2019).
3. Durkheim (1995).
4. To this, there may be at least two critiques. First, I recognize a distinct possibility that I could be accused of committing a rather serious offense: universalizing the experiences of U.S. workers. This is by no means my intention, and that is why I refer to this theory as a map or, perhaps better, a set of markers meant to aid in

making sense of the current situation in which creative labor finds itself. Particular political economies will, of course, contain distinctive assemblages of these markers, but, nevertheless, I think this map may prove conceptually relevant beyond the empirical contexts from which my theoretical points emerged. The second, perhaps less consequential, criticism may come from fellow ethnographers, especially those who bristle at the mere mention of "capitalism" or any other macrolevel abstraction when discussing ethnographic observations. I ask those scholars to please note the level of detail in my ethnographic rendering of work while reading with an open mind.

5. Boutang (2011).
6. Mould (2018).
7. Vercellone (2005).
8. Fuchs (2014, 268).
9. Virno (2004).
10. Scholz (2016).
11. George Lukács famously criticized the Frankfurt School as being a bit too comfortable in their contemplation of what Adorno called "damaged life." Lukács called them residents of the "Grand Hotel Abyss," happy to theorize but not to change the world. While I do not fully agree with Lukács, I do think a variety of critical theorists, some Marxist, some not, paint rather hopeless pictures of seamless capitalisms. As Fredric Jameson writes in *Postmodernism, or The Cultural Logic of Late Capitalism*, "Insofar as the theorist wins, therefore, by constructing an increasingly closed and terrifying machine . . . he loses, since the critical capacity of his work is thereby paralyzed . . . and the impulses of negation and revolt . . . are increasingly seen as vain or trivial in the face of the model itself" (1990, 5).
12. Berardi (2009); e.g., Gregg (2011); Ross (2004, 2009, 2013).
13. Here, I refer to aesthetic labor, a term that emerged from the research literature on organizational aesthetics. Anne Witz and her colleagues (2003) describe organizational aesthetics as a combination of artifacts/objects/technologies and workers. Over the last decade, sociologists of labor focused on aesthetic labor to great effect, but at the expense of theorizing the relationship between labor and objects in organizational life (e.g., Gruys 2012; Williams and Connell 2010).
14. Massumi (2002, 2015); Berardi (2009); Hardt and Negri (2005).
15. See Gill and Pratt (2008) for review and critique.
16. Bucher (2018).
17. To be clear, my argument for a politics of judgment is an argument for workers' ability to determine the ends to which they put their means, essentially a call for workers' creative control rather than capitalist control over creative labor. The mention of judgment in contrast to a politics of affect may cause some to recall Deleuze's (1998) discussion of judgment, in which he said, "Judgment prevents the emergence of any new mode of existence. . . . What expert judgment, in art, could ever bear on the work to come?" (135). There, he seemed to be taking issue with institutional judgments, the heavy hands of bureaucrats and other "expert" authorities of the state. As he went on to say in the same paragraph, "It is not a question of judging other existing beings, but of sensing whether they agree or disagree with us, that is, whether they bring forces to us, or whether they return us to the miseries of war, to the poverty of the dream, to the rigors of organization."

Though open to interpretation, Deleuze clearly stands against judgments of the state and powerful institutions, of those who might prevent the building of new ways of being, new assemblages for living. I take no issue with such a stance, only that people deserve some say as to the desirability of those new assemblages, a chance to reflect upon their sensed (dis)agreement.

18. Bourdieu (2000).
19. See Lazzarato (2011).
20. Turco (2016).
21. Mazzarella (2010, 299).
22. Dijck, Poell, and Waal (2018).
23. Conger and Scheiber (2020).
24. Grazian (2019).
25. Srnicek (2016).
26. Bourdieu (1993).
27. Taylor (2014).
28. Couldry and Hepp (2018); Dijck, Poell, and Waal (2018, 2).
29. Biernacki (1997).
30. Cf. Rosenblat (2018).
31. See Gregg (2011); Snyder (2016); Wajcman (2016); Wajcman and Rose (2011).
32. E.g., Scholz (2016); Srnicek (2016); Taylor (2014).
33. Lewis (2018).
34. Standing (2014); Scholz (2016); Srnicek (2016).
35. Alexander (2019); Ghaffary (2019); Gurley (2019).

METHODOLOGICAL APPENDIX: ATTENDING TO DIFFERENCE IN SIMILARITY AND GENDER'S ACCESS

1. Duffy (2017); Mears (2011); Neff (2012).
2. Grindstaff (2002).
3. Baudrillard (1989).
4. Abu-Lughod (2008).
5. Burawoy (1998).
6. Bennett (2003).
7. See Siciliano (2016).
9. Frenette (2013); Halle (1987).
10. See Siciliano and O'Connor (2012); Varner (2007).
11. Though this accurately describes my experiences, I am also aware of how much this statement echoes Michael Burawoy's *Manufacturing Consent* (1982), in which he discusses participating in shopfloor "games" despite himself.

REFERENCES

Abbott, Andrew. 1988. *The System of Professions: An Essay on the Division of Expert Labor*. Chicago: University of Chicago Press.

Abu-Lughod, Lila. 2008. "'Writing Against Culture.'" *Cultural Geography Reader*, March 3. https://doi.org/10.4324/9780203931950-13.

Adler, Paul S. 2001. "Market, Hierarchy, and Trust: The Knowledge Economy and the Future of Capitalism." *Organization Science* 12 (2): 215–34. https://doi.org/10.1287/orsc.12.2.215.10117.

Adler, Paul S., and David Obstfeld. 2007. "The Role of Affect in Creative Projects and Exploratory Search." *Industrial and Corporate Change* 16 (1): 19–50. https://doi.org/10.1093/icc/dtl032.

Adorno, Theodor W. 1991. "On the Fetish Character in Music and the Regression of Listening." In *The Culture Industry : Selected Essays on Mass Culture*, edited by J. M. Bernstein. London: Routledge.

——. 2004. *Aesthetic Theory*. London: Continuum.

Ahmed, Sara. 2006. *Queer Phenomenology: Orientations, Objects, Others*. Durham, NC: Duke University Press.

Albergotti, Reed. 2020. "Black Creators Sue YouTube, Alleging Racial Discrimination." *Washington Post*, June 18. https://www.washingtonpost.com/technology/2020/06/18/black-creators-sue-youtube-alleged-race-discrimination/.

Alexander, Julia. 2019. "YouTubers' First Organizing Attempt, the Internet Creators Guild, Is Shutting Down." *The Verge*, July 11. https://www.theverge.com/2019/7/11/20688929/internet-creators-guild-shutting-down-hank-green-youtube-copyright-claims-monetization.

Amabile, Teresa M., Sigal G. Barsade, Jennifer S. Mueller, and Barry M. Straw. 2005. "Affect and Creativity at Work." *Administrative Science Quarterly* 50 (3): 367–403. https://doi.org/10.2189/asqu.2005.50.3.367.

Amin, Ash, and Nigel Thrift. 2013. *Arts of the Political: New Openings for the Left*. Durham: Duke University Press.

Aneesh, A. 2009. "Global Labor: Algocratic Modes of Organization." *Sociological Theory* 27 (4): 347–70. https://doi.org/10.1111/j.1467-9558.2009.01352.x.

Anteby, Michel. 2008. "Identity Incentives as an Engaging Form of Control: Revisiting Leniencies in an Aeronautic Plant." *Organization Science* 19 (2): 202–20. https://doi.org/10.1287/orsc.1070.0343.

Arthur, Michael Bernard, and Denise M. Rousseau. 2001. *The Boundaryless Career: A New Employment Principle for a New Organizational Era*. Oxford: Oxford University Press.

Baker, Phyllis. 1991. *Bored and Busy: An Analysis of Formal and Informal Organization in the Automated Office*. New York: Peter Lang International Academic.

Ball, Matthew. 2014. "Redef Original: How YouTube MCNs Are Conquering Hollywood." *Redef*, December 15. http://redef.com/original/how-youtube-mcns-are-conquering-hollywood.

Barbrook, Richard, and Andy Cameron. 1995. "The Californian Ideology." *Mute* (September). http://www.metamute.org/editorial/articles/californian-ideology.

Barley, Stephen R., and Gideon Kunda. 2011. *Gurus, Hired Guns, and Warm Bodies: Itinerant Experts in a Knowledge Economy*. Princeton, NJ: Princeton University Press.

Barnwell, Ashley. 2017. "Durkheim as Affect Theorist." *Journal of Classical Sociology* (May). http://journals.sagepub.com/doi/10.1177/1468795X17702917.

Baudrillard, Jean. 1981. *Simulacra and Simulation*. Trans. Sheila Faria Glaser. Ann Arbor: University of Michigan Press.

——. 1989. *America*. London: Verso.

Baym, Nancy K. 2015. "Connect with Your Audience! The Relational Labor of Connection." *Communication Review* 18 (1): 14–22. https://doi.org/10.1080/10714421.2015.996401.

Becker, Howard Saul. 1963. *Outsiders: Studies in the Sociology of Deviance*. Glencoe, IL: Free Press.

——. 1982. *Art Worlds*. Berkeley: University of California Press.

Bell, Daniel. 1976. *The Coming of Post-Industrial Society: A Venture in Social Forecasting*. Reissue ed. New York: Basic Books.

Bennett, Andy. 2003. "The Use of 'Insider' Knowledge in Ethnographic Research on Contemporary Youth Music Scenes." In *Researching Youth*, ed. Andy Bennett, Mark Cieslik, and Steven Miles, 186–99. London: Palgrave Macmillan UK. https://doi.org/10.1057/9780230522466_12.

Benson, Rodney Dean, and Érik Neveu. 2005. *Bourdieu and the Journalistic Field*. Cambridge: Polity.

Berardi, Franco. 2009. *The Soul at Work: From Alienation to Autonomy*. Los Angeles: Semiotext(e).

Berg, Heather, and Constance Penley. 2016. "Creative Precarity in the Adult Film Industry." In *Precarious Creativity: Global Media, Local Labor*, ed. Michael Curtin and Kevin Sanson, 159–71. Berkeley, CA: University of California Press.

Berlant, Lauren. 2011. *Cruel Optimism*. Durham, NC: Duke University Press.

Biernacki, Richard. 1997. *The Fabrication of Labor Germany and Britain, 1640–1914*. Berkeley: University of California Press.

Blauner, Robert. 1967. *Alienation and Freedom: The Factory Worker and His Industry.* Chicago: University of Chicago Press.

Boellstorff, Tom. 2010. *Coming of Age in Second Life: An Anthropologist Explores the Virtually Human.* Princeton, NJ: Princeton University Press.

Boltanski, Luc, and Ève Chiapello. 2005. *The New Spirit of Capitalism.* London: Verso.

Bourdieu, Pierre. 1993. *The Field of Cultural Production: Essays on Art and Literature.* New York: Columbia University Press.

——. 2000. *Distinction: A Social Critique of the Judgment of Taste.* Cambridge, MA: Harvard University Press.

Boutang, Yann Moulier. 2011. *Cognitive Capitalism.* Cambridge: Polity.

Braverman, Harry. 1974. *Labor and Monopoly Capital: The Degradation of Work in the Twentieth Century.* New York: Monthly Review Press.

Bucher, Taina. 2018. *If . . . Then: Algorithmic Power and Politics.* Oxford: Oxford University Press.

Burawoy, Michael. 1982. *Manufacturing Consent: Changes in the Labor Process Under Monopoly Capitalism.* Chicago: University of Chicago Press.

——. 1985. *The Politics of Production: Factory Regimes Under Capitalism and Socialism.* London: Routledge.

——. 1998. *The Extended Case Method.* Berkeley: University of California Press.

Bureau of Labor Statistics. 2015. "OES Survey Data." 2015. http://data.bls.gov/pdq /SurveyOutputServlet.

——. 2016. "Union Members Summary." 2016. http://www.bls.gov/news.release /union2.nr0.htm.

Burgess, Jean, and Joshua Green. 2009. "The Entrepreneurial Vlogger: Participatory Culture Beyond the Professional-Amateur Divide." In *The YouTube Reader,* ed. Pelle Snickars and Patrick Vonderau, 89–107. Stockholm: National Library of Sweden.

Burgess, Jean, Joshua Green, Henry Jenkins, and John Hartley. 2009. *YouTube: Online Video and Participatory Culture.* Cambridge: Polity.

Cable, Daniel M., Francesca Gino, and Bradley R. Staats. 2013. "Breaking Them In or Eliciting Their Best? Reframing Socialization Around Newcomers' Authentic Self-Expression." *Administrative Science Quarterly* 58 (1): 1–36. https://doi.org/10.1177 /0001839213477098.

Caldwell, John Thornton. 2008. *Production Culture: Industrial Reflexivity and Critical Practice in Film and Television.* Durham, NC: Duke University Press.

Callon, Michel. 1998. "An Essay on Framing and Overflowing: Economics Revisited by Sociology." In *Laws of the Markets,* ed. Michel Callon, 244–69. New York: Wiley.

Callon, Michel, and John Law. 1982. "On Interests and Their Transformation: Enrolment and Counter-Enrolment." *Social Studies of Science* 12 (4): 615–25.

Cash, Hilarie. 2011. "The Online Social Experience and Limbic Resonance." *Psychology Today.* http://www.psychologytoday.com/blog/digital-addiction/201112/the -online-social-experience-and-limbic-resonance.

Castells, Manuel. 2010. *Rise of the Network Society.* Vol. 1 of *The Information Age: Economy, Society, and Culture.* Oxford: Wiley-Blackwell.

Caves, Richard E. 2000. *Creative Industries: Contracts Between Art and Commerce.* Cambridge, MA: Harvard University Press.

Cetina, Karin Knorr. 2009. "The Synthetic Situation: Interactionism for a Global World." *Symbolic Interaction* 32 (1): 61–87. https://doi.org/10.1525/si.2009.32.1.61.

Cetina, Karin Knorr, and Urs Bruegger. 2000. "The Market as an Object of Attachment: Exploring Postsocial Relations in Financial Markets." *Canadian Journal of Sociology* 25 (2): 141–68. https://doi.org/10.2307/3341821.

——. 2002. "Inhabiting Technology: The Global Lifeform of Financial Markets." *Current Sociology* 50 (3): 389–405. https://doi.org/10.1177/0011392102050003006.

Chambers, Nick, Elnaz Kashefpakdel, Jordan Rehill, and Christian Percy. 2018. *Drawing the Future*. London: Education and Employers.

Chun, Wendy Hui Kyong. 2005. "On Software, or the Persistence of Visual Knowledge." *Grey Room* 18:26–51.

——. 2011. *Programmed Visions: Software and Memory*. Cambridge, MA: MIT Press.

Clough, Patricia Ticineto, and Jean Halley, eds. 2007. *The Affective Turn: Theorizing the Social*. Durham, NC: Duke University Press.

Cohen, Nicole S., and Greig de Peuter. 2018. "'I Work at VICE Canada and I Need a Union': Organizing Digital Media." In *Labour Under Attack: Anti-Unionism in Canada*, ed. Stephanie Ross and Larry Savage. Halifax: Fernwood.

Comaroff, Jean, and John L. Comaroff. 2000. "Millennial Capitalism: First Thoughts on a Second Coming." *Public Culture* 12 (2): 291–343.

Conger, Kate, and Noam Scheiber. 2020. "The Great Google Revolt." *New York Times Magazine*, February 19. https://www.nytimes.com/interactive/2020/02/18/magazine/google-revolt.html.

Copeland, Cooper. 2014. "Maker Studios & MCNs: The New Hollywood—Campus Circle." October 2. http://www.campuscircle.com/review.cfm?r=20542.

Costas, Jana, and Peter Fleming. 2009. "Beyond Dis-Identification: A Discursive Approach to Self-Alienation in Contemporary Organizations." *Human Relations* 62 (3): 353–78. https://doi.org/10.1177/0018726708101041.

Couldry, Nick, and Andreas Hepp. 2018. *The Mediated Construction of Reality*. New York: John Wiley & Sons.

Craig, David, and Stuart Cunningham. 2019. *Social Media Entertainment: The New Intersection of Hollywood and Silicon Valley*. New York: New York University Press.

Csikszentmihalyi, Mihaly. 1990. *Flow: The Psychology of Optimal Experience*. New York: Harper Perennial.

Curtin, Michael, and Kevin Sanson. 2016. *Precarious Creativity: Global Media, Local Labor*. Berkeley: University of California Press.

Damarin, Amanda Kidd. 2013. "The Network-Organized Labor Process: Control and Autonomy in Web Production Work." In *Networks, Work and Inequality*, Research in the Sociology of Work 24, 177–205. Emerald Group Publishing Limited.

Debord, Guy. 1981. "Report on the Construction of Situations and on the International Situationist Tendency's Conditions of Organization and Action." In *Situationist International Anthology*, ed. Ken Knabb, 17–28. Bureau of Public Secrets.

Deleuze, Gilles. 1998. "To Have Done with Judgment." In *Essays Critical and Clinical*, 126–35. London: Verso.

Deleuze, Gilles, and Felix Guattari. 1987. *A Thousand Plateaus: Capitalism and Schizophrenia*. Minneapolis: University of Minnesota Press.

DeNora, Tia. 2000. *Music in Everyday Life*. Cambridge: Cambridge University Press.

——. 2003. *After Adorno: Rethinking Music Sociology.* Cambridge: Cambridge University Press.

Deuze, Mark. 2007. *Media Work.* Cambridge: Polity.

——. 2019. "On Creativity." *Journalism* 20 (1): 130–34. https://doi.org/10.1177/1464884918807066.

Dewey, John. 2005. *Art as Experience.* New York: Berkeley.

Dijck, José van. 2013. *The Culture of Connectivity: A Critical History of Social Media.* New York: Oxford University Press.

Dijck, José van, Thomas Poell, and Martijn de Waal. 2018. *The Platform Society: Public Values in a Connective World.* Oxford: Oxford University Press.

Duffy, Brooke Erin. 2017. *(Not) Getting Paid to Do What You Love: Gender, Social Media, and Aspirational Work.* New Haven, CT: Yale University Press.

Duffy, Brooke Erin, and Elizabeth Wissinger. 2017. "Mythologies of Creative Work in the Social Media Age: Fun, Free, and 'Just Being Me.'" *International Journal of Communication* 11:20.

duGay, Paul, ed. 2005. *The Values of Bureaucracy.* Oxford: Oxford University Press.

Durkheim, Émile. 1995. *The Elementary Forms of Religious Life.* Trans. Karen E. Fields. New York: Free Press.

Edwards, Richard C. 1979. *Contested Terrain: The Transformation of the Workplace in the Twentieth Century.* New York: Basic Books.

Economist. 2014. "Not What It Seemed." *Economist,* April 14. http://www.economist.com/blogs/charlemagne/2014/04/frances-6pm-e-mail-ban.

Eikhof, Doris, and Chris Warhurst. 2013. "The Promised Land? Why Social Inequalities Are Systemic in the Creative Industries." *Employee Relations* 35 (5): 495–508. https://doi.org/10.1108/ER-08-2012-0061.

Endrissat, Nada, Gazi Islam, and Claus Noppeney. 2015. "Enchanting Work: New Spirits of Service Work in an Organic Supermarket." *Organization Studies* 36 (11): 1556–76.

Farrow, Ronan. 2017. "From Aggressive Overtures to Sexual Assault: Harvey Weinstein's Accusers Tell Their Stories." *New Yorker,* October 10. https://www.newyorker.com/news/news-desk/from-aggressive-overtures-to-sexual-assault-harvey-weinsteins-accusers-tell-their-stories.

Fine, Gary Alan, and Michaela de Soucey. 2005. "Joking Cultures: Humor Themes as Social Regulation in Group Life." *Humor—International Journal of Humor Research* 18 (1): 1–22. https://doi.org/10.1515/humr.2005.18.1.1.

Finnegan, Ruth. 1989. *The Hidden Musicians: Music-Making in an English Town.* Middletown, CT: Wesleyan University Press.

Fisher, Max, and Amanda Taub. 2019. "On YouTube's Digital Playground, an Open Gate for Pedophiles." *New York Times,* June 4. https://www.nytimes.com/2019/06/03/world/americas/youtube-pedophiles.html.

Fleming, Peter, and Andrew Sturdy. 2011. "'Being Yourself' in the Electronic Sweatshop: New Forms of Normative Control." *Human Relations* 64 (2): 177–200.

Florida, Richard L. 2002. *The Rise of the Creative Class.* New York: Basic Books.

Foucault, Michel. 2010. *The Birth of Biopolitics: Lectures at the Collège de France, 1978—1979.* New York: Picador.

——. 2012. *Discipline and Punish: The Birth of the Prison.* New York: Knopf Doubleday.

Fouch, Rayvon. 2006. "Say It Loud, I'm Black and I'm Proud: African Americans, American Artifactual Culture, and Black Vernacular Technological Creativity." *American Quarterly* 58 (3): 639–61.

Frank, Thomas. 1998. *The Conquest of Cool: Business Culture, Counterculture, and the Rise of Hip Consumerism.* Chicago: University of Chicago Press.

Frenette, Alexandre. 2013. "Making the Intern Economy: Role and Career Challenges of the Music Industry Intern." *Work and Occupations* 40 (4): 364–97. https://doi .org/10.1177/0730888413504098.

Friedman, Andrew. 1977. "Responsible Autonomy Versus Direct Control Over the Labour Process." *Capital & Class* 1 (1): 43–57. https://doi.org/10.1177/03098168770 0100104.

Fuchs, Christian. 2010. "Labor in Informational Capitalism and on the Internet." *Information Society* 26 (3): 179–96. https://doi.org/10.1080/01972241003712215.

——. 2011. "Cognitive Capitalism or Informational Capitalism? The Role of Class in the Information Economy." In *Cognitive Capitalism, Education, and Digital Labor,* ed. Michael A. Peters and Elgin Bulut, 75–122. New York: Peter Lang.

——. 2013. "Class and Exploitation on the Internet." In *Digital Labor: The Internet as Playground and Factory,* ed. Trebor Scholz, 211–24. New York: Routledge.

——. 2014. *Digital Labour and Karl Marx.* New York: Routledge.

Gagliardi, Pasquale. 1996. "Exploring the Aesthetic Side of Organizational Life." In *Handbook of Organization Studies,* ed. Stewart R. Clegg, Cynthia Hardy, and Walter Nord. London: Sage.

Gahan, Brendan. 2014. "Limbic Resonance—The Science Behind the Success of YouTubers." *YouTube Marketing—Brendan Gahan* (blog). December 2. http:// brendangahan.com/limbic-resonance-science-behind-success-youtubers/.

Gell, Alfred. 1992. "The Technology of Enchantment and the Enchantment of Technology." In *Anthropology, Art, and Aesthetics,* ed. Jeremy Coote and Anthony Shelton, 40–63. Oxford: Clarendon.

——. 1998. *Art and Agency: An Anthropological Theory.* Oxford: Clarendon.

Gerardi, Matt. 2017. "Take a Trip to the Automated Hellscape of YouTube Videos Aimed at Kids." *AV Club.* https://www.avclub.com/take-a-trip-to-the-automated -hellscape-of-youtube-video-1820196139.

Gerber, Alison. 2017. *The Work of Art: Value in Creative Careers.* 1 ed. Stanford, CA: Stanford University Press.

Gershon, Ilana. 2017. *Down and Out in the New Economy: How People Find (or Don't Find) Work Today.* Chicago: University of Chicago Press.

Ghaffary, Shirin. 2019. "Tech Workers Have Been Reluctant to Unionize, but Google Contractors Just Changed That." *Vox.* September 24. https://www.vox.com/recode /2019/9/24/20880727/google-workers-unionized-contractors-hcl-tech-activism.

Gielen, Pascal. 2013. *Creativity and Other Fundamentalisms.* Amsterdam: Ram.

Gill, Rosalind, and Andy Pratt. 2008. "In the Social Factory?" *Theory, Culture & Society* 25 (7–8): 1–30. https://doi.org/10.1177/0263276408097794.

Gillespie, Tarleton. 2010. "The Politics of 'Platforms.'" *New Media & Society* 12 (3): 347–64. https://doi.org/10.1177/1461444809342738.

——. 2014. "The Relevance of Algorithms." In *Media Technologies: Essays on Communication, Materiality, and Society,* ed. Tarleton Gillespie, Pablo J. Boczkowski, and Kirsten A. Foot, 167–93. Cambridge, MA: MIT Press.

Godart, Frédéric, Sorah Seong, and Damon Phillips. 2020. "The Sociology of Creativity: Elements, Structures, and Audiences." *Annual Review of Sociology* 46 (1). https://doi.org/10.1146/annurev-soc-121919-054833.

Goffman, Erving. 1959. *The Presentation of Self in Everyday Life*. New York: Doubleday.

Gouldner, Alvin Ward. 1964. *Patterns of Industrial Bureaucracy*. New York: Free Press.

——. 1982. *The Dialectic of Ideology and Technology: The Origins, Grammar, and Future of Ideology*. New York: Oxford University Press.

Granovetter, Mark S. 1973. "The Strength of Weak Ties." *American Journal of Sociology* 78 (6): 1360–80.

Gray, Mary L., and Siddharth Suri. 2019. *Ghost Work: How to Stop Silicon Valley from Building a New Global Underclass*. Boston: Houghton Mifflin Harcourt.

Grazian, David. 2019. "Thank God It's Monday: Manhattan Coworking Spaces in the New Economy." *Theory and Society*, October. https://doi.org/10.1007/s11186-019 -09360-6.

Gregg, Melissa. 2011. *Work's Intimacy*. New York: Wiley.

——. 2018. *Counterproductive: Time Management in the Knowledge Economy*. Durham, NC: Duke University Press.

Gregg, Melissa, and Gregory J. Seigworth. 2010a. "An Inventory of Shimmers." In *The Affect Theory Reader*, ed. Gregg and Seigworth, 1–28. Durham, NC: Duke University Press.

——. 2010b. *The Affect Theory Reader*. Durham, NC: Duke University Press.

Griffith, Terri, John Sawyer, and Margaret Neale. 2003. "Virtualness and Knowledge in Teams: Managing the Love Triangle of Organizations, Individuals, and Information Technology." *Management Information Science Quarterly* 27 (2): 265–87.

Grimes. 2011. *Oblivion*. 4AD.

Grindstaff, Laura. 2002. *The Money Shot: Trash, Class, and the Making of TV Talk Shows*. Chicago: University of Chicago Press.

Grint, Keith, and Steve Woolgar. 1997. *The Machine at Work: Technology, Work, and Organization*. Cambridge: Polity.

Gruys, Kjerstin. 2012. "Does This Make Me Look Fat? Aesthetic Labor and Fat Talk as Emotional Labor in a Women's Plus-Size Clothing Store." *Social Problems* 59 (4): 481–500. https://doi.org/10.1525/sp.2012.59.4.481.

Gurley, Lauren Kaori. 2019. "Here's What the CEO of Kickstarter Said to Creators About Firing Union Organizers." *Vice* (blog). September 27. https://www.vice.com /en_us/article/a35jpg/heres-what-the-ceo-of-kickstarter-said-to-creators-about -firing-union-organizers.

Hall, Stuart, and Tony Jefferson, eds. 1975. *Resistance Through Rituals: Youth Subcultures in Post-War Britain*. London: Routledge.

Halle, David. 1987. *America's Working Man: Work, Home, and Politics Among Blue Collar Property Owners*. Chicago: University of Chicago Press.

Hanlon, Patrick. 2006. *Primalbranding: Create Zealots for Your Brand, Your Company, and Your Future*. New York: Simon and Schuster.

Haraway, Donna J. 1991. "Situated Knowledges: The Science Question in Feminism and the Privilege of Partial Perspective." In *Simians, Cyborgs, and Women: The Reinvention of Nature*, 183–201. New York: Routledge.

Hardt, Michael. 2005. "Immaterial Labor and Artistic Production." *Rethinking Marxism* 17 (2): 175–77. https://doi.org/10.1080/08935690500046637.

Hardt, Michael, and Antonio Negri. 2001. *Empire*. Cambridge, MA: Harvard University Press.

——. 2005. *Multitude: War and Democracy in the Age of Empire*. New York: Penguin.

Haug, Wolfgang Fritz. 1987. *Commodity Aesthetics, Ideology & Culture*. International General.

Hebdige, Dick. 1978. *Subculture: The Meaning of Style*. New Accents. London: Methuen.

Hennekam, Sophie, and Dawn Bennett. 2017. "Sexual Harassment in the Creative Industries: Tolerance, Culture, and the Need for Change." *Gender, Work & Organization* 24 (4): 417–34. https://doi.org/10.1111/gwao.12176.

Hern, Alex. 2016. "How Alphabet Became the Biggest Company in the World." *The Guardian*, February 2. http://www.theguardian.com/technology/2016/feb/01/how-alphabet-made-google-biggest-company-in-the-world.

Hesmondhalgh, David, and Sarah Baker. 2010. " 'A Very Complicated Version of Freedom': Conditions and Experiences of Creative Labour in Three Cultural Industries." *Poetics* 38 (1): 4–20. https://doi.org/10.1016/j.poetic.2009.10.001.

——. 2011. *Creative Labour*. London: Taylor & Francis.

——. 2015. "Sex, Gender, and Work Segregation in the Cultural Industries." *Sociological Review* 63 (S1): 23–36. https://doi.org/10.1111/1467-954X.12238.

Highmore, Ben. 2010. *Ordinary Lives: Studies in the Everyday*. New York: Routledge.

Hirsch, Paul M. 1972. "Processing Fads and Fashions: An Organization-Set Analysis of Cultural Industry Systems." *American Journal of Sociology* 77 (4): 639–59.

Hochschild, Arlie Russell. 2003. *The Managed Heart: Commercialization of Human Feeling*. Berkeley: University of California Press.

Horkheimer, Max. 1947. *Eclipse of Reason*. New York: Oxford University Press.

Horkheimer, Max, and Theodor Adorno. 1947. "The Culture Industry: Enlightenment as Mass Deception." In *Dialectic of Enlightenment*, trans. John Cumming. New York: Herder and Herder.

Horkheimer, Max, and Theodor W. Adorno. 2007. *Dialectic of Enlightenment*. Stanford, CA: Stanford University Press.

Horning, Susan Schmidt. 2013. *Chasing Sound: Technology, Culture, and the Art of Studio Recording from Edison to the LP*. Baltimore, MD: Johns Hopkins University Press.

Hull, Frank M., Nathalie S. Friedman, and Theresa F. Rogers. 1982. "The Effect of Technology on Alienation from Work Testing Blauner's Inverted U-Curve Hypothesis for 110 Industrial Organizations and 245 Retrained Printers." *Work and Occupations* 9 (1): 31–57. https://doi.org/10.1177/0730888482009001003.

Huws, Ursula. 2014. *Labor in the Global Digital Economy: The Cybertariat Comes of Age*. New York: New York University Press.

Irani, Lilly. 2015a. "Difference and Dependence Among Digital Workers: The Case of Amazon Mechanical Turk." *South Atlantic Quarterly* 114 (1): 225–34.

——. 2015b. "The Cultural Work of Micro-Work." *New Media & Society* 17 (5): 1–21.

——. 2019. *Chasing Innovation: Making Entrepreneurial Citizens in Modern India*. Princeton, NJ: Princeton University Press.

Jameson, Fredric. 1990. *Postmodernism, or The Cultural Logic of Late Capitalism*. Durham, NC: Duke University Press.

Jenkins, Henry. 1992. *Textual Poachers: Television Fans and Participatory Culture.* New York: Routledge.

———. 2006. *Convergence Culture: Where Old and New Media Collide.* New York: New York University Press.

Joas, Hans. 1997. *The Creativity of Action.* Trans. Jeremy Gaines and Paul Keast. Chicago: University of Chicago Press.

Joas, Hans, Richard Sennett, and Antje Gimmler. 2006. "Creativity, Pragmatism, and the Social Sciences." *Distinktion: Journal of Social Theory* 7 (2): 5–31. https://doi.org/10.1080/1600910X.2006.9672927.

Johnson, David, Christopher Voce, and Clare Garberg. 2017. "Engineer Your Technology Environment to Improve Employee Productivity and Flow." In *Landscape: The Workforce Enablement Playbook.* Cambridge, MA: Forrester. https://www.forrester.com/report/A+Crisis+Of+Attention+Technology+Productivity+And+Flow/-/E-RES113826#AST977121.

Jones, Angela. 2020. *Camming: Money, Power, and Pleasure in the Sex Work Industry.* New York: New York University Press.

Kalleberg, Arne L. 2009. "Precarious Work, Insecure Workers: Employment Relations in Transition." *American Sociological Review* 74 (1): 1–22. https://doi.org/10.1177/000312240907400101.

———. 2011. *Good Jobs, Bad Jobs: The Rise of Polarized and Precarious Employment Systems in the United States, 1970s–2000s.* Russell Sage Foundation.

Kant, Immanuel. 1951. *The Critique of Judgment.* Trans. J. H. Bernard. New York: Hafner.

———. 1986. *Philosophical Writings.* Continuum International Publishing Group.

Karpik, Lucien. 2010. *Valuing the Unique: The Economics of Singularities.* Trans. Nora Scott. Princeton, NJ: Princeton University Press.

Kealy, Edward R. 1974. "The Real Rock Revolution: Sound Mixers, Social Inequality, and the Aesthetics of Popular Music Production." PhD diss., Northwestern University.

———. 1979. "From Craft to Art: The Case of Sound Mixers and Popular Music." *Work and Occupations* 6 (1): 3–29. https://doi.org/10.1177/009392857961001.

Klobas, Jane E., and Paul D. Jackson. 2007. *Becoming Virtual: Knowledge Management and Transformation of the Distributed Organization.* New York: Springer.

Knights, David. 1990. "Subjectivity, Power, and the Labour Process." In *Labour Process Theory*, ed. David Knights and Hugh Willmott. London: Macmillan.

Kozlowski, Michal, Agnieszka Kurant, and Jan Sowa, eds. 2014. *Joy Forever: The Political Economy of Social Creativity.* London: MayFlyBooks/Ephemera.

Kracauer, Siegfried. 1963. *The Mass Ornament.* Frankfurt: Suhrkamp Verlag.

Latour, Bruno. 2007. *Reassembling the Social: An Introduction to Actor-Network-Theory.* Oxford: Oxford University Press.

Lazzarato, Maurizio. 2011. "The Misfortunes of the 'Artistic Critique' and of Cultural Employment." In *Critique of Creativity: Precarity, Subjectivity, and Resistance in the "Creative Industries,"* ed. Gerald Raunig, Gene Ray, and Ulf Wuggenig, 41–56. London: MayFlyBooks/Ephemera.

———. 2014. *Signs and Machines: Capitalism and the Production of Subjectivity.* Trans. Joshua David Jordan. Los Angeles, CA: Semiotext(e).

Leiter, Jeffrey. 1985. "Worker Alienation in the Textile Industry Reassessing Blauner." *Work and Occupations* 12 (4): 479–98. https://doi.org/10.1177/0730888485012004005.

Lerum, Kari. 2004. "Sexuality, Power, and Camaraderie in Service Work." *Gender & Society* 18 (6): 756–76. https://doi.org/10.1177/0891243204269398.

Levitt, Steven D., and Sudhir Alladi Venkatesh. 2000. "An Economic Analysis of a Drug-Selling Gang's Finances." *Quarterly Journal of Economics* 115 (3): 755–89.

Lewis, Rebecca. 2018. "Alternative Influence: Broadcasting the Reactionary Right on YouTube." *Data & Society.* https://datasociety.net/wp-content/uploads/2018/09/DS_Alternative_Influence.pdf.

Leys, Ruth. 2011. "The Turn to Affect: A Critique." *Critical Inquiry* 37 (3): 434–72.

Lingo, Elizabeth L., and Siobhán O'Mahony. 2010. "Nexus Work: Brokerage on Creative Projects." *Administrative Science Quarterly* 55 (1): 47–81. https://doi.org/10.2189/asqu.2010.55.1.47.

Linstead, Steve. 1985. "Jokers Wild: The Importance of Humour in the Maintenance of Organizational Culture." *Sociological Review* 33 (4): 741–67. https://doi.org/10.1111/j.1467-954X.1985.tb02447.x.

Lloyd, Richard D. 2006. *Neo-Bohemia: Art and Commerce in the Postindustrial City.* New York: Routledge.

Lukács, György. 1971. *History and Class Consciousness: Studies in Marxist Dialectics.* Cambridge, MA: MIT Press.

Madrigal, Alexis C. 2018. "Raised by YouTube." *The Atlantic,* November. https://www.theatlantic.com/magazine/archive/2018/11/raised-by-youtube/570838/.

Marazzi, Christian. 2011. *Capital and Affects: The Politics of the Language Economy.* Trans. Giuseppina Mecchia. Los Angeles: Semiotext(e).

Marx, Karl. 1978a. "Economic and Philosophic Manuscripts of 1844." In *The Marx-Engels Reader,* 2nd ed., ed. Robert Tucker. New York : Norton.

——. 1978b. "Grundrisse." In *The Marx-Engels Reader,* 2nd ed., ed. Robert Tucker. New York: Norton.

——. 1978c. "The German Ideology." In *The Marx-Engels Reader,* 2nd ed., ed. Robert Tucker. New York: Norton.

Massumi, Brian. 2002. *Parables for the Virtual: Movement, Affect, Sensation.* Durham, NC: Duke University Press.

——. 2015. *Politics of Affect.* Cambridge: Polity.

Mayer, Vicki. 2011. *Below the Line: Producers and Production Studies in the New Television Economy.* Durham, NC: Duke University Press.

Mazzarella, William. 2010. "Affect: What Is It Good For?" In *Enchantments of Modernity: Empire Nation Globalization,* ed. Dube Saurabh. London: Routledge.

——. 2017a. "Sense out of Sense: Notes on the Affect/Ethics Impasse." *Cultural Anthropology* 32 (2): 199–208. https://doi.org/10.14506/ca32.2.04.

——. 2017b. *The Mana of Mass Society.* Chicago: University of Chicago Press.

McRobbie, Angela. 2016. *Be Creative: Making a Living in the New Culture Industries.* Cambridge: Polity.

Mears, Ashley. 2011. *Pricing Beauty: The Making of a Fashion Model.* Berkeley: University of California Press.

Melville, Herman. 1856. "Bartleby, the Scrivener: A Story of Wall-Street." In *The Piazza Tales.* New York: Dix & Edwards.

Menger, Pierre-Michel. 1999. "Artistic Labor Markets and Careers." *Annual Review of Sociology* 25:541–574.

Miège, Bernard. 1989. *The Capitalization of Cultural Production.* International General.

Mills, C. Wright. 1951. *White Collar*. Oxford: Oxford University Press.

Molotch, Harvey. 2004. *Where Stuff Comes From: How Toasters, Toilets, Cars, Computers, and Many Other Things Come to Be as They Are*. London: Routledge.

Mould, Oli. 2018. *Against Creativity*. New York: Verso.

Müller, Eggo. 2009. "Where Quality Matters: Discourses on the Art of Making a YouTube Video." In *The YouTube Reader*, ed. Pelle Snickars and Patrick Vonderau, 126–39. Stockholm: National Library of Sweden.

Muniesa, Fabian, Yuval Millo, and Michel Callon. 2007. "An Introduction to Market Devices." *Sociological Review* 55:1–12. https://doi.org/10.1111/j.1467-954X.2007.00727.x.

Napoli, Philip M. 2003. *Audience Economics: Media Institutions and the Audience Marketplace*. New York: Columbia University Press.

Neff, Gina. 2012. *Venture Labor: Work and the Burden of Risk in Innovative Industries*. Cambridge, MA: MIT Press.

Negus, Keith. 1999. *Music Genres and Corporate Cultures*. London: Routledge.

Newell, Sasha. 2018. "The Affectiveness of Symbols: Materiality, Magicality, and the Limits of the Antisemiotic Turn." *Current Anthropology* 59 (1): 1–22. https://doi.org/10.1086/696071.

Noble, Safiya Umoja. 2018. *Algorithms of Oppression: How Search Engines Reinforce Racism*. New York: New York University Press.

Nover, Scott, and Rachel Winicov. 2020. "Black Creators File Class-Action Lawsuit Against YouTube." *Adweek*, June 19. https://www.adweek.com/digital/black-creators-class-action-lawsuit-youtube-google/.

Nowotny, Stefan. 2011. "Immanent Effects: Notes on Cre-Activity." In *Critique of Creativity: Precarity, Subjectivity, and Resistance in the "Creative Industries,"* ed. Gerald Raunig, Gene Ray, and Ulf Wuggenig, trans. Aileen Derieg, 9–22. London: MayFlyBooks/Ephemera.

O'Connor, Alan. 2008. *Punk Record Labels and the Struggle for Autonomy: The Emergence of DIY*. Critical Media Studies. Lanham, MD: Lexington.

Oldenziel, Ruth. 1999. *Making Technology Masculine: Men, Women, and Modern Machines in America, 1870–1945*. Amsterdam: Amsterdam University Press.

Pang, Laikwan. 2012. *Creativity and Its Discontents: China's Creative Industries and Intellectual Property Rights Offenses*. Durham, NC: Duke University Press.

Pasquale, Frank. 2015. *The Black Box Society*. Cambridge, MA: Harvard University Press.

Peuter, Greig de. 2011. "Creative Economy and Labor Precarity." *Journal of Communication Inquiry* 35 (4): 417–25. https://doi.org/10.1177/0196859911416362.

Plester, Barbara. 2009. "Crossing the Line: Boundaries of Workplace Humour and Fun." *Employee Relations* 31 (6): 584–99. https://doi.org/10.1108/01425450910991749.

Porter, Theodore M. 1996. *Trust in Numbers: The Pursuit of Objectivity in Science and Public Life*. Princeton, NJ: Princeton University Press.

Powell, Walter. 1990. "Neither Market nor Hierarchy: Network Forms of Organization." *Research in Organizational Behavior* 12:295–336.

Quinn, Ryan W. 2005. "Flow in Knowledge Work: High Performance Experience in the Design of National Security Technology." *Administrative Science Quarterly* 50 (4): 610–41. https://doi.org/10.2189/asqu.50.4.610.

Raunig, Gerald, Gene Ray, and Ulf Wuggenig, eds. 2011. *Critique of Creativity: Precarity, Subjectivity, and Resistance in the "Creative Industries."* London: MayFlyBooks/Ephemera.

Reich, Robert B. 1991. *The Work of Nations*. New York: Knopf.

Rennstam, Jens. 2012. "Object-Control: A Study of Technologically Dense Knowledge Work." *Organization Studies* 33 (8): 1071–90. https://doi.org/10.1177/0170840612453527.

Rey, P. J. 2012. "Alienation, Exploitation, and Social Media." *American Behavioral Scientist* 56 (4): 399–420. https://doi.org/10.1177/0002764211429367.

Rosenblat, Alex. 2018. *Uberland: How Algorithms Are Rewriting the Rules of Work*. Berkeley: University of California Press.

Ross, Andrew. 2004. *No-Collar: The Humane Workplace and Its Hidden Costs*. Philadelphia: Temple University Press.

——. 2009. *Nice Work If You Can Get It: Life and Labor in Precarious Times*. New York: New York University Press.

——. 2013. "In Search of the Lost Paycheck." In *Digital Labor: The Internet as Playground and Factory*, ed. Trebor Scholz, 13–32. New York: Routledge.

Rossman, Gabriel, Nicole Esparza, and Phillip Bonacich. 2010. "I'd Like to Thank the Academy, Team Spillovers, and Network Centrality." *American Sociological Review* 75:31–51.

Roy, Donald. 1953. "Work Satisfaction and Social Reward in Quota Achievement: An Analysis of Piecework Incentive." *American Sociological Review* 18 (5): 507–14. https://doi.org/10.2307/2087434.

——. 1959. "'Banana Time': Job Satisfaction and Informal Interaction." *Human Organization* 18 (4): 158–68.

Rutherford, Danilyn. 2016. "Affect Theory and the Empirical." *Annual Review of Anthropology* 45 (1): 285–300. https://doi.org/10.1146/annurev-anthro-102215-095843.

Sallaz, Jeffrey J. 2015. "Permanent Pedagogy: How Post-Fordist Firms Generate Effort but Not Consent." *Work and Occupations* 42 (1): 3–34. https://doi.org/10.1177/0730888414551207.

Saval, Nikil. 2015. *Cubed: A Secret History of the Workplace*. New York: Knopf Doubleday.

Scholz, Trebor, ed. 2013. *Digital Labor: The Internet as Playground and Factory*. New York: Routledge.

——. 2016. *Uberworked and Underpaid: How Workers Are Disrupting the Digital Economy*. New York: John Wiley & Sons.

Schumpeter, Joseph A. 2008. *Capitalism, Socialism, and Democracy*. 3rd ed. New York: Harper Perennial.

Sedgwick, Eve Kosofsky, and Adam Frank. 2003. *Touching Feeling: Affect, Pedagogy, Performativity*. Durham, NC: Duke University Press.

Sennett, Richard. 2000. *The Corrosion of Character: The Personal Consequences of Work in the New Capitalism*. New York: Norton.

——. 2007. *The Culture of the New Capitalism*. New Haven, CT: Yale University Press.

Sewell, Graham. 1998. "The Discipline of Teams: The Control of Team-Based Industrial Work Through Electronic and Peer Surveillance." *Administrative Science Quarterly* 43 (2): 397–428. https://doi.org/10.2307/2393857.

——. 2005. "Nice Work? Rethinking Managerial Control in an Era of Knowledge Work." *Organization* 12 (5): 685–704. https://doi.org/10.1177/1350508405055943.

Siciliano, Michael. 2016. "Control from On High: Cloud Computing, Skill, and Acute Frustration Among Analytics Workers in the Digital Publishing Industry." *Research in the Sociology of Work* 29 (1): 125–54.

Siciliano, Michael, and Alan O'Connor. 2012. "MAXIMUMSOCIALSCIENCE: A Conversation/Interview with Alan O'Connor." In *Punkademics*, ed. Zack Furness, 91–104. Brooklyn, NY: Autonomedia.

Simmel, Georg. 1995. "The Metropolis and Mental Life." In *Metropolis: Center and Symbol of Our Times*, 30–45. New York: New York University Press.

Simondon, Gilbert. 2012. "On Techno-Aesthetics." *Parrhesia* 1 (14): 1–8.

Situationist International. 1981. "The Bad Days Will End." In *Situationist International Anthology*, ed. Ken Knabb, 82–87. Bureau of Public Secrets.

Smythe, Dallas. 1977. "Communications: Blindspot of Western Marxism." *Canadian Journal of Political and Social Theory* 1 (3): 1–27.

Snyder, Benjamin H. 2016. *The Disrupted Workplace: Time and the Moral Order of Flexible Capitalism*. Oxford: Oxford University Press.

Social Blade. 2017. "Top 5000 YouTubers." February 21. http://socialblade.com/youtube /top/5000.

Srnicek, Nick. 2016. *Platform Capitalism*. Cambridge: Polity.

Standing, Guy. 2014. *A Precariat Charter: From Denizens to Citizens*. A&C Black.

——. 2016. *The Precariat: The New Dangerous Class*. London: Bloomsbury.

Stewart, Kathleen. 2007. *Ordinary Affects*. Durham, NC: Duke University Press.

Storey, John, Graeme Salaman, and Kerry Platman. 2005. "Living with Enterprise in an Enterprise Economy: Freelance and Contract Workers in the Media." *Human Relations* 58 (8): 1033–54. https://doi.org/10.1177/0018726705058502.

Strati, Antonio. 2003. "Knowing in Practice: Aesthetic Understanding and Tacit Knowledge." In *Knowing in Organizations: A Practice-Based Approach*, ed. Davide Nicolini, Silvia Gherardi, and Dvora Yanow. New York: Routledge.

Stuart, Forrest. 2020. *Ballad of the Bullet: Gangs, Drill Music, and the Power of Online Infamy*. Princeton, NJ: Princeton University Press.

Suchman, Lucy. 2007. *Human-Machine Reconfigurations: Plans and Situated Actions*. Cambridge: Cambridge University Press.

Swedberg, Richard. 2011. "The Role of Senses and Signs in the Economy." *Journal of Cultural Economy* 4 (4): 423–37. https://doi.org/10.1080/17530350.2011.609703.

Taylor, Astra. 2014. *The People's Platform: Taking Back Power and Culture in the Digital Age*. New York: Henry Holt.

Terranova, Tiziana. 2017. "Platform Capitalism and the Government of the Social. Facebook's 'Global Community.'" *TRU* (blog). February 21. http://www.technoculture.it /en/2017/02/21/platform-capitalism-and-the-government-of-the-social/.

Théberge, Paul. 2016. "The End of the World as We Knew It: The Changing Role of the Studio in the Age of the Internet." In *The Art of Record Production: An Introductory Reader for a New Academic Field*, ed. Simon Zagorski-Thomas and Simon Frith. New York: Routledge.

Tolbert, Pamela. 2001. "Occupations, Organizations, and Boundaryless Careers." In *The Boundaryless Career: A New Employment Principle for a New Organizational Era*, ed. Michael Bernard Arthur and Denise M. Rousseau, 331–45. Oxford: Oxford University Press.

Tronti, Mario. 2019. *Workers and Capital*. London: Verso.

Tufekci, Zeynep. 2018. "Opinion | YouTube, the Great Radicalizer." *New York Times*, June 8. https://www.nytimes.com/2018/03/10/opinion/sunday/youtube-politics-radical .html.

Turco, Catherine. 2016. *The Conversational Firm: Rethinking Bureaucracy in the Age of Social Media*. New York: Columbia University Press.

Turkle, Sherry. 1997. *Life on the Screen: Identity in the Age of the Internet*. New York: Simon & Schuster.

Umney, Charles, and Lefteris Kretsos. 2015. "'That's the Experience': Passion, Work Precarity, and Life Transitions Among London Jazz Musicians." *Work and Occupations*, February. https://doi.org/10.1177/0730888415573634.

U.S. Bureau of Labor Statistics. 2013a. "Union Affiliation Data for Motion Pictures and Sound Recording Industries." http://data.bls.gov/timeseries/LUU0204918700?data_tool=XGtable.

——. 2013b. "Sound Recording Industries—May 2013 OES Industry-Specific Occupational Employment and Wage Estimates." http://www.bls.gov/oes/current/naics4_512200.htm.

——. 2016. "Table 5. Median Years of Tenure with Current Employer for Employed Wage and Salary Workers by Industry, Selected Years, 2006–16." September 22. https://www.bls.gov/news.release/tenure.t05.htm.

USA Today. 2014. "France Bans Work E-Mail After 6 p.m." *USA Today*. http://www.usatoday.com/story/money/business/2014/04/11/newser-france-work-email-ban/7592125/.

Vallas, Steven Peter, and Michael Yarrow. 1987. "Advanced Technology and Worker Alienation Comments on the Blauner/Marxism Debate." *Work and Occupations* 14 (1): 126–42. https://doi.org/10.1177/0730888487014001007.

Vaneigem, Raoul. 2001. *Revolution of Everyday Life*. Trans. Donald Nicholson-Smith. London: Rebel.

Varner, Stewart. 2007. "Youth Claiming Space: The Case of Pittsburgh's Mr. Roboto Project." In *Youth Cultures: Scenes, Subcultures, and Tribes*, ed. Paul Hodkinson and Wolfgang Deicke, 161–74. London: Routledge.

Venturi, Robert, Steven Izenour, and Denise Scott Brown. 1977. *Learning from Las Vegas—The Forgotten Symbolism of Architectural Form*. Rev. ed. Cambridge, MA: MIT Press.

Vercellone, Carlo. 2005. "The Hypothesis of Cognitive Capitalism." In *The Hypothesis of Cognitive Capitalism*. London: Birkbeck College and SOAS. https://halshs.archives-ouvertes.fr/halshs-00273641.

——. 2007. "From Formal Subsumption to General Intellect: Elements for a Marxist Reading of the Thesis of Cognitive Capitalism, in Historical Materialism." *Historical Materialism* 15 (1): 13–36.

Virno, Paolo. 2001. "General Intellect." Trans. Arianna Bove. http://www.generation-online.org/p/fpvirno1.htm.

——. 2004. *A Grammar of the Multitude: For an Analysis of Contemporary Forms of Life*. Cambridge, MA: MIT Press.

Vonderau, Patrick. 2009. "Writers Becoming Users: YouTube Hype and the Writer's Strike." In *The YouTube Reader*, ed. Pelle Snickars and Patrick Vonderau, 108–25. Stockholm: National Library of Sweden.

Wajcman, Judy. 2016. *Pressed for Time: The Acceleration of Life in Digital Capitalism*. Chicago: University of Chicago Press.

Wajcman, Judy, and Emily Rose. 2011. "Constant Connectivity: Rethinking Interruptions at Work." *Organization Studies* 32 (7): 941–61. https://doi.org/10.1177/01708 40611410829.

Wallenstein, Andrew. 2012. "Media Bigs Flock to YouTube Power Players." *Variety*, November 21. http://variety.com/2012/digital/news/media-bigs-flock-to-youtube -power-players-1118062549/.

Wamsley, Laurel. 2017. "Is YouTube's Algorithm Endangering Kids?" *NPR.org*. 2017. https://www.npr.org/sections/thetwo-way/2017/11/27/566769570/youtube-faces -increased-criticism-that-its-unsafe-for-kids.

Warren, Samantha. 2008. "Empirical Challenges in Organizational Aesthetics Research: Towards a Sensual Methodology." *Organization Studies* 29 (4): 559–80. https://doi.org/10.1177/0170840607083104.

Washington Post. 2016. "France Might Pass a Law That Makes It Illegal to Send After-Hours Work Emails." https://www.washingtonpost.com/news/the-switch/wp/2016 /05/12/france-might-pass-a-law-that-makes-it-illegal-to-send-after-hours-work -emails/.

Weber, Max. 1978. *Economy and Society: An Outline of Interpretive Sociology*. Berkeley, CA: University of California Press.

Weiss, Geoff. 2019. "Hank Green's Internet Creators Guild to Shutter, Citing No 'Path to Financial Stability.'" *Tubefilter* (blog), July 10. https://www.tubefilter.com/2019 /07/10/internet-creators-guild-to-shutter/.

——. 2020. "A Lot of YouTube Creators Just Disclosed Their Declining AdSense Rates Amid the Coronavirus Pandemic. Most Are Down at Least 20%, with a Few Bright Spots." *Tubefilter* (blog), April 16. https://www.tubefilter.com/2020/04/16/creators -disclose-declining-adsense-rates-coronavirus/.

Whyte, William H. 1956. *The Organization Man*. Philadelphia: University of Pennsylvania Press.

Williams, Christine, and Catherine Connell. 2010. "Looking Good and Sounding Right." *Work and Occupations* 37 (3): 349–77. https://doi.org/10.1177/0730888410 373744.

Williams, Raymond. 1978. *Marxism and Literature*. New York: Oxford University Press.

——. 1981. *The Sociology of Culture*. Chicago: University of Chicago Press.

——. 1983. "Culture." In *Keywords*, 87–93. New York: Oxford University Press.

Willis, Paul E. 1978. *Profane Culture*. London: Routledge.

——. 1990. *Common Culture: Symbolic Work at Play in the Everyday Cultures of the Young*. Boulder, CO: Westview.

Witz, Anne, Chris Warhurst, and Dennis Nickson. 2003. "The Labour of Aesthetics and the Aesthetics of Organization." *Organization* 10 (1): 33–54. https://doi.org/10 .1177/1350508403010001375.

Wright, Erik Olin. 1998. *Classes*. London: Verso.

YouTube. 2017. "Statistics—YouTube." https://www.youtube.com/yt/press/statistics .html.

Zafirau, Stephen. 2007. "Reputation Work in Selling Film and Television: Life in the Hollywood Talent Industry." *Qualitative Sociology* 31 (November): 99–127. https:// doi.org/10.1007/s11133-007-9083-8.

Zysman, John, and Martin Kenney. 2014. "Sustainable Growth and Work in the Era of Cloud and Big Data: Will Escaping the Commodity Trap Be Our Undoing?" Berkeley Roundtable on the International Economy Working Paper 6.

INDEX

Adorno, Theodor: on aesthetic experiences, 93, 125; on alienated judgment, 261n40; on autonomous art, 34, 35, 36, 44; on color-coding, 265n63; and creativity discourses, 34, 35, 36; on damaged life, 269n11; on heteronymous cultural production, 153; on pleasure in technology, 91

advertising: and creativity as business buzzword, 7, 29; by social media platforms, 7, 8, 42–43, *42, 142,* 143

aesthetic agency: and aesthetic experiences, 97, 98; and aesthetic landscape, 68–69, 168; and The Future staff, 210; and human-machine assemblages, 77, 93–94; and pleasure in technology, 80, 87, 158, 159; and sound engineers, 71, 74–75, 77–79; and survivor art, 168–69; and technical expertise, 72–73; and technical expertise acquisition, 91–92. *See also* autonomy

aesthetic enrollment: and alienated judgment, 120, 125; and conceptual map of creative labor, 226–27; and

content creators, 158; and contradictions of creative labor, 69, 119; and data visualizations, 144; defined, 87, 258n26; Durkheim on, 12; and human-machine assemblages, 94; instability of, 95, 97, 123; and instrumental pragmatism, 98, 163, 228; and labor regimes, 182; and platform discipline, 182–83; and stockbrokers, 266n71. *See also* contradictions of creative labor

aesthetic experiences: and aesthetic agency, 97, 98; and alienation, 121, 125; and content creators, 161–63, 264n43; definitions of, 11, 92–93, 259n49; and The Future staff, 17, 178–79, 180, 181, 210; as games, 264–65n47; and human-machine assemblages, 75, 257n16; and instrumental pragmatism, 163, 228; and politics of judgment, 231; and SoniCo office staff, 97–98; and stockbrokers, 266n71; and technical expertise acquisition, 91. *See also* contradictions of creative labor

aesthetic labor, 269n13

GPSR Authorized Representative: Easy Access System Europe, Mustamäe tee 50, 10621 Tallinn, Estonia, gpsr.requests@easproject.com